Special Kids for Special Treatment?

or

How special do you need to be to find yourself in a special school?

Helen Phtiaka

 The Falmer Press

(A member of the Taylor & Francis Group)
London • Washington, D.C.

UK   Falmer Press, 1 Gunpowder Square, London, EC4A 3DE
USA   Falmer Press, Taylor & Francis Inc., 1900 Frost Road, Suite 101,
        Bristol, PA 19007

First published in 1997

A catalogue record for this book is available from the British Library

ISBN 0 7507 0725 9 cased
ISBN 0 7507 0618 X paper

Library of Congress Cataloging-in-Publication Data are available on request

Jacket design by Caroline Archer

Typeset in 10/12pt Times by
Graphicraft Typesetters Ltd., Hong Kong.

Printed in Great Britain by Biddles Ltd., Guildford and King's Lynn on paper which has a specified pH value on final paper manufacture of not less than 7.5 and is therefore 'acid free'.

Special Kids for Special Treatment?

Dedication

To Kyriacos
who supported me
throughout my venture:
'Of course I'll help you darling
if your switch over to IBM[1]'

                              and

                                        to Costas
                              who badly wanted it:
                              'You do realize
                    you never dedicated anything
                                        to me!'

both special kids in their own right!

---

1   Just for the record, *I didn't!*

Contents

List of Tables

Acknowledgments

A very cordial 'thank you' to Malcolm Clarkson for keeping a long held promise and giving me a chance. To Bob Burgess who taught me all I know about book proposals and to Sara Delamont who gave me a fresh presentation idea and kindly agreed to write a foreword for the book. Based on such advice, how can it fail to be a success?

Warning!

This is not a 'how to' book. Quite often when we are dealing with classroom problems 'God only knows how to!' *I* certainly don't, given that I am not even there! The one who knows best after God is you (the teacher)! You know, or you should know, the pupils and their own special way, you have access to people who taught them before and others who will teach them after you. You have all the information you need at your fingertips. Use it. Where this book may help is by providing the means for you to obtain a deeper understanding of the way your pupils think by showing how other pupils in similar situations did think. If (heaven forbid!) I have to give practical advice to my reader by suggesting an essential tool for a teacher faced with lack of cooperation from a pupil, I would say this: It is my firm belief that the one single trait a teacher need possess to not only survive, but also succeed in her job, is love leading to reflective thinking. We are all so well tuned to react defensively and think the worst of a pupil reaction which is out of the ordinary or seems to dispute what we say!

I often remember Jason[1] who taught me a very good lesson. I was young in age and new to the researcher's job, and on top of that a female foreigner in a rather rough school — well as rough as you could get in a shire county. I stood in front of a year 10 class I hardly knew and tried to enthuse them about my questionnaire. I had spent so many hours on it, I had argued with my supervisor over where the commas should be, I had written a touching foreword, my damned PhD depended on them filling in this questionnaire! I encouraged and pleaded and cajoled. I heard a groan! I looked around. It was Jason. Body language all negative, unspoken words you could guess on his lips. I did not know him then. I looked at him. I thought 'He must be one of them deviants I am looking for! He is going to give me trouble! I had better watch him closely!' What a proper little teacher I was — and I had not even trained as one! So, while the others were doing their best filling in what must have looked to them as an enormous questionnaire of ten pages, I 'casually' approached Jason — I was almost whistling!. I accidentally dropped an eye on his left — he hid the left side of his paper. I dropped one on his right — he hid the right side of his paper. I stood over him like an ogre and kindly asked if he needed help. He mumbled something I did not hear or remember, possibly — not me! It's you who said needed help mate! I offered to help anyway. He did not welcome my help. From looking at his scribles and from what I managed to extract from him it finally

---

1 All names mentioned in this book, apart from my own, are, of course, pseudonyms.

clicked! Jason could not read! Year 10 maybe, but he could not read and he could hardly write. The last thing he wanted was everyone, even an outsider, who by the sounds of it could read in two languages, to find out his secret! I backed up in a state of shock leaving Jason to struggle with the questionnaire and retain as much pride and dignity he could. Poor Jason! Deviant! Trouble! Need to watch him! For your sake, I hope you learned to read, but I doubt you did if your teachers shared my first impression of you . . .

A Private Story Told in Public

Academic writers, much like novelists, are faced with a dilemma little known to other professions. They start work in the privacy of their own nest, possibly in their pyjamas, looking casual and relaxed and at the same time too awful to be seen. They can listen to music and dance while they are thinking, they can be munching away something terribly unhealthy while they are writing, they can spill coffee all over their papers, they can happily swear for this paragraph that does not convey what it is meant to, or they can bang the desk causing a minor earthquake when they have finally 'got it'! They can even take their work for a walk, to the mountain or to the sea, as if it were a pet! A privileged group of people you'd think. Not many professionals can afford to do that. Most working women have to get up extremely early, rush into the bathroom, rush out of it, choose an outfit for the day, become beautiful (somehow) and rush out of the house. Most working men have to fight with the razors in the morning, but this is an area less well known to me, so I shall not elaborate . . . Most working women and men are also tied to their desk. They cannot secretly hide in the privacy of their own bedroom under a big pile of blankets and read. They cannot take their work with them somewhere private. They have to be seen to be working in the public eye looking their best, in a specified public area.

Yet, there is nothing more public than a piece of academic writing! If you have never met the person writing, you may not know how old they are, how pretty they look, how they carry themselves or how they dress, but you do know their innermost thoughts and beliefs, their life principles and their most secret ideas. This is a haunting idea! It is particularly haunting for a beginner who has enjoyed the privileged privacy of the writing part of the work to arrive at the public outcome. This is a step worth thinking about.

I have been thinking about it, for some years now.

When I first arrived in Scotland thirteen years ago, I had the excitement, the curiosity and the anxiety of a very young research student, a foreigner even, trying to survive in an unknown environment and at the same time make the most of her stay there. I did survive. In fact I thrived. I had a great time as a student both in Scotland and in England and I finally completed what I thought at the time was a brilliant piece of work. It was. Or so the examiners thought, because after giving me a fair time at the viva, they shook my hand smiling. You don't forget such moments, and I will not forget Sara Delamont shaking my hand and saying wittingly: 'It is a pity that University regulations do not allow us to announce to you the outcome of this conversation. It would have been nice to be able to finish a viva congratulating the candidate on their PhD.'

That was enough.

I got out of the building, to a London that was not my place, neither my University. I was once again a foreigner in a foreign place. There was no internal examiner or supervisor with me in my viva. I was in a University other than my own, in a non-familiar city where I knew nobody, faced with people I was meeting for the first time in my life in the full knowledge that they had the power to determine my future.

London had never looked as warm and friendly as it did that afternoon!

I am no longer a research student, and I no longer consider my PhD work as the mortal answer to all immortal questions. I still consider it as a bloody good piece of work and one I have to share with others. I am still puzzled by this private/public issue. But I no longer live in Britain. The kids I studied are now young men and women working, or otherwise, in various areas of Britain. One of them wrote to me a few months back announcing the birth of her second daughter and telling me off for not having a family myself, especially considering how old I was!

I am not this old. But I am old enough. I am no longer a student. I have students of my own. And the kids I wrestled with for the piece of work contained in this book are no longer kids. I did promise to make them famous if they gave me some of their time. I have not kept that promise so far. Fame is no longer a danger to them, and they may well enjoy seeing themselves portrayed on paper under new names.

For them, and for me, and for all of you who may find this book useful, or stimulating, or interesting, or simply fun, this very private part of my life, has to become public at last.

Helen Phtiaka
August 1996

Preface

School deviance has been an area of educational interest for a long time. In past years two basic models have been used to interpret and explain it, each one associated particularly with one academic tradition. Psychologists have attempted to use a diagnostic model, and sociologists have tried to explore the pupils' own thinking. Neither discipline has succeeded in offering an adequate explanation of the phenomenon. In the meantime school deviance continues to be dealt with by legislation informed by inadequate models, mainly diagnostic, and pupils continue to be classified, and at times discriminated against, because of behaviour which is not fully understood.

This book offers a new perspective on the subject by adopting an interdisciplinary approach in an effort to achieve a more complete understanding of the phenomenon of school deviance and to answer the question: Are behaviour differences between deviant pupils within and without mainstream education such as to justify a division?

The book is highly topical given the recurring conflict within recent legislation regarding treatment of children with special needs, (Education Act 1981 v Education Reform Act 1988), and between thoughtful regulating and legislation resulting from years of research in the area of special needs as well as international influences such as the UN Convention of the Rights of the Child held in 1989 (Education Act 1981; Children Act 1989) and financial and political pressures resulting mainly from the ERA pressurizing schools to boost their public profile, even at the expense of pupils who require their help.

Foreword

In *Hooligan* Geoffrey Pearson (1983) has shown that for over a century the middle and upper class in Britain have feared social unrest stemming from lower class males (hooligans, yobs, louts), and have blamed schools and teachers for failing to civilize or pacify them. As I write this, a perfect example of such a moral panic (centred on knives and discipline in schools) is gripping England, and the government is promising schools in England and Wales more powers to exclude and refuse admission to, troublesome pupils.

The publication of Helen Phtiaka's research in which she compares the behaviour of deviant/rebellious/resistant adolescents in a mainstream school and in a special unit for those expelled from the mainstream, is therefore timely. Her central point is that the realities of discipline problems in schools are much more complex than current rhetoric allows. Her research includes adolescents who were too much for a normal school to cope with but settled happily into a small specialist centre, contrasted with those still 'trapped' miserably in the mainstream system. At the heart of her analysis is an ironic contrast: the specialist centre held the adolescents' loyalty and got their attendance but at the cost of teaching them nothing. Adolescents at the centre were not taught the subjects of the core curriculum, left full time education without exam passes, got no credentials, acquired few marketable skills. They would not have acquired these things in the mainstream schools which expelled them either, and at least at the centre they were happy and off the street, but it is clear that neither setting works academically for those adolescents.

As a moral panic swirls through Britain those unheard are the adolescents themselves: the great strength of the book is that Helen Phtiaka has given these unhappy, and disruptive, adolescents a space to tell their stories: to be heard calling through the sound barrier of the adult rhetoric.

Sara Delamont
Cardiff 1996

Part I

The Literature

The first part of the book presents the central question of the study and highlights the issues involved. It also attempts to give a clear picture of the way these issues have been dealt with in the past and explains why a new approach is necessary. The first chapter outlines the development of compulsory schooling and special education in Britain from the first piece of educational legislation right up to the 1981 Education Act, focusing on the category of maladjustment. It deals with models currently used to interpret deviant behaviour in school, and points out their limitations. Finally, it suggests a model which can overcome these limitations and provides a more global understanding of the phenomenon of deviant behaviour.

Chapter 1

Looking Back . . .

Introduction

Handicapped people have often in the past been treated with disrespect and suspicion. The example of ancient Spartans, who used to dispose of handicapped newborn babies by throwing them from a cliff, is perhaps extreme, but attitudes towards handicapped adults and children have been, for a long period in European history, unfriendly, even hostile. The Christian church was one of the first institutions to take an interest in the welfare of such adults and children, but its approach has often been mistaken and it has retrospectively been accused of a slow reaction to a social need (Tomlinson, 1982), and occasional condemnation of handicapped people as 'a curse from God' (Pritchard, 1963). Nevertheless the church has played a crucial role in changing attitudes towards handicapped people and has forced the State to do the same (Tomlinson, 1982). State and public attitude is now different, to the extent that proper care and provision for the weakest members of society is acknowledged as a sign of a civilized culture. European countries, and Britain in particular, have attempted, in the last fifty years, to show their interest towards handicapped citizens by developing very sophisticated systems of care. In the last twenty years, however, these systems have come under severe criticism.

In Britain the education of the handicapped first became a State concern in the nineteenth century (Education Acts, 1870–1904). The State, under the influence of democratic and liberal ideas of the time, attempted to ensure that handicapped children were entitled to education, like all children (Morrish, 1970). Education was provided, however, for them in separate schools and institutions excluding handicapped children from the mainstream schools that 'normal' pupils attended. The more sophisticated the special education system became, the more children were removed away from the mainstream school (Ford *et al*, 1982). The division between 'mainstream' and 'special' education, initially motivated, according to some (Upton, 1992) by a wish to help the handicapped children providing a sheltered and well equipped environment[1], very soon became problematic. This drew attention and criticism to existing systems of provision.

The dividing line between mainstream and special education gave serious cause for concern because it often proved to be arbitrary, particularly with non-normative categories of handicap, such as behavioural problems and 'maladjustment'. The reason traditionally offered for providing children with an alternative education was that they could not take full advantage of the mainstream system and they needed

Table 1:   Number of special schools in ILEA

Type of school	Schools/units	Pupils
Visually impaired	5	367
Hearing impaired	4	214
Motor impaired	8	473
Delicate	13	1172
Emotional/Behavioural difficulties	34	1289
Moderate learning difficulties	24	2519
Severe learning difficulties	16	1381
Autistic	7	122
Hospical	2	106
Units for hearing impaired	13	314
Units for language impaired	7	110
Total	**133**	**8067**

Source: ILEA Research and Statistics Report, 1984

further help (Tomlinson, 1982; Ainscow, 1993). Removal from the mainstream was not seriously questioned while the number of children removed remained small and people remained convinced that this was to the children's advantage. As the system grew more sophisticated and the number of withdrawals increased, it gradually became clear that naming a pupil deviant and transferring him/her outside the mainstream was neither easy, nor straightforward. It also became apparent that it was very difficult to decide which children gave enough reason for concern to make special educational provisions necessary. At that point the relative ease which seemed to characterize decision for transfer gave rise for concern (Tomlinson, 1981a). Because of its unique features the case of maladjustment presents a special interest and will be my main focus.

After the Second World War, educational provisions for handicapped children increased in Britain. The increase rate reached its peak in the 1970s, which is particularly ironic as it coincided with the move towards comprehensive education (Morrish, 1970; Coulby, 1984). For schools and units of children with behavioural problems, this increase was phenomenal (Ford *et al*, 1982). This can be clearly demonstrated by the distribution of different handicaps in special education schools and units.

In table 1 there appears to be no shortage of special schools and units in the London area. Particularly noteworthy is the percentage of schools and units for children with behavioural problems. The number of these schools, including schools or units for autistic children, is both larger than the total number of provisions for all other categories, and larger even than any single category, if they are grouped in categories for physical, learning and health problems. If one considers that it is often hard to distinguish between learning and behavioural problems in special schools placements (Smith, 1992; Davie, 1993; Gulliford, 1992), then the number of children with behavioural or emotional problems becomes even greater. This makes the percentage of disturbed children in British schools surprisingly high.

The sharpest increase in the variety and the numbers of provisions for such children, has been observed in the last twenty years. It is possible that this reflects an increase in the number of problem children, in which case we need to examine the reasons behind this dramatic increase. It may also be the result of other factors. It is possible, for example, that pressures relating to comprehensivization seriously tested mainstream schools' ability to cope. This led to requests for help, which were met with an increase in special schools and units. Alternatively it is possible that changes in legislation shifted the dividing line between mainstream and special education, and allowed more children to be classified as disturbed.

Two social science disciplines have traditionally adopted two very different kinds of explanations for the causes of deviant behaviour in school, the need for expansion of special provisions, and the reasons favouring such an expansion. Each one has adopted different approaches, and has concentrated on different questions, and so they have succeeded in developing in a parallel way, almost ignoring each other, while dealing with very similar problems.

Psychologists and sociologists developed an interest in deviant behaviour within **mainstream schools** in the late sixties, each discipline for its own reasons. The psychologists' interest was partly a response to criticism of the medical model of individual pathology applied in special schools (Levitt, 1957 and 1963). Sociologists, on the other hand, were interested in applying deviance theories dating back to Durkheim's notion of anomie (Durkheim, 1968) to the school. Research on deviant behaviour in the mainstream was dominated by sociologists as different models attempted, in closely focused case studies, to explain the pupils' social world and the phenomenon of school deviance.

On the other hand, literature on deviant behaviour and maladjustment in **special schools and units** followed one of two main trends. The first described case studies of 'special' children or special schools (Wills, 1945; Redl and Wineman, 1951; Dockar-Drysdale 1968 and 1971), and the work done with them, emphasizing individual pathology and concentrating on therapeutic techniques[2]. Information and advice on coping with special 'categories' of children was offered in books based on the author's past experience and expert knowledge (Stott, 1956; Gulliford, 1971; Rutter, 1975; Laslett, 1977; Stott, 1982), rather than particular research projects. This trend, exclusively followed by psychologists, established the authority of the profession in the field of special education.

The second trend, developed much later, was distanced from pupils and schools, concentrating on special education policy making, its philosophy and politics (Galloway and Goodwin, 1979; Barton and Tomlinson, 1981; Swann, 1981; Booth, 1982; Ford *et al*, 1982; Galloway *et al*, 1982; Tomlinson, 1982; Booth and Potts, 1983; Barton, 1988 and 1993). Sociologists dominated the second trend. Psychologists' interest in policy making was limited, and directly related to the Warnock Report (1978) and the subsequent 1981 Education Act. Their concern was for the integration of handicapped pupils into the mainstream system, wanting perhaps to ensure that integration did not threaten their position and did not damage their professional status. Sociological interest in special education policy seemed to be an extension of interest in the notion of deviance in education. Sociologists were critical of developments in special education, seriously questioning basic assumptions made by the Warnock Report, such as the notion of 'special needs', and arguing that such suggestions originated from mistaken premises and perpetuated old, undesirable ideas (also Norwich, 1993).

Given the long psychological dominance in special education it is easy to appreciate the sociologists' need to highlight new questions, apparent in the second trend described above. It is, nonetheless, difficult to understand the absence of case study sociological research in special education (with very few exceptions: Sewell, 1981; Atkinson *et al*, 1981). Concentrating on special education pupils rather than structures may appear to the unsuspected to be subscribing to the medical model. Nevertheless, findings originating from this research could prove to be a very useful tool in sociological hands. By examining pupils directly, sociologists could prove that the distinction between normal and special, particularly in the non-normative categories such as maladjustment, is as unjustified and unnecessary, as they argue it to be harmful and ethically questionable.

It is hard to speculate the reasons for the sociologists' reluctance to research special schools. Tomlinson (1982) argues that lack of research in such schools only reflects the hierarchical value placed on different types of school in our society, as research on girls coming much later than research on boys, reflects the inferior position of women in this society. One wonders, however, whether lack of sociological studies in special schools is also a result of a power structure which inhibits access to sociologists, reflecting psychologists' strong hold over these establishments. It might also be proof that psychological theories have penetrated far enough to persuade sociologists that pupils in special schools are beyond their reach and require expertise they do not possess.

Whatever the reasons, ethical questions about special education cannot be fully answered until more is known about children who attend special education premises. The best way to evaluate the ethics for the existence of such units is by examining the need for them. This book wishes to raise questions of ethics, as well as questions regarding the need for and the efficiency of the special education system as it exists in Britain today with particular reference to behaviour problems. It does not propose to do this by merely examining its historical development, its structure and the politics behind it. Before questions of ethics can be answered satisfactorily, a deeper knowledge of pupils attending special schools and units is necessary. By examining their thinking and decision making, we can best identify their differences from or similarities to deviant pupils within the mainstream and judge their placement in a special school or unit. This book will therefore attempt to evaluate the need for a division between mainstream and special education deviance through a comparison of deviant pupils from both sides of the dividing line. Before this can be done, an examination of the development of British legislation on matters of compulsory and special education is necessary. It is also necessary to examine critically physhological and sociological research contributions to deviant behaviour inside and outside mainstream education. Given the complicated nature of the phenomenon, an understanding of both disciplines' theories and findings is necessary before we can evaluate policy on school deviance.

It would be useful to define 'school deviance' at this point. The term, as used in this book, implies types of behaviour that upset and/or hinder classroom or school functioning in any way. Such forms of behaviour can be: breaking the school rules, disobeying, challenging or threatening teachers, disrupting lessons and playing truant. It may also involve arguments and fights with other pupils. Since most pupils can be expected to present such forms of behaviour to some extent at some time during their school careers, let me clarify that the pupils chosen for this study have exhibited deviant behaviour to an extent that has repeatedly brought them to school attention and on occasion resulted in rejection from the mainstream. The forms of misbehaviour used are directly linked with school, and do not involve outside agencies like the police.

The Development of Compulsory Schooling and Special Education in Britain 1870–1988

It is important to study the development of compulsory education in Britain[3], as well as the changing legislative framework of special education, if we are to understand a situation where the majority of pupil referrals to special schools and units[4] takes place during the last years of compulsory schooling.

The first official concern for compulsory education in Britain appeared with the Elementary Education Act 1870. The Act established the school boards, and empowered them to make bye-laws requiring the parents of children of no less than 5 and no more than 13 years of age, to 'cause them to attend school unless there is some reasonable excuse' (Education Acts, 1870–1904). The creation of this decentralized system, which was used in Britain almost unchanged until the Education Reform Act came along, was a flexible political compromise of a government challenged by the opposition and the National Educational League to introduce compulsory education, but faced with a very small number of schools and a very negative public opinion[5].

It took two more steps for compulsory education to become a law: the Education Act 1876, and the Education Act 1880. The Education Act 1876 made parents legally responsible for their child's school attendance:

It shall be the duty of the parent of every child to cause such a child to receive efficient elementary instruction in reading, writing and arithmetic, and if such parent fail to perform such duty, he shall be liable to such orders and penalties as are provided by this Act. (Education Acts, 1870–1904)

The Education Act 1880 made the educational authorities legally responsible for the existence of bye-laws concerning compulsory schooling:

It shall be the duty of the Local Authority of every school district in which bylaws respecting the attendance of children at school under Section 74 of the Education Act 1870 are not the passing of this Act in force, forthwith to make bye-laws under that section for such district. (*Ibid*).

From 1760 onward a number of charity special schools had been functioning, as individuals had expressed an interest in training handicapped pupils. The first official recognition of the problem by the State was signified in 1893, when parents were obliged by law to send some of these children to school along with the others. The first move towards this direction was the Elementary Education (Blind and Deaf Children) Act 1893[6], which, obviously only catered for blind and deaf children:

> The efficient elementary instruction which, under the Elementary Education Act 1876, a parent must cause his child to receive, shall in the case of a blind or deaf child be construed as including instruction suitable to such a child, and the fact of a child being blind or deaf shall not in itself, except in the case of a deaf child under 7 years of age, be a reasonable excuse for not causing the child to attend school, or for neglecting to provide efficient elementary instruction for the child. (Elementary Education (Blind and Deaf Children) Act 1893)

In 1899 two new categories of handicap appeared in the legislation, the 'defective' and 'epileptic' children. The 1899 Act specified that the school authority had the power to determine which children were defective or epileptic and so 'incapable of receiving proper benefit from the instruction in the ordinary public elementary benefit from the instruction in the ordinary public elementary schools' (Elementary Education (Defective and Epileptic Children) Act, 1899). As long as the children were not 'imbeciles' or 'merely dull or backward', the authority, according to the Act, was obliged to give them the opportunity of 'receiving benefit from the instruction in such special classes or schools as are in this Act mentioned'. And the Act continued, specifying the way special classes should function. The term 'special' was already well established by that time. However, the categories included in the term were to undergo big changes. First, the term 'defective', originally referring only to mental defect, was expanded with the 1918 Education Act (The Fisher Act) to include physically defective children. The school leaving age was also raised by the same Act to 14. The legislation regarding the five existing special categories became more detailed and explicit with the Education Act 1921. More categories of handicap were not introduced until 1944.

The 1944 Education Act (1944 EA) was a very important stage in the development of special education in Britain, as it completely reconsidered and restructured the field. According to this Act, the local education authorities (LEAs) were required to make provisions for children who suffered any disability of mind or body, by providing special educational treatment for them: i.e. education by special methods appropriate to their handicap. At the same time the Secretary of State was given the responsibility of 'defining the several categories of pupils requiring special educational treatment, and making provision as to the special methods appropriate for the education of pupils of each category' (1944 EA). The same Act introduced the ideal of education for all children from 5 to 16 years, and demanded an increase of two years in the school leaving age. The purpose of this increase was argued to be 'to deal with the problem of juvenile delinquency, and protect the demoralization of character which arises from premature entry into industry' (Kandel, 1951). The 1944 Education Act gave the Minister the power to raise the school leaving age to 16 as soon as he was satisfied that this was practicable. Even the raise to 15, however, was to be delayed for a few years, because of 'inadequate school accommodation and lack of trained teachers' (Morrish, 1970). The school leaving age was finally raised to 15 in April 1947.

In the Handicapped Pupils and School Health Regulations published in 1945, as a consequence of the 1944 EA, eleven categories of handicapped pupils were listed: (i) blind; (ii) partially sighted; (iii) deaf; (iv) partially hearing; (v) delicate; (vi) diabetic; (vii) educationally subnormal; (viii) epileptic; (ix) maladjusted; (x) physically handicapped; (xi) those suffering from speech defects. Depending on the severity of the handicap, the authority had to provide special educational treatment in special schools, in any school of the authority, or in a school 'not so maintained but suitable'. The authority was also free to establish schools in hospitals or to allow for education to be given in the institution without necessarily the existence of a school. The term 'maladjusted' appeared for the first time in British educational legislation in these Regulations, and so its definition there was of great importance. The definition given by the Handicapped Pupils and Schools Health Regulations in 1945 read: 'Maladjusted are pupils that show evidence of emotional instability or psychological disturbance, and require special educational treatment in order to effect their personal, social or educational readjustment'.

In the years that followed only minor alterations were made regarding special education. In the case of maladjustment, the Report of the Committee on Maladjusted Children (The Underwood Report), published by the Ministry of Education in 1955, was of major importance. This Committee was appointed in 1950 with the remit of investigating the new category and giving its opinion[7]. In its effort to explain what was meant by 'maladjusted child' the Committee attempted to review the arrangements available for treating and preventing maladjustment at that time. They recommended that efforts should be made to prevent the problem arising in the family, and they emphasized the role of psychological treatment. The next step in the development of special education was the Education (Handicapped Children) Act of 1970. The main concern of this Act were hospitalized children, especially the long-stay patients, who were believed not to receive appropriate education. With this Act the responsibility for the education of these children was shifted from the local health authorities, to the LEAs. The Secretary of State was asked to 'make such provisions as appears to him to be necessary or expedient in consequence of the Act' (1970 EA). Also in 1970 another act, the Chronically Sick and Disabled Persons' Act, introduced three new categories of handicap: (i) deaf-blind; (ii) autistic; and (iii) dyslexic, and placed them too under the responsibility of their LEA.

On 1 September 1972 the long-held objective of compulsory education for all pupils from 5 to 16 years, first expressed in the 1944 Education Act, became reality, as the school leaving age was raised to 16. This modification, which came in effect on 1 September 1973, was initially met with apprehension by teachers, who feared that more demands were made on them without more resources becoming available (NAS, 1973). It was nevertheless proclaimed a success by a DES report on education based on a series of school visits made four years later (DES, 1979). In 1976, section 10 of the 1976 Education Act suggested that LEAs should provide special education in normal schools when possible, but the section was never implemented (Tomlinson, 1982).

Much more important was the impact of the 1981 Education Act, which equalled the 1944 Act as a source of radical changes regarding special education. This Act, exclusively concerned with special education, was the government's response to the Warnock Report, published in 1978 by the Warnock Committee, which was set up in 1973 'to inquire into the education of handicapped children and young people'. In line with the Warnock Report's radical new ideas, the existing special education categories were abolished, and the idea of 'special educational needs' was introduced. The aim was to drop the distinction between handicapped and non-handicapped children and so to free special education from the stigma attached to it, indicating that as many as one in five children might need special educational help at some stage of their school career. According to the new proposals, the role and the structure of special education would change, and mainstream schools would undertake educational responsibility for the majority of children that would have been recommended for special schooling under the previous Acts. However, special schools were not destined to disappear, as both the Warnock Report and the 1981 Act recognized that there would still be at least three groups of children who could not benefit from the ordinary school system, and would continue to be in need of special schooling. One of the suggested groups, was 'those (pupils) with severe emotional or behavioural disorders who have difficulty in forming any relationships or whose behaviour is so extreme and unpredictable that it causes disruption in an ordinary school or prevents other children from benefiting from education' (Warnock Report, 1978).

The 1981 Education Act was followed by a number of Acts, (Mental Health Act, 1983; Disabled Persons [Services, Consultation and Representation] Act, 1986; 1988 Education Reform Act; Children Act, 1989; National Health Service and Community Care Act, 1990; 1992 Further and Higher Education Act; 1993 Education Act) all of which are relevant to children and young people with special educational needs (Friel, 1995), but none of which has paralleled its impact. The Education Reform Act of 1988 has naturally exercised the most influence, establishing, as it did, the legal right of access to a common curriculum for all pupils. It has also instigated the most dangers, by focusing on competition between schools and thus by definition excluding children who are not academically competitive. Exclusion rates and statements have both risen (Solity, 1992; Beveridge, 1993), as schools appear unable to compromise the need to cater for all pupils with the demand to be competitive in the market.

The process of the development of special education provision thus becomes clear. Starting as an area provided for by charities, the education of the handicapped soon became a serious State concern and a field of professional specialization. Unorganized and random in the beginning, it reached a high degree of sophistication with the 1944 Education Act. Thirty years later, under the influence of more liberal ideas and financial pressures, this sophisticated structure was dismantled to help accommodate individual needs, bridge the gap between handicapped and non-handicapped pupils and avoid the stigma attached to 'special' pupils. A few years after that, and before such practices had a chance of being developed properly, financial pressures appear to be leading to the pre-1980s situation, victimization of pupils with special needs and segregation from the main educational body.

This has, in brief, been the development of legislation regarding special education in Britain[8]. It is time now to concentrate on the case of maladjustment from 1944 onwards, and examine the development of relevant research. Before proceeding to do so it would be helpful to clarify the term 'maladjusted', its definition and use.

The Term 'Maladjusted'

It is useful to examine the categorization of the phenomenon of maladjustment and the term itself, in order to appreciate early attitudes towards it.

Categorization

From the ten special categories established with the 1944 Education Act[9], eight were concerned exclusively with physical handicaps. One, the 'educationally subnormal' was dealing with intelligence, and one, the 'maladjusted' was addressing problems of personality. The important role of the medical model in dealing with all categories is evident. Where there was a handicap, there was a cause that could be identified, and a treatment that could be applied. In the case of maladjustment, the cause was placed in the individual and its family, and the treatment aimed to produce the pupil's social readjustment (The Underwood Report, 1955).

The term

According to the Oxford English Dictionary, a maladjusted person is one who is 'not satisfactorily adjusted to his environment and conditions of life'. And so maladjustment was by implication a problem which lay in the individual as he/she failed to adjust to a given environment. Also, by implication, the environment itself was considered blameless and was not examined. It is worth remembering here that when the term was introduced a fully developed compulsory schooling system was operating in the country[10], and the school leaving age was 14 years of age, soon to be raised to 15. The age of 14 to 15 apparently created the need for some legal restraint on pupils. This legislation must no doubt have come to aid of teachers who found teenagers difficult to control.

The definition of maladjustment

It is finally worth noting here the vagueness of the definition of maladjustment given in the Handicapped Pupils and Schools Health Regulations[11], especially when bearing in mind its importance for the assessment of maladjustment, and its implications for the education and even the life of pupils diagnosed as maladjusted. A vague term in itself, 'maladjusted' was interpreted and explained with two equally — if not more — vague terms, 'emotional instability' and 'psychological disturbance'. This definition, instead of helping to clarify the term, left it open to a number of interpretations. Categorization of maladjustment as a handicap, interpretation as individual sickness and vagueness of definition, created a powerful combination which could, and did, prove a very effective tool of social control. It gave psychiatrists and psychologists enormous power, as it allowed them to be the only experts able to identify, diagnose and cure maladjustment. In this way, the two professions were established as the true authority in the field, and their work was seen as a philanthropic response to a genuine need and remained beyond criticism for a considerable amount of time (Bowman, 1981).

The Development of Research and Thinking

The section will attempt to summarise existing theories and views, to point out the intentions and inadequacies of specific paradigms, and to indicate why a combination of approaches is necessary for an evaluation of the division between mainstream and special school deviance. Presentation of the studies will follow a chronological order, and will be structured on the basis of study area. The medical model will examine early psychological work in special schools and units, and the educational model will examine their work in the mainstream during the seventies. The presentation of the sociologists' work will follow the opposite order, as their interest first developed in relation to mainstream schools and has only recently expanded to include special education.

The Psychological-Medical Model

Early research and thinking in the area of maladjustment was dominated by psychiatrists and psychologists, and this had a unique influence on the development of provision and treatment methods. The medical model being the only explanation available in the middle forties, became the 'true and only' explanation of maladjustment.

Aetiology

The philosophy underlying the model was mainly based on psychoanalytical theories of the unconscious and disturbed mother-infant relationships[12]. Bad mothering, rejection, early maternal deprivation, lack of love and feeling unwanted were argued to be some of the main causes of maladjustment.

According to Redl and Wineman (1951)[13], a particular kind of behaviour develops in an individual because of the interaction of two sets of variables. One is the impulsive system, which includes impulses, desires and needs and which seems to push the individual in a direction of gratification and goal attainment. The other is the control system, which has the function and the power to decide which desires will be permitted to reach the level of behavioural action. The maladjusted child suffers from lack of control. One part of his[14] ego is helpless. The other part, which is delinquent by definition, can react with great efficiency. It is this delinquent ego that is responsible for the highly manipulative behaviour of the maladjusted child.

Stott (1956) introduced the concept of executive reactions. According to this concept the purpose of the executive reactions is to 'ensure that the basic personality needs of the individual are satisfied, as fully as possible in the circumstances, or to minimize the bad effects when they can not be avoided'. In any unfavourable situation these reactions operate instinctively to produce the necessary readjustment either in the person or in his environment. When the individual finds himself in an unfavourable situation without being able to take any effective counteraction, anxiety arises. The individual becomes fretful and restless, and is unable to settle down and pursue other interests. This restlessness becomes chronic in children who have been subjected to long periods of family insecurity and is common to all stages of maladjustment. Stott later recognized two major causes of maladjustment: environmental reasons, such as broken or unhappy families, and congenital reasons, such as stress or accidents during pregnancy and birth (Stott, 1982).

But Laslett had already stated that it is important to recognize multiple causation of maladjustment (Laslett, 1977). According to Laslett, even if physical or genetic causes contribute to maladjustment, it is usually the absence or the breakdown of the fundamental support systems essential for the satisfactory emotional development of a child, which causes maladjustment. Maladjustment in children is seen by Laslett as a typical result of inadequate responses to a child's basic needs, such as love, safety, self-esteem and self-actualization.

Categories

Various categories of maladjustment were also recognized. Wills (1945) distinguished between punishment seekers and truants; Dockar-Drysdale (1968) introduced the 'frozen' children; and more sophisticated categorizations of maladjusted types of behaviour were developed by Rutter (1967) and Stott (1982). According to Stott maladjustment was expressed in three major forms: (i) withdrawal, shyness from any human attachment for fear of a new rejection; (ii) hostility, arising when the child could no longer bear the anxiety and so brought about the feared breach with his behaviour; and (iii) avoidance, consisting of a compulsion to seek exciting diversions as a means of forgetting the loss of the loved parent figure. The Bristol Social Adjustment Guides, (Stott, 1966) and the Children's Behaviour Questionnaire (Rutter, 1967), were the most common questionnaires used for screening in an effort for early identification and treatment of maladjustment. In both instruments a similar method of categorization was used with a main distinction between conduct and neurotic disorders. Various other criteria were also used to help identify the presence of maladjustment, such as the persistence, the frequency and the severity of the child's symptoms (Rutter, 1975).

Treatment

There was complete agreement between psychologists regarding treatment. Whatever the causes, they argued it was possible to cure maladjustment by providing sincere love and a lot of care. The first aim of the treatment was thus the creation of a secure environment, where the child would feel loved and wanted, his value as a member of the group would be emphasized, and he would stop feeling inferior (Bettelheim, 1955; Stott, 1956). Opportunities for successful relationships were also emphasized, as they could change the child's view of himself and others (Redl and Wineman, 1951; Bettelheim, 1955). Redl and Wineman (1951) also argued that children quite often developed a conflict because of the unexpected new situation. Their repertoire of behaviours did not include any way of dealing with love and respect, and it was of vital importance for the therapist to discharge this conflict at the beginning of the treatment.

The aim of the treatment was to return children to normal life as soon as possible. According to some therapists, a minimum of two years in a special school was required before this could be possible (Wills, 1945; Redl and Wineman, 1951; Bettelheim, 1955; Dockar-Drysdale, 1968). Special schools were mostly residential because the children did not have supportive homes to back up the efforts of a day school, and also because this was a controlled environment facilitating psychological therapy.

The therapists' expectations were not always high:

> We must realize that the sub-culture of the child's personality will always remain weak. The foundation for his personality development was laid in infancy and early childhood. We may be able to strengthen it here and there, but we can not give the child a new subculture. On this basically weak foundation we must try to help the child develop sufficient ego strength and personality integration to enable his limited inner resources to carry him along, even if external conditions fail him. (Bettelheim, 1955)

A number of techniques were used for treatment, based entirely on psychological and medical theories: individual psychotherapy; group therapy; different types of behaviour therapy; counselling and play therapy. Various types of drugs, including tranquilizers and anti-depressants were also used (*Ibid*; Rutter, 1975; Laslett, 1977), although in 1982 Stott condemned their use with maladjusted children as 'unacceptable'.

Evaluation

A dark area in the history of psychological treatment of maladjusted children was the evaluation of the effectiveness of this treatment. As early as 1957 criticism arose about the effectiveness of psychotherapy with children (Levitt, 1957). Levitt examined thirty-five studies showing results of psychotherapy with children, and he stated that his results did not support the hypothesis that recovery from neurotic disorder was facilitated by psychotherapy. The experimental groups, that had been receiving treatment, and the control groups, that had not, showed roughly the same percentage of improvement. Furthermore, time had proven to be an important factor of improvement in the follow up studies.

In 1963 Levitt launched another criticism on the same issue (Levitt, 1963). He stated again that available evaluation studies did not support the hypothesis that psychotherapy facilitates recovery from emotional illness in children. His new data also suggested that the improvement rate was lowest for cases of delinquency and anti-social acting out, and highest for identifiable behavioural symptoms like enuresis and school phobia. He attempted to explain this finding by stating that spontaneous remission rate might also be lower for delinquents and higher for special symptoms, and that the differences in therapy might simply reflect these facts.

In spite of these results Levitt, being a psychologist himself, did not suggest abandonment of psychotherapy with children. Instead, he stated the need for an appropriate way of evaluating the treatment, which would help researchers 'to find the personality or the process which makes for successful treatment'. And although he invited further criticism of the use of psychotherapy, he failed to question whether the treatment was not working because the problem was not entirely, or even not at all, with the 'patient'. Even without doing so, however, he gave rise to important questions which contributed to changes in research direction.

Levitt's was the first in a series of criticisms on provision and treatment for the maladjusted which became increasingly stronger. Criticism initially came from psychologists and psychiatrists (Eisenberg *et al*, 1965; Wright *et al*, 1976), but soon expanded to include educational psychologists (Rutter *et al*, 1979; Galloway and Goodwin, 1979; Topping, 1983), and eventually sociologists (Booth, 1978; Tomlinson, 1981b; Tomlinson, 1982; Ford *et al*, 1982).

As is evident so far, in the medical model deviance is located within the individual pupil who remains detached from his school. The only concession made by some researchers is that these problems are not inherited but created by a stressful home environment. We will now go on to examine a view which also argues for the influence of the environment but defines it in terms of school attended and not home background.

The Educational Model

Having been very influential in the field of school deviance for nearly thirty years, the medical model finally received a severe blow in the seventies, when the research focus was transferred by the psychologists themselves, from the individual child and his home background to the mainstream school, in an effort to identify the institution's role in the development and possible perpetuation of deviance.

One reason for the change of focus appears to have been the medical model's inability to adequately explain and treat school deviance. This inability became increasingly apparent through lack of evidence of success with individual treatment. Psychologists were the first to criticize the medical model and suggest ways of improving it. Lack of satisfaction with the existing medical model demanded new research enquiries. School conditions at the time forced these enquiries in a specific direction. Life circumstances in British homes had considerably improved on those which had inspired the legislation of 1944. Consequently the arguments of the individual pathology approach, heavily relying on poor home and family conditions, were no longer fully applicable, and able to explain the ever increasing need for provisions. In the 1970s, twenty-six years after the 1944 Education Act, the category of maladjustment was well established and the number of provisions for the maladjusted had significantly increased[15]. Even this increased number of facilities was, however, not considered large enough to adequately cater for the needs of the secondary schools. Schools argued that indiscipline was reaching a crisis point, and teachers felt left to cope with it unaided (Gillham, 1981a; Galloway, *et al*, 1982). School worries can be better understood in the context of major changes taking place in secondary education as comprehensive schools were slowly replacing grammar and secondary modern schools.

Pressure from schools coupled with concern for the dramatic increase of facilties for the maladjusted and the disruptive, forced researchers to seek new explanations for deviance which, ironically, questioned the schools themselves. In their search for explanations, researchers became aware of two critical points. First, maladjusted behaviour was a result of interaction between the child and people around it, so the child could not be studied in isolation. Second, many children who presented problems in school did not do so at home (Galloway and Goodwin, 1979).

Due to expansion in provision, the population of special schools and units for maladjusted and disruptive pupils had grown (Bowman, 1981). The individuals studied in the seventies appear on occasion very different from those reported in earlier studies[16]. Expansion in 'objects' of study, as well as change in research attitude, called for new terminology. Researchers in the seventies avoided the term 'maladjusted' and used less ambiguous and more behaviour specific terms instead. So pupils became disruptive, difficult, truant and withdrawn, always described in terms of behaviour within school premises. Children labelled with any of these terms could be found in schools and behavioural units for the maladjusted.

Another characteristic of research of this period was the concentration on secondary school studies. In secondary education school demands for help were acute, and special provisions were increasing to satisfy such demands. Moves toward secondary school studies reflected the weakening influence of psychoanalysis, as researchers no longer considered early identification and diagnosis essential, possibly taking into account the spontaneous remission factor reported by critics of the psychoanalytical method (Robins, 1966 and 1972; Mitchell and Rosa, 1981). These studies, as well as those mentioned earlier, (Levitt, 1957 and 1963; Eisenberg *et al*, 1965; Wright *et al*, 1976) appeared to have allowed behaviouristic ideas to become more dominant, by suggesting that psychotherapy was particularly ineffective with children, and by showing that a big percentage of individuals who had received psychotherapy for acting out behaviour as children, continued their deviant career as adults. They reported that these individuals were more likely to receive in-patient psychiatric treatment as adults, as they presented new psychological problems, and were more likely to be in confrontation with the police, to have a long history of unemployment etc. The behavioural model allowed for hope suggesting that deviant behaviour resulted from bad schooling, owing to inappropriate balance of positive and negative reinforcements. School factors being considered crucial for pupil behaviour, therapy could easily be provided by modifying school ethos.

The first to provide statistical evidence that schools exercise an influence on pupil behaviour, was Michael Power (Power *et al*, 1967). He claimed to find large differences in delinquency rates between secondary schools, which he could not attribute solely to differences in delinquency rates in the school catchment areas. He argued that some of the schools he studied may have helped to prevent delinquency, while others may have in fact contributed to its development. Although Power was severely criticised (Baldwin, 1972) and was refused permission to carry out further research in the same LEA, researchers very quickly focused on the points he made, and produced new results.

Reynolds' research (1976) showed a direct correlation between a school's rank position and the unemployment record of its school leavers. This was important in indicating that aspects of the education system and particular characteristics of schools actively function to create rather than prevent delinquency. Nonetheless Reynolds was particularly anxious to point out that research findings which simply related children from disadvantaged homes with educational failure were inadequate if not unhelpful.

It was Rutter's work that was probably the most influential study of the educational model (Rutter *et al*, 1979), partly because it was conducted in a more systematic way (differences in school intake were better controlled), and partly because, Rutter being an important figure in psychological circles, his book was widely read. In his study of secondary schools in an Inner London Borough it was shown that schools varied considerably with respect to pupil behaviour, attendance, exam success and delinquency rate. The important finding was that differences between schools remained after differences in school intake were taken into account. Variations in the outcome were systematically and strongly associated with characteristics of schools as social institutions, reflecting a causal relationship. This suggested that schools had an important influence on pupil behaviour and attainment.

In a study carried out a few years later (Galloway *et al*, 1982), the evidence also pointed towards the importance of school processes as critical variables both in development and management of disruptive behaviour. Without denying the severity of problems presented by pupils who were eventually placed outside the mainstream school, Galloway and his colleagues emphasized the role of the processes within school in the prevalence and severity of disruptive behaviour. Galloway, like Rutter, concluded that disruptive behaviour within a school reflects the unwritten and often unspoken attitudes and practices within the school, the 'school ethos'.

As a consequence of these research findings mainstream school came under attack. Teacher responsibilities towards pupils were emphasized, and suggestions for improvement of school structure and teaching strategies were offered to minimize deviance. The educational psychologists' role was reassessed (Topping, 1983; Gillham, 1981b). Good school environment, consistent teacher behaviour and the role of the teacher as a behaviour model was stressed. Teacher personality and behaviour towards pupils was emphasized. Classroom processes were closely examined and attention was paid to management strategies used by teachers (Corrie *et al*, 1982). Advice for more efficient classroom management also became available (Laslett and Smith, 1984).

Slowly teachers appeared to replace parents in bearing the sole responsibility for pupil misbehaviour. Attention on classroom processes inevitably put a lot of pressure on teachers, as they were held responsible for labelling pupils as 'maladjusted' and expelling them from the mainstream. On the positive side, it drew attention to teacher working conditions and the problems faced as a consequence of pupil misbehaviour. Having at first received the blame for pupil behaviour, teachers were suddenly perceived to be in need of help, and seen as new research targets. Asked what caused them concern in the classroom they identified four major problems: (i) controlling pupil behaviour; (ii) achieving curriculum goals; (iii) contributing to pupil learning; and (iv) keeping pupil interest alive (Corrie *et al*, 1984). From this point onwards a new research path was open, that of 'teacher stress' (Kyriacou and Sutcliffe, 1977), as the excessive amount of different skills required from teachers became apparent. Seen from this perspective, the need for assistance with difficult pupils became evident and external provisions were occasionally thought of as the most desired form of assistance.

By concentrating heavily on school the educational model indicated its belief that school can influence deviant pupil behaviour utilising expertise and skills already available in its premises (Galloway *et al*, 1982). Deviant pupils were considered to be at the end of a continuum, their behaviour resulting from confusion, misunderstanding, displeasure or lack of control. Maximizing school efficiency in an effort to satisfy all parties involved appeared thus to be the main goal of this model.

We now turn to a radically different tradition of educational research which does not subscribe to the view that misbehaviour in school requires treatment, but rather sees it as a conscious individual or group response to an authoritarian regime. This tradition perceives special education not as a legitimate (successful or unsuccessful) means of helping individual pupils, but as an ethically disputed method of social control.

Sociological Models

This section will attempt to present briefly studies of deviance in mainstream schools based on a sociological tradition. It will deal with a range of approaches which will appear later on in this book when behaviour of mainstream and special unit pupils will be described.

The sociological concept of school as a social system was introduced in the late sixties when the idea of school as an institution was beginning to dominate the psychological tradition. The two concepts had a very different background. Sociological theories of the school system had their roots in Emile Durkheim's idea that deviance is not irrational, but can be seen as a response to specific social circumstances. Researchers were not interested in passing judgment on pupil behaviour, but rather in understanding the logic of this behaviour and the thinking behind it. Within the sociological perspective, the story was told, as far as that was possible, from the pupils' point of view. Schools were questioned as independent organizations with their own goals and values. Forms of deviance examined in this context were very similar to those of the previous model. The pupils dealt with regularly broke rules imposed by school or teachers, were disruptive in the classroom, often to the extent of being rude or threatening towards teachers, played truant and missed occasional lessons or whole school days. Three main models were followed by sociologists in their school research. The adaptation model, originating from Merton's work, the sub-cultural model developed by Albert Cohen, and the interactionist approaches.

The adaptation model

The first to use a sociological theory of deviance for research in a British school was Wakeford (1969). Using Merton's adaptation of the original Durkheim theory of anomie, Wakeford distinguished five principal ways of adaptation for the pupils of a boarding school: conformity; colonization; retreatism; intransigence and rebellion. According to Merton's theory (Merton, 1957), there are, on the one hand, the culturally defined goals, purposes and interests that are the legitimate objectives of society members. On the other hand there is an element of cultural structure which defines, regulates and controls the acceptable means of reaching these objectives. Individuals are rational beings and can make choices. They may either accept or reject the cultural goals and they may either accept or reject the institutional means. On the basis of this distinction between goals and means and acceptance and rejection, five models of adaptation arise. Wakeford's categories of adaptation were somewhat different from the original Merton categories. According to Wakeford, a pupil can be a conformist, in which case he accepts both the goals and the means of the school and tries to do his best. He can also adopt a colonizing attitude, which combines an ambivalence about formal rules and regulations with an indifference to school goals. Alternatively he can be a retreatist, where he shows indifference or even rejection for school goals and means without replacing them with anything else. Intransigence would consist of a clear rejection of school means accompanied by an indifference to its goals. In the final case, that of rebellion, the pupil rejects both the goals and the means of the school, and substitutes them with his own goals and means.

With Woods (1979) the adaptation model became richer, with the introduction of new models of conformity. Woods found Wakeford's typology weak, for while it allowed twenty-four spaces for non-conformity, it only provided one for conforming adaptations. According to Woods, when applied to a possibly benevolent institution like school, conformity is not necessarily restricted to 'sucking up' or 'creeping', as

Wakeford had suggested. Woods named the negative compliance Wakeford referred to, 'ingratiation'. He argued that pupils who adopt this mode show 'indulgence' to the school's goals and means, and they are the ones Wakeford called 'creeps'. A more moderate response to goals and means he called 'identification'. Identification leads to another form of conformity called 'compliance'. There are two types of compliance, the optimistic compliance, that comes from an air of hope and expectancy from new pupils, and the instrumental compliance, where pupils are not interested in the subjects themselves, but in the opportunities the subject offers them. Another form of conformity, brought back from the original typology of Merton by Woods, is that of 'ritualism', where pupils accept the fact that school has certain official norms of behaviour, and they just conform. The last kind of conformity mentioned by Woods is 'opportunism'. This is a 'trying out' phase before settling into another style of adaptation during which conformity represents the basic mode. Woods made it clear that most pupils display varying responses to schools, teachers and subjects, and do not follow only one way of adaptation.

The adaptation model refined by Wakeford and Woods, although representing a sociological point of view, pointed heavily to the individual. Pupils were believed to be rational and free individuals able to make their own choices. They were all considered to have equal opportunities for choice, regardless of background and life outside school, and were seen as simply responding to demands made on them by the institution.

The sub-cultural model

The sub-cultural model went a step further, recognizing the importance of pupil social background in choice of adaptation form followed within school. The idea of subcultural grouping originated from Cohen's work on Chicago gangs (Cohen, 1955), but the model was redeveloped for use within school as an alternative to Merton's theory. Cohen originally believed that — as Merton had argued — everybody was trying to achieve the values stated by society. It soon became obvious to him that these values were not dictated by a random sample of the population, but rather the minority in power, which was the middle class. These values therefore were not of a neutral nature. They were middle class values. The question arose whether working class people internalized such values. Cohen, unable to fit delinquency in any of Merton's categories of adaptation, argued that working class boys were almost by definition unable to succeed in middle class terms, because they lacked the necessary resources. This inability to succeed produced a status frustration which led to a reaction against conventional middle class values. Academic success being the most important value of this kind in school, pupils reacted to it and created a subculture within which status was derived from factors other than academic success.

Differences between the adaptation and sub-cultural models are apparent in the implications these theories have when applied to school. Wakeford argued that there is an inherent truth in school values, and a pupil has a choice to accept or reject them. Whilst according to the sub-cultural model, the individual might have a completely different code of values and might be very limited indeed in his/her choice. Yet similarities with Wakeford's last category, rebellion, can be detected, the difference being that in Wakeford's category the decision is taken rationally and in a social vacuum.

Hargreaves (1967) was the first researcher to apply the sub-cultural model to a British school. His study attempted to explore the importance of the school social system, and especially the structure of peer groups, in relation to the educational process. In that effort he was faced with the phenomenon of a strong association between low academic streams and high deviance rates. Hargreaves tried to explain this phenomenon by arguing that because of the streaming system a sub-cultural differentiation takes place in school. All this occurs in the context of adolescence, at a time when the individual is trying to find an identity rejecting parental and teacher authority, and has a strong need of peer support. In the middle of all this uncertainty, the low stream boys in Hargreaves' school perceived a status deprivation within school, and realized the implications of the extension of this low status into their future careers. Their response to this failure was to create their own sub-culture, where achievement of a high status was still possible. Hargreaves' work showed very clearly how school facilitates pupil realization of their deprived status by failing them twice: first in the 11+ examination, (a result that led them to a secondary modern school), and later by placing them in low streams. The school also encouraged formation of sub-cultural groupings by forcing pupils within streams to socialize only with each other and by imposing on them the worst teachers. Hargreaves concluded that the existence of significantly larger number of deviant pupils in the low streams was as much the result of school and peer group influence, as it was the result of accumulation of a certain personality type in each specific stream.

Subscribing to the same theory, Lacey (1970) tried to examine what happens in a grammar school where all pupils are by definition high achievers in academic work. The result was fascinating. Lacey showed how the school facilitated formation of an anti-school sub-culture out of an initially very conformist group of pupils. He used two terms to describe the phenomenon: differentiation and polarization. Differentiation in Lacey's terms meant separation and ranking of pupils according to a multiple set of criteria constituting the value system of a grammar school. The differentiation process was carried out by the school system in the face of teachers. Polarization was a process which took place within the student body, and was partly a result of differentiation, but was also influenced by the pupils themselves and had an autonomy of its own.

The process of change in the development of pupil sub-culture as Lacey described it was very dramatic. Pupils, who had never experienced school failure before and were happy and proud to be amongst the best of their primary schools, faced with harsh competition and failure for the first time developed emotional and neurotic disorders. These were expressed by symptoms such as bursting into tears, refusing to go to school, having sleepless nights, bedwetting, truanting, or even suffering from mild epilepsy fits. These reactions were evident mainly in the first year and to a lesser extent in the beginning of the second year. Lacey states that the true anti-school group started to emerge in the second year, and developed markedly in the third and fourth years.

In the late seventies the 11+ exam lost its importance as comprehensive education became more popular and spread throughout the country. Given the new circumstances Hargreaves' and Lacey's studies ceased to be topical, and there was a need for research in the new setting. Ball (1981) attempted to study the development of sub-cultural groupings in a comprehensive school. Interestingly enough, Beachside Comprehensive had tried to replace the streaming system of the old secondary modern with a similar banding system. Ball discovered that the most important consequence of the introduction of the banding system was the creation of discipline and control problems in the lower bands as pupils were expected to perform specific kinds of behaviour. Bad classroom behaviour appeared to be reinforced by the banding and non-existent in mixed ability classes.

Differentiation of pupil behaviour between lessons was so obvious that the headteacher admitted there was more anti-school feeling in the low bands than there had been in the low streams before the school had become comprehensive. Pupils were classified into bands on the basis of their academic ability and it was obvious, according to Ball, that the processes of polarization and differentiation were taking place in Beachside Comprehensive. Evidence for this was the specific distribution of friendship choices, the existence of a clique membership and the changes within it, and also changes in distribution of academic success. Teacher perception of pupils was clearly influenced by pupil behaviour in the classroom, and classroom behaviour often appeared to be of greater significance than academic performance in pupil ranking. The existence of mixed ability classes in school enabled Ball to make a comparison between pupil behaviour in them and pupil behaviour in the banded classes. He found that differences between the two were so striking, that they had initiated amongst staff support for mixed ability classes in the hope to facilitate classroom control.

Both sociological explanations examined so far, view deviant behaviour in school as a normal and legitimate pupil response to school authority. Both models accept that motivation for appropriate pupil behaviour comes from subscription to academic success, and is generalized in different contexts, academic success being considered as the only value of the school system. Both models also accept that pupils have some choice, the only difference being that the sub-cultural model accepts the possibility of a pupil sub-culture created quite independently from the official school culture and functioning as an alternative to it. There is, however, a sociological approach that does not consider academic failure the sole reason for the creation of a pupil sub-culture, and this we shall now examine.

Interactionism

The third main model of sociological research of deviant behaviour in school is interactionism. Interactionism arose as a reaction to the two previous models and their generalizations concerning pupil orientations. Werthman (1963) was probably the first researcher to argue that in the school he studied there was no relationship between academic performance and deviance. Deviance seemed to take place in some classes but not in others, and with some teachers but not with others, outside the classroom as well as inside. In order to answer the questions arising, Werthman tried to explore the pupils' own subjective views of school, leaving aside school goals and values. What he found was that pupils were organized in gangs which included pupils of various academic abilities who did not accept teacher authority a-priori, but on the basis of certain criteria. Describing these criteria Werthman emphasized the importance of the teacher being 'straight', meaning showing respect for the gang's autonomy, and restricting him/herself to teaching situations.

Gannaway (1976) expanded on Werthman's idea by building a decision making model of the way pupils evaluate teachers. According to this model pupils ask three main questions about their teachers: (i) can the teacher keep order?; (ii) can he/she have a laugh?; (iii) does he/she understand pupils? If the teacher passes all three tests successfully, the only demand remaining to be satisfied is how interesting and relevant their lesson is.

Furlong (1976) contributed to the movement by introducing the concept of 'interaction sets'. His concern was that pupil behaviour was not rigidly structured and thus a more flexible approach was needed in order to understand it. According to Furlong, the pupils who constituted the interaction set perceived what was happening in the classroom in a very similar way and communicated their perception to each other. He stated that interaction sets changed rapidly as the situation changed, and he concluded that pupil interaction was not a product of an overall orientation to school, but varied according to a particular context.

Turner (1983) tried to combine the adaptation model[17] with the interactionist approach, and he introduced the concept of pupil goals. He accepted Furlong's idea that pupil actions are likely to vary significantly depending on the context and the circumstances, but argued that each pupil has a main positive or negative orientation to school. Turner emphasized the importance of motivation in pupil decision making, and the importance of the decision making process in the quest for the pupil's overall orientation to school. He stated that knowledge of pupil long and short term goals is necessary before a pupil can be taken as accepting, rejecting, or being ambivalent about school goals. Pupil orientations change, he argued, as their careers develop, but even so pupils do not accept or reject school values in total. Instead they react to them selectively on the basis of their own goals and interests. Of considerable importance, according to Turner, is the context where the decision making process takes place. Decisions are not taken in a social vacuum, and home background exercises significant influence on them. School official policies and informal pressures operating within it are also of major importance for pupil decision making. Turner concluded that all these factors provide a framework around which pupils negotiate their school careers, and, although outcomes are uncertain, it can be shown that some outcomes are far more probable than others.

The labelling theory

In the context of interactionism a new theory developed rested on the assumption that deviance only becomes important when recognized and named as such. It was argued (Becker, 1963) that all pupils break the school regulations at some point or other, but only those who are perceived and defined as doing so by someone in power, usually a teacher, become deviant. According to this theory particular pupils and behaviours are picked out for special treatment (Kitsuse, 1962). Lemert (1967) introduced the concepts of primary and secondary deviance. Primary deviance occurs when rule breaking goes unnoticed and can be easily normalized. In the case of secondary deviance, the child is detected and labelled as deviant. What is important here is that he/she accepts the deviant label, makes it part of his/her identity and lives up to it. An important consequence of the labelling process is thus a drastic change in pupil identity. Another consequence is that under the weight of the stigma the pupil turns for support to pupils that bear a similar label, and a deviant sub-culture is born.

Hargreaves and his colleagues (Hargreaves *et al*, 1975) describe the factors that lead some pupils to 'stand out' from the rest, and be given a 'typing'. The first factor is the 'sibling phenomenon', which occurs when the teacher has taught one of the pupil's siblings in the past. A second factor is staffroom discussion, where teachers receive from each other information about a particular pupil. A third is a particular problem the child might have which may be widely disseminated among teachers. All these factors can make a child who might have just started school and would otherwise have been treated like the others, 'stand out' from his/her peers, and attract school staff attention. The fact that a pupil 'stands out' does not, however, in itself make them deviant. Deviant pupils, according to Hargreaves and his colleagues, emerge as distinct individuals, each one with his/her own deviant methods and particular motives. Yet they all are 'trouble makers', for they all present teachers with practical problems. Teachers acquire a certain knowledge about these pupils, based on multitudinous events, most of which are forgotten, and built over time into a coherent and resistant opinion. It is this opinion that is influential for pupil identity.

Bird (1980), however, showed that the influence of a label is significantly minimized by factors like school size, sophistication of understanding of pupil needs by staff and the position school occupies in the pupil's life. She emphasized the importance of academic labelling, as academic opinions are more systematically communicated to pupils through bands, sets or simply grades for their work, and are therefore more likely to influence pupil identity.

This has been a brief and selective account of sociological studies of deviant behaviour in school. The difference from the psychological approaches is clear, as these researchers do not judge pupil behaviour but are rather interested in understanding and explaining it. They also show that deviance is not an inherent condition, but rather a pupil response to school. This view, very different from that of the medical model, retains a similarity with the educational model, as it points to school environment for an explanation of pupil behaviour. A major difference from that model is that sociologists do not seek to influence or 'improve' pupil behaviour, as they do not consider this behaviour to be a result of misunderstanding or lack of control, but believe it to be conscious and deliberate.

There are, of course, sociological studies of deviance which adopt a completely different viewpoint and interpret deviance as a product of social class, race or gender response to school (Fuller, 1980; Willis, 1977; Rex and Tomlinson, 1979; Corrigan, 1979; Furlong, 1984). Such approaches derive, as Furlong (1985) in his critical account puts it, 'from neo-Marxist work in which education is seen in the context of the "social and cultural reproduction" of society', and appear rather distant from explanations of school deviance presented so far. We shall therefore refrain from presenting them here and comparing them to approaches already examined.

Having examined sociological studies of deviance in the mainstream school, we should now turn to sociological studies dealing with deviance outside the mainstream system.

Sociological Studies of Special Education

Finding sociological studies which deal with special school deviance, to parallel those of the psychologists mentioned earlier in this chapter, is not an easy task. For, as stated in the beginning of the chapter, sociologists have never attempted case studies in special education premises similar to those they conducted in the mainstream. This has already been explained as a result of the dominance of psychologists in these areas, and as an outcome of the fact that sociologists were interested in posing and answering different questions about special education.

Sociology of special education, however, does exist. A new field, it has already raised important questions and has provided considerable cause for thought by challenging a very strong status quo and exposing another side of a discipline which had for long been respected as purely altruistic and humanitarian. Sociologists have argued that special education is nothing but a method of social control, and have attempted a critical examination of its development in an effort to prove this (Bowman, 1981; Tomlinson, 1982).

Sociologists were first attracted to special education by the dramatic increase of special provisions which in the seventies forced psychologists to direct their attention to the mainstream. At approximately the same time the two disciplines became interested in what was until then each other's field. Sharp and Green (1975) appeared to be the first sociologists to focus on 'peculiar' children, the type that psychologists had been concentrating on until then. Their aim was to show, by concentrating on individual pupils, how classroom processes structure pupils' social identities, and how these identities are the initial stages of the institutionalization of social selection. They suggested that early success and failure in the classroom is of crucial importance for entering the occupational structure, and hence the social class structure, at different levels. And they concluded, like Bernstein five years before them (Bernstein, 1970), that education can not be expected to 'make a difference' until the secret messages about social position that teachers unwillingly pass on to their pupils are controlled and eliminated. Sharp and Green's main interest was not in special education, but rather in the mainstream, in an effort to show that hopes of comprehensivization could not be materialized unless more radical measures were taken. They did, however, do a major service to special education, and that is why they are mentioned here, as their individual approach, different from those of

Hargreaves (1967) and Lacey (1970), produced very detailed in-depth case studies of specific children. By presenting a well argued case of rational explanation for these children's behaviour, they pioneered a new way of interpreting deviant behaviour on an individual level. They showed that types of behaviour which had for a long time been considered to be beyond reason, could be interpreted in a perfectly valid rational mode.

Perhaps unsurprisingly, teachers were the first to feel the need to publicly show that the children they were working with, were, given a chance interesting, co-operative and happy individuals (Wakefield, 1977; White and Brockington, 1978; Grunsell, 1978, 1980a and 1980b; White, 1980). In this way they were the first to imply that it was the school and not the pupils that were at fault. Writers such as Wakefield, White, Brockington and Grunsell, were not simply interested in describing their work with children, and the children's improvement, but gave lively portraits of the pupils, which generated interest within sociological circles, and encouraged psychologists to question their previous assumptions. In this respect their writings, written on the basis of experience rather than research, and addressed to the general public, contributed greatly to diverting research to a different path and influenced psychologists to turn to the mainstream, and sociologists to concentrate on special schools. Some of their suggestions however, by emphasizing the role of special centres and recommending the establishment of more such units and schools (White and Brockington, 1978), did not contribute much to the cause of sociological notions against separatism.

Galway (1979) appears to have been the first person working in special education premises to have requested the opinion of the pupils in a special unit about that unit. In her paper, which bears the 'provocative' title 'What pupils think of special units', Galway unashamedly reported the pupils' own point of view, although very briefly. Tattum (1982), by categorizing, as well as describing, the opinions of pupils attending a special unit, went even further. He argued that, contrary to prevailing theories, the pupils' behaviour in school had been rational. He attempted to highlight this rationality by presenting the pupils' own views and explanations of their actions. Tattum was thus the first researcher to interpret deviant behaviour outside the mainstream according to a sociological view of deviance. For that he needed to accept pupil accounts at face value, and so he did. This is an interesting approach, for it is of course vital to treat the pupils as rational beings if one is to offer a rational explanation for their deviant behaviour; only a psychological approach which is interested in arguing that pupils have no control over their behaviour could possibly interpret their accounts in any different way. It does, however, present some methodological problems. In mainstream schools the researcher has plenty of opportunity to verify pupil accounts, either by direct observation or through teacher interviews. Such possibilities are limited for a researcher in a special unit when enquiring about events that have taken place in the mainstream. He/she has to rely heavily on pupil accounts. Pupils placed in a special unit however have every reason to justify their position, by lying if necessary. So, it is not enough — if one is interested in discovering the reasons for the pupils' placement there — to ask the pupils. A variety of other methods, such as pupil observation and teacher interviews in the unit, as well as consultation of school records, are necessary in order to overcome the constraints of post-hoc interviewing. I will later suggest a model which tries to overcome these methodological problems. More recently Cooper (1993) conversed with 'deviant pupils' in residential special schools. He claims that the pupils found the experience rewarding and personally enriching, having experienced improvement in their self-esteem and having improved their sense of control over their lives. This may well be so, but the danger of pupil rationalization needs to be kept in mind. Furthermore, rewarding and enriching experiences is what these pupils should have been offered in the mainstream school. An education system is failing badly if pupils are required to move onto special schools in order to achieve such educational experiences. We should, however, return to sociologists' contribution to special education

Although studies like the ones mentioned above greatly facilitated a shift from a pathological explanation of deviant behaviour to an understanding of it, sociological case studies of special schools and pupils never appeared, as sociologists continued to remain distant from case studies in special education. Their interest, when expressed, focused on decision and policy making in special education (Booth, 1978; Barton and Tomlinson, 1981; Bowman, 1981; Ford *et al*, 1982; Tomlinson, 1982). By questioning the historical development of special education, its establishment as a discipline, and the struggles behind policy making and the formulation of recent legislation, sociologists attempted to expose the inadequacies of the medical model which had dominated the field until then. They also tried to expose the politics behind what was until then widely recognized as a humanitarian, benevolent and altruistic approach. This was a novel method of studying special education, and it requires particular attention.

Coming at a time when the medical model, having dominated the area for over thirty years had achieved no apparent results — except for multiplying the number of special provisions, and thus perhaps securing the experts' position, the criticism of the medical model approach was necessary and refreshing, if not welcome[18]. It was necessary because the principles on which the medical model rested had never before been challenged, and it was refreshing because it allowed for new theories and novel approaches. Sociology has undoubtedly an important role to play in special education and its participation is vital for the establishment of a dialogue and a balance. It is possible, however, that in their effort to challenge the practices and the implications of the medical model, sociologists sometimes went too far, criticizing both policy and practice in special education with equal severity. It is, of course, necessary to point out that special education pioneers were not faultless, and personal ambitions played an important role in their work. It is, however, rather harsh to misconstrue their motivation examining their actions retrospectively in the light of what we know today. Finally, it is very problematic to offer criticism but no alternative options to an applied area with urgent needs such as special education. To demonstrate these points more fully I will examine some of the arguments used by sociologists in their questioning of policy and practice in special education.

In their critical accounts of the development of special education as a discipline, Bowman (1981) and Tomlinson (1982) point out that the education of the handicapped and the disabled was initially mainly vocational. They later use this argument to support the suggestion that the motivation of the businessmen who initially ran special schools was based on profit expectations. They also argue that the motivation behind the later decision of the State to establish special schools was based on an effort to decrease the amount of State money spent on the handicapped. This is most probably true. It is interesting, however, to compare the Victorian view of 'training the handicapped to earn a living' with the modern view of independent living for the handicapped and the disabled, put forward by unions for the disabled. It is perhaps reasonable to argue that a century or two ago disabled people had the same wish for self-sufficiency they have now. Seen in the light of this comparison the idea of 'forced work' could be interpreted as a coincidence of interests between the State and the handicapped, the main difference being the possibly unfavourable terms of conditions of work.

Another argument used as proof for lack of humanitarian aims in the development of special education, is the professional conflicts that are shown to have influenced the decision making and the legislation of special education in Britain (Ford *et al*, 1982; Tomlinson, 1982). This, although undoubtedly true, is not a phenomenon unique to special education. It could furthermore be argued that such conflicts were not merely those of professional interests, but rather differences of opinion and philosophy. This phenomenon would not be surprising in a new field where ethical dilemmas are so sharp.

Tomlinson (1982) also argues that psychologists usually fail to take into account the lack of 'cultural capital' when categorizing children of lower classes as deviant. This way they overlook the fact that working class children are severely disadvantaged when competing in spheres where middle class resources are needed. A counter-argument could be that it is perhaps the lack of 'cultural capital' one tries to compensate for, when offering 'training' or even 'therapy', and talking about empowering pupils with new skills. It is perhaps valid to argue that the role of special education, in a competitive society where achievement plays such an important role, might well be to bridge the 'cultural capital' gap, and ensure that all pupils have similar opportunities to achieve. Psychologists would consequently be accused of prescribing to a given type of society and not attempting to change it, which, of course, would be true. May we then accuse caring professions of helping to maintain the status quo? Should we abolish them in order to facilitate social change? These questions are beyond the scope of this book, but need to be asked here to indicate the complexity of the issues we are dealing with.

Because of this complexity criticism should perhaps concentrate on special education practice rather than motivation. The motives of psychologists as a profession could well have been altruistic and humanitarian[19]. The profession can still be held responsible for very serious mistakes, such as the use of descriptive terms as normative ones, and the degradation of functional provisions to discriminatory and disadvantaging facilities, and also for their reluctance to cooperate with other disciplines to solve the problem at hand. However sociologists, by being so critical of the motivation and intentions of those subscribing to the medical model, have not facilitated the discussion either. Matters of politics and power in special education, like those raised by Barton and Tomlinson (1981) (see also Tomlinson 1981b and 1982), are of major importance, but do not necessarily prove the guilt of the motivation behind all those subscribing to the medical model. Furthermore, the pupils' own viewpoint is an important aspect. Instead of being ignored, as it has been so far, it should be examined before statements about the pupils' 'position in the receiving end of the decision making' (Barton and Tomlinson, 1981), or their powerlessness (Tomlinson, 1982) are to be considered of any value. As Sewell (1981) points out, 'structural explanations which show segregation as a form of class or ethnic repression might have a general validity, but they do not do justice to the full complexity of individual cases'. Neither does any method so far. Let us see if we can find a methods which does.

We have now examined a wealth of research paradigms which have dealt with deviant pupil behaviour inside as well as outside the mainstream school. It is evident, from the diversity of the explanations and the severe criticism between disciplines, that serious problems are still at hand relating to issues of special education policy, and particularly to the division between mainstream and special education deviance. This appears to be owing to a lack of communication between the two disciplines which have been dealing with the issue. Those who have suffered as a result are mainly the pupils themselves, whom both disciplines appear to have wanted to help. Since special education is an applied field, research into it should have realistic goals which aim to solve the very real problems facing pupils and teachers involved in it. Cooperation and exchange of ideas is necessary for this. It seems that an alternative approach, empowered with the strengths of both disciplines, but free of their misconceptions, is needed in order to evaluate the existing policies. The next section will attempt to present such an approach.

Post 1981 Education Act

The 1981 Education Act was a landmark in British educational legislation for children with special needs for three reasons. First, because it dealt exclusively with them and was the first Education Act since 1944 to pay such detailed attention to their needs. Second, because it relied heavily on the recommendations of the 1978 Warnock Report and introduced dramatic changes to the concept of special needs and a specific assessment procedure for dealing with children with such needs by the school. Third, because by placing the child in the centre of the assessment process, and by giving the child and its parents a voice, it gave a significant boost to studies which aimed at listening to what the children had to say. This is obvious in the literature after the 1981 Act. The Act itself clearly states that 'The feelings and perceptions of the child should be taken into account and the concept of partnership should, wherever possible, be extended to older children and young persons.' (1981 Education Act) thus legitimizing, for the first time in the history of special education, the pupil's voice. A number of studies looking closely into children's thinking in a variety of settings follows, (Armstrong, Galloway and Tomlinson, 1993; Lloyd-Smith, 1993; Garner, 1994). Joint conclusion: neither children nor parents are seriously listened to and taken into account, despite the new legislation. This is not just true for Britain. America (Ware, 1994) and Cyprus (Phtiaka, 1996) have similar incidents to exhibit where parents, or children, or both are put aside and crucial decisions are taken on their behalf. It is perhaps more striking in Britain, however, where conflicting pieces of legislation are concurrently produced, and ambivalence is created and maintained by conflicts within a given piece of legislation. Deviant behaviour is a case in point as the 1981 Education Act 'specifically excludes from the statementing process those pupils who are referred to special units on the grounds of their problem behaviour in school' (Lloyd-Smith, 1993, p. 23), and the Draft Circular of 1993 draws a distinction between exclusion and special needs (Garner, 1994).

A New Model

As stated above, a pupil's transfer from mainstream to special education has been interpreted by researchers in two main ways. On the one hand, it has been seen as a necessity provoked by behaviour disturbance in the person, be this due to genetic or environmental factors. This is the view that has mainly been supported by psychologists. On the other hand, sociologists have on the whole interpreted this transfer as a political decision forced on a defenceless and powerless individual. It has been argued so far that each one of these arguments alone is inadequate and oversimplistic as a single explanation of the phenomenon, because each one has been arrived at through the examination of only one set of variables. Both will therefore be challenged.

It is worthwhile to outline here the process of the research undertaken, and to examine how theoretical reservations about the validity of either view came to be confirmed by the research findings. The nature of the study described in this book has been primarily exploratory. The research question of what the differences between deviant pupils within and without mainstream school are, if any, initially left room for a number of possible explanations. It was, however, largely expected that the deviant pupils inside and outside the mainstream would exhibit very similar behaviour patterns and would be very much in control of their own behaviour and fate. The findings formed a far more complex picture. It was found, and it will be shown, that deviant behaviour in school does, contrary to what psychologists argue, have its own logic when seen from the pupils' point of view. Some pupils will be seen to be fully aware of the regulations and restrictions limiting them. It will be shown that when they break them, they do so for a particular reason. Their behaviour can not therefore be considered irrational. These pupils appear to be in control, and their referral to outside agencies, far from being imposed on them, will be seen to be consciously provoked by the pupils themselves.

It will also be shown, however, that, in contrast with what sociologists believe, there is a number of deviant pupils who can not be said to be in control of their own behaviour, as they do not appear to be at all aware of the consequences of this behaviour, and seem to have no long-term plans to aim towards. These pupils will indeed be seen to be in need of help, although it will be argued that outside agencies are far from ideal for providing this help.

It will, therefore, become evident that it is as inadequate, unsatisfactory and patronizing to argue the pupils' point for them in ignorance of their opinion (Tomlinson, 1982), as it is to dismiss them as ill (Stott, 1982). Deviant pupils within and without the mainstream have very strong and interesting points to make regarding their behaviour, and they should be asked. These pupils are a very important source of insight into the thinking behind deviant behaviour in school, even if there is a need for their views to be carefully evaluated. To discover what pupils themselves think and how they explain their own behaviour one has to ask them first. After that, in order to ensure against lying or memory failure, it is necessary, to scrutinize their accounts and measure them up against all other evidence. This will indicate if they are rationally justified or simply a product of a rationalization process.

Research carried out in a mainstream or a special school alone, cannot, because of its limitations, offer adequate explanations to questions regarding the dividing line between the two. Even so, a comparison between the two has never been attempted. Researchers have not been interested in defining the line, either because they have taken it for granted, or because they have totally rejected it. This line appears nonetheless to be the cause of serious concern amongst psychologists and sociologists alike. It is suggested that by concentrating on it, very crucial questions can be answered. For this, research in mainstream as well as special school premises, and direct comparison between the two is needed. This method, despite the difficulties it entails, is argued here to be the best for exploring differences in behaviour of deviant pupils inside and outside the mainstream, and so defining the limits of the dividing line. The findings could facilitate understanding between the two schools of thought in this area. They could also help justify the need or otherwise for the existence of special educational provisions for problems of behaviour, and possibly explain the reasons for the spectacular recent expansion of the latter. This study is a step towards this direction and it has three main aims:

(i) To identify the similarities and the differences between deviant pupils on either side of the dividing line.

(ii) By discovering the extent of these differences or similarities, to assess the justification of the division between mainstream and special school deviance.

(iii) If the case be proved of behaviour differences (or simply behaviour problems) which need to be catered for, to question how this could be best achieved.

It is necessary here to summarize the theoretical model within which these three questions will be answered.

Individual children arrive at secondary school[20] possessing specific personality traits, different cultural and ethnic backgrounds, and a variety of primary school experiences. It appears that at this point specific factors play an important role in increasing or decreasing the individual pupil's possibilities of being treated as an age pupil. Such vulnerability factors appear to be the gender of the pupils, their ~~cultural~~ and home background, and their previous school experience. The ethos of the particular secondary school pupils enter can also contribute to the vulnerability of their position. These factors seem to exercise an important influence on pupils' school life for two reasons: first because they can direct their opinion about school (in general and in particular) to a certain path, and second because they can provoke a specific kind of response from teachers. The quality of these factors can increase or decrease the risk of the pupils 'being noticed and picked out'. It has been shown (ILEA Research and Statistics Report), that belonging to an ethnic minority group[21], or being working class, increases the probabilities of a clash between a pupil and a school, and a consequent referral. Being a boy, or coming from a broken home, or even attending a school with low behaviour tolerance, are factors which appear to have the same effect. It also appears that the more of these negative factors are present in a particular case, the greater the risk for the individual pupil.

Once the pupils are in school, they are confronted with school demands and have to respond to them. Pupils usually make use of all available ways of responding (Turner, 1983), using different modes to fit the demands of a particular situation and a particular teacher (Furlong, 1976). In this process of interaction between the pupils and the school system, pupil decision making is crucial. Pupils are free to take their own decisions, their freedom only being limited by the vulnerability factors. So the decision making process is very much influenced by these factors, but not determined by them. Not surprisingly, pupils, having tried a variety of ways of responding, finally choose specific ones, and at some point in their school career there is evidence of a major orientation towards school (Hargreaves, 1967; Ball, 1981), although variability of responses still exists, and pupils' major orientation is open to change (Turner, 1983).

Although the factors mentioned play an important role in pupil decision making for reasons that have been explained, it is argued that it is mainly the pupils' decision making itself which formulates the differentiation process within the classroom, first initiated by the vulnerability factors, even further. In extreme cases this results to the exclusion of a pupil from the mainstream system. Hence examination of pupil decision making is expected to indicate the differences between a deviant pupil in a mainstream school and a pupil who attends a special school or unit for reasons of misbehaviour. The term 'pupil decision making' covers the everyday decisions pupils are confronted with, such as: to go to school, to arrive on time, to wear a school uniform, to be quiet in the classroom, to work when they are asked, to complete homework etc. As suggested already, researchers have in the past given different interpretations to the thinking behind the pupils' decision making. Wakeford (1969) and Woods (1979) have argued that pupil reactions to school demands are based on their adoption of a particular mode of adaptation. Researchers like Werthman (1963) and Furlong (1976), however, have shown that pupils' reactions are not so straightforward, and they do in fact vary significantly, not only between individuals, but also within the same individual at different times. On the basis of this evidence, Turner (1983) has rejected the suggestion of the adaptation model about an overall acceptance or rejection of school. Instead of attempting to identify overall modes of adaptation, he has tried to investigate specific pupil actions, such as response to teacher demands. Turner also introduced the interesting notion of pupil goals (see the previous section on sociological models). He argued that depending on their short term aims pupils adopt a variety of approaches at a given moment, but it is their long-term goals that appear to shape their overall orientation towards school. If this new variable is taken into account, it appears that pupils must indeed have a major orientation to school, in spite of their variable reactions at given instances. This is the perspective that will be pursued in this study.

The pupils' short-term aims will be explored in an effort to explain the variety of responses produced by a single pupil in different situations. Their long-term goals will also be sought in an attempt to understand their decision making at crucial moments as an expression of a major orientation to school.

It has been argued that the pupils' deviant career in school is very much influenced by various vulnerability factors, but is finally determined by their own decision making process. It can thus be explained why not all pupils who would be considered 'at risk' are finally transferred to a special school or unit, while establishing that the pupils who are in such provisions, tend, in their overwhelming majority, to possess one or more of these factors. It will be seen however that where pupil decision making is weak or lacking, the vulnerability factors play a crucial role in the development of the pupil's school career.

Research Design

Having posed the research question and explained the theoretical model within which this question will be answered, it is time to examine a more detailed suggestion of the research design. It has been argued that in an effort to judge the necessity for the existence of special provisions for deviant pupils, this study will attempt to compare deviant pupils within the mainstream to deviant pupils who have been transferred to a special unit. Direct comparison of the behaviour of these pupils is expected to indicate if the differences in their behaviour are such in quality or degree, as to justify a division. It has been argued in the previous section (see 'A new model'), that the decision making process of the pupils is considered more important than factors related to their home and school background, and so the study will concentrate on uncovering this process through an examination of pupil behaviour. Two areas of study will be used; a mainstream school and a special unit. Various methods such as questionnaires and observation will be used to identify the most deviant group of pupils within the mainstream school. Closer observation and interviews, as well as other secondary methods described later will be used to closely examine the behaviour of the selected pupils. Observation is expected to give direct evidence of pupils' daily behaviour patterns, and pupil interviews are hoped to give some insight into the pupils' thinking. The two methods will be used to check each other, as will other indirect methods such as teacher interviews, school records, etc. The incidents recorded and the themes drawn from the interviews will then be scrutinized, and the pupils' deeper thinking and decision making will be revealed.

Similar research methods will be used in the special unit. Identification of the deviant pupils will not be attempted there, as all pupils, having been transferred outside the mainstream, will be considered to qualify as deviant. Observation and interviews will be used to explore pupil behaviour patterns and identify their decision making. Certain methodological modifications will be issued to accommodate the different context. The specific problems involved will be discussed in detail in the methodology regarding the special unit. The pupils' motivation and thinking will then be discussed in detail and specific incidents as well as quotations will be used to illustrate the arguments. Comparisons between the various deviant groups of pupils will finally be attempted in an effort to answer the main and the secondary questions of the study.

Conclusion

School deviance has so far been shown to be an issue of interest for a number of disciplines. It has been pointed out that research in this field has been extensive and has adopted a variety of approaches. These approaches have however been criticised here as inflexible and incomplete. A new model has been presented, which attempts to combine the strengths of the old ones while avoiding their limitations, in an effort to present a more complete view of the problem of school deviance and thus produce a more satisfactory answer to the questions involved.

Postscript

On a new critical reading I can clearly see my painful effort to follow two traditions through and formulate a personal understanding adopting an attitude which somehow resembles sitting on a bench. Clearly, the two traditions of psychology and sociology have grown and developed quite separately and are based on altogether different assumptions. The closest parallel I can find is in Visser and Upton (1993), where Baroness Warnock and Len Barton are to be found a few pages apart arguing the most diverse of arguments:

Several of the chapters below hint at the revival of the sociological doctrine prevalent in the 1970s which held that the concept of special educational needs was a kind of a social construct imposed by a hierarchical and conformist society upon children who, apart from this perception of them, had no identifiable needs. Such a theory seems to me mistaken and also damaging. It is true that life in an advanced industrial society demands of people a level of competence which in turn calls for education. But it is then a fact, not a manipulative 'perception', that there are those who need special educational provision if they are to reach that level. It is important to distinguish the false belief that society creates the category of 'special needs' from the true belief that many children's special

needs arise out of poor social conditions, out of homelessness, ignor-
ance, violence and abuse in their backgrounds. (pp. viii-ix)

To this comes later the reply, and it remains for you to match the quotation
to the author:

For those of us who are committed to a comprehensive system of
education which is sufficiently resourced and offers an inclusive
form of policy and practice, one of the greatest dangers is that of
complacency. The struggle we face is both difficult and urgent. It
does require setting the issue of special needs within a sociopolitical
perspective. Decisions over who gets what, how, when and why,
within a context of limited resources, are essentially political. We
need to recognize the extent and stubbornness of institutional dis-
crimination and seek to pursue an alternative vision. (p. 39)

The first quotation belongs, of course, to Baroness Warnock (Warnock, 1993)
and the second to Len Barton (Barton, 1993). To this annoying 'hint at the
revival of the sociological doctrine prevalent in the 1970s', and naturally
presumed dead, comes the reply in the form of a 'barmy theory':

. . . the problem of special needs is to a large extent a problem of
poverty and social disadvantage. The fact that this is not generally
recognised reflects the high profile of children with physical, sens-
ory and cognitive disabilities who tend to come from all sections of
society and whose parents can organise powerful lobbies to defend
the interests of their children. (Mittler, 1993, p. 22)

Evidently the question has not been answered yet — not only because I did
not publish my work earlier — and will perhaps never be answered. In one
sense it is a wonder how one can go so far and yet remain on the same spot.
It is also worth questioning the notion of accepting a given 'advanced industrial society' or 'poor conditions, homelessness, ignorance, violence and abuse'
without examining their origins or wishing to alter them. Mittler (1993) is
quite right — and not the only one — to be alarmed at the government's
failure to listen.

   Where I perhaps identify with the first quotation is in the implied question of 'what do we do as educators? How do we bridge the gap in the
meantime?' — apart from being vigilant and demanding towards the state —
which is my first priority as the second quotation suggests. Some form of
immediate intervention seems to me essential, alongside political debate and
pressure. In that I do not remain unmoved by the practitioner's plea that at
the end of the day a teacher has to teach and a pupil has to learn, (Visser,
1993) without sharing his conviction that classroom differentiation practices
are more important than policy and provision debates.

   For these reasons, and because of what I perceive as a highly complex
dilemma, I seem to still largely identify with the contents of chapter 1. In the

> *same fashion as the previous authors I too seem to have travelled a long way without yet moving far from my initial spot.*

Notes

1 Sociologists have seriously questioned the humanitarian motivation behind the development of the field, as we shall see later on.

2 School case studies were also written by teachers, (Wakefield, 1977; White and Brockington, 1978; Grunsell, 1978, 1980a and 1980b; White, 1980) following a very different tradition.

3 For two very detailed, as well as very different, accounts of the historical development of special education in Britain, see Pritchard (1963) and Tomlinson (1982). Ford *et al*, (1982) also provides a very good critical account.

4 Topping (1983) gives a very good critical account of the special education provisions available for secondary school pupils in Britain.

5 Humphries (1981) describes in detail the struggles of working class parents and children against compulsory education. See also Furlong (1985).

6 The London School Board had already established a separate school for the deaf in 1874 (Tomlinson, 1982), and this date is often considered to signify the beginning of State provision for special education in England and Wales.

7 It is interesting that the term was first officially established and then explored. It is hard to imagine how the Underwood Committee, being under pressure to discover who the maladjusted child was, could possibly have suggested that such a child did not exist.

8 The account has intentionally been uncritical so far. Sociologists have tried to show that the development of special education has not been the benevolent act of a caring State but an effort for social control directed by a continuous struggle between professions (Bowman, 1981; Tomlinson, 1982). It is, however, important to emphasize at this point that regardless of professional ambitions and political struggles, a real concern for handicapped pupils was expressed, and the intentions of the individuals involved did not lack care.

9 The two categories of diabetic and delicate became one in 1953 and the total number of special categories was reduced to ten.

10 See Furlong (1985) for a detailed account of the process towards compulsory schooling and the reasons behind its introduction.

11 As already stated in the previous section, this definition read: 'Maladjusted are pupils that show evidence of emotional instability or psychological disturbance, and require special educational treatment in order to effect their personal, social or educational readjustment'.

12 Another force in the psychological explanation of maladjustment and deviance was the learning theory. Bandura (1971), the main theorist interested in the effects of deviant behaviour learning on children, was particularly concerned with anti-social behaviour arising when children are influenced by violent behaviour but not taught how to distinguish between appropriate and inappropriate occasions for its use. The influence of the learning theory was indicated in teacher handbooks for classroom control based on learning theory principles (Poteet, 1974), and implemented in school intervention on a larger scale (ILEA, 1983). Its influence was mainly felt in the enrichment of 'treatment' methods, but it never had the impact of psychoanalysis.

13 Psychology and psychiatry were also flourishing in America at that time and American theories and treatment methods were very influential in Britain.

14 The masculine gender used reflects the predominant gender of the children, but also the widespread sexism in special education literature.

15 See Ford *et al*, (1982) and Topping (1983).

16 There is in fact less difference amongst pupils than suggested by research. Observed differences are mainly owing to the research perspective, the deviant acts being very similar.

17 Turner (1983) modified the adaptation model to fit responses to specific teacher demands. He suggested that there are six possible alternatives: compliance, which is to carry out the teacher's demand as requested; distanced compliance, where the pupil complies in such a manner that he/she distance themselves from the act of conforming; disguised deviance, where the pupil appears to conform but is in fact behaving in a deviant way; withdrawal, where the pupil switches off, becomes lethargic or falls asleep; sabotage, where the pupil tries to wreck a lesson and possibly undermine the teacher's authority; and, finally, refusal, where the pupil refuses to comply with the teacher, or disobeys a command.

18 It was in fact perceived as a big threat to the educational model, and was initially described as 'doomwatch' (Gilham, 1981b), because it was considered damaging to the newly proposed school mission. According to the prevalent view of the time, schools had an important role to play in changing attitudes and limiting disruption within their premises. Claims that schools can make no difference to the wider society (Bernstein, 1970; Sharp and Green, 1975) were supposed to be very damaging to teacher moral.

19 Ford *et al*, (1982) emphasize that contribution of individuals in the early work in the field should not be underestimated, and Tomlinson (1982) also allows for individual exceptions, but they both go on to criticize the motivation of psychologists as a profession.

20 Following the tradition of the majority of research, this study will concentrate on secondary school pupils of fourteen years of age and above, as this appears to be the time when the problem of referral and transfer outside the mainstream becomes more acute Gillham (1981b), Galloway *et al*, (1982).

21 For special reference to ethnic minorities see Tomlinson (1983).

Part II

Burleigh High

The purpose of this part is to present the work undertaken in the mainstream school, Burleigh High. Chapter 2 describes in detail the methodology used there. Chapter 3 presents the behaviour patterns and the views of one group of deviant pupils, group A, and chapter 4 deals with the behaviour and the views of the other deviant group identified in the mainstream, group B.

Chapter 2

How Did I Do It? I:
Methodology Used in Burleigh High

The School

A variety of methodological approaches were used in the mainstream school, first to identify the most deviant out of 131 fourth year pupils[1], and later for the closer study of the pupils identified. They included questionnaires, observation and interviewing of pupils and teachers. Before describing these methods it is necessary to describe the school where the study was carried out.

Brief History

Burleigh High was chosen for this study because it was the most representative school of the town people. Situated in a working class area, the school drew its intake from families of manual workers, and had a slight reputation of being 'rough'. School teachers were very aware of their role in the wider community of Burleigh, and their responsibility towards it. Burleigh High was the product of the union of two secondary modern schools established in the late fifties, Burleigh Boys School and Burleigh Girls School. The two schools had functioned side by side in separate buildings for about a decade, sharing only a common dining hall used at different times of the day. In the early seventies they were united to form a co-educational secondary modern, which in the middle seventies was turned into a comprehensive[2]. The school had been threatened with closure in the mid-eighties, due to falling rolls, and had been saved thanks to a Burleigh community campaign. Its size, however, had been reduced to 1000 pupils, (approximately two-thirds of its previous size), and major compromises (such as use of the buildings by evening and further education colleges) had to be made in order to save it[3]. The academic year 1984/85, when the fieldwork took place, was a Silver Jubilee year for Burleigh High which celebrated with special joy the rescue of the school.

Buildings

The school grounds, having catered for two schools, were extensive, including games fields and football pitches. Despite partial use by other colleges agreed in the academic year 1983/84, the school retained an adequate number of classrooms and laboratories. There was also a large dining hall, a large theatre hall, an indoor gym, a sick bay and a number of other facilities. Fifth and fourth year students had their own private social areas. The staffroom, inaccessible to pupils, was a new building, recently rebuilt after a fire caused by ex-pupils. The condition of the school buildings was very good, all damage immediately repaired not allowing time for vandalism to accumulate. Classrooms and corridors were tidy and clean with no graffiti, walls decorated with art work and murals painted by pupils. Each teacher had his/her own classroom, and so pupils had to move between classrooms for their lessons.

Ethos

The school had a very clearly defined set of rules (see appendix 1) documented in its pamphlet. There was great emphasis in maintaining these rules and regulations. Pupils failing to do so were immediately corrected and often punished. School uniform was strictly enforced and pupils arriving at school in inappropriate clothes were sent home to change. There was a clearly defined and regularly enforced punishment system, which included lines, detentions, reports, letters to parents and, ultimately, suspensions from school.

However, the school atmosphere was very friendly, and despite their large number, the pupils were on the whole well catered for and looked after. The school's pastoral system was very effective allowing year tutors to follow a year's intake through to the end of their schooling, and become familiar with each individual child. As a rule, tutors and teachers were interested in pupils' problems and provided help and support when necessary. This friendly atmosphere appeared to result from the fact that a number of teachers had been in the school for many years, and had a deep commitment to the pupils and their families, as well as insight and compassion with the problems of the area. They considered the school and the area 'their own', and took a special interest in it.

Curriculum and Timetable

A considerable variety of subjects was on offer, as the school tried to cater for diverse needs. During the first three years a broad range of subjects was taught, all of which were compulsory, allowing the pupils no choice. In the fourth and fifth year there was a division between compulsory subjects, (English and maths), and six options chosen from four groups of subjects[4]. Pupils chose options after individual interviews and meetings involving them and their parents, but there were limitations imposed by teacher opinion of pupil abilities, or shortage of places[5]. In addition, a non-exam life skills course involving careers, social and moral education, politics and keyboard skills was available, and recreational activities were also on offer. All pupils were expected to take some examination in their last term, and there were no non-examination groups in the school.

The school day began with registration and assembly, followed by four lesson periods in the morning, and four in the afternoon. The lessons were usually taught in double periods, although the occasional single period was allowed in the first and second years. There were two year assemblies a week for each year, all other mornings spent with class tutors.

Below is a detailed timetable of the school day:

9.00 – 9.10	Registration
9.10 – 9.25	Class time
9.25 – 10.00	Period one
10.00 – 10.35	Period two
10.35 – 10.50	Break
10.50 – 11.25	Period three
11.25 – 12.00	Period four
12.00 – 1.00	Lunch time
1.00 – 1.05	Registration
1.05 – 1.40	Period five
1.40 – 2.15	Period six
2.15 – 2.30	Break
2.30 – 3.05	Period seven
3.05 – 3.40	Period eight

Other Information

The school had a very busy social life, including a school orchestra, play performances, a wealth of extra-curricular activities and a youth club. A lot of time and effort was spent organizing events such as Christmas plays or pantomimes, and an 'activities week' at the end of the academic year. During the Jubilee year, special celebrations were also organized, including art exhibitions, school history, sporting activities, fireworks and a theatre review. Old pupils were invited to contribute, and parental involvement gave the whole community a very strong feeling of togetherness.

Burleigh High proudly exhibited its achievements, celebrating not only its past twenty-five years of history, but also its future after the recent rescue. Despite its relatively 'rough' reputation in West Town and all the hazards it had been through, Burleigh High was providing a major service to its community, by keeping it together, and making it take both an interest and a pride in its school.

Methodology Used — General Information

Having described the school, it is time to concentrate on the methodology used[6]. Two methodological problems were met very early on.

The research question — differences between deviant pupils within and without the mainstream — ambitious and without a precedent, posed serious methodological problems. The first was the choice of school. Two fields of study were obviously required, a mainstream school and some form of special school. The latter was required to be structurally as close to the former as possible, if comparisons between the two were to be of some validity. For this reason, residential special schools were excluded, as they represented a very different type of institution, and their pupils' faced serious problems at home as well as school (ILEA Research and Statistics Report, 1984). The closest possible structure was a special unit for pupils with 'behavioural problems'. Pupils attending this kind of provision lived at home, and their placement in the unit had required minimum administrative procedures and time[7].

Another methodological problem was the choice of pupils to study within the mainstream school. It was necessary here to differentiate, as comparisons between pupils attending the special unit and a random group of pupils in the mainstream would maximize differences and not serve the purpose of the study. In order to identify the most deviant pupils within the mainstream school a point of reference was needed, against which pupil attitude and performance would be measured. Sociologists have traditionally used sociograms to identify deviant groups in school (Pollard, 1984), but in this case a sociogram would have been of no use, as it would only identify sub-cultural grouping, with groups likely to include pupils of various degrees of deviance and would not provide a 'ranking of deviance'. Teacher testimony was also rejected, as teachers did not teach all pupils and would be unable to comment on some of them, and also because it has repeatedly been shown (Werthman, 1963; Furlong, 1976) that teachers do not experience the whole range of pupil behaviour. It was therefore decided to use a questionnaire to assess deviant behaviour, and facilitate choice of deviant pupils to study within the mainstream school[8].

The need for a questionnaire presented new problems, as no valid and standardized questionnaire existed which could be used. A new questionnaire was constructed making every effort to ensure that it was valid and efficient. Direct observation would help compensate for possible inadequacies. The combined use of questionnaire and observation was expected to give a reliable ranking of deviant behaviour, and help produce a differentiation of pupils suitable and adequate for the purposes of the study.

Fieldwork in Burleigh High lasted seven months. The first two weeks were spent in general observation and familiarizing with the premises the teachers and the pupils. By the end of this period I was familiar with twenty-six out of thirty-seven teachers, and forty-one out of 131 fourth year pupils, twenty-four of whom were later included in the sample. During these two weeks the questionnaire was prepared for the pilot study and the observation sheet took its final form. The methods used to produce the desired group differentiation in Burleigh High will be described first, and those which concentrated on the study of the deviant pupils identified, will follow.

Identification of the Deviant Pupils

Eleven weeks were exclusively devoted to this task using observation and a questionnaire.

Questionnaire — General Information

Pupils in special schools or units usually admit to having had problems in school and retain strong negative views about the mainstream (Tattum, 1982). In order to be comparable, the most deviant pupils in the mainstream were expected:

(i)   to possess an overall negative attitude towards school;
(ii)   to express this attitude with overt misbehaviour in the classroom and the playground; and
(iii) thus to have repeatedly been punished, having acquired a reputation and a 'bad' school record.

To meet these requirements the questionnaire should have four different sections teasing out: (i) the pupil's **orientation** towards school; (ii) their **behaviour**; (iii) their **reputation** and possible connections between the three. A fourth section was also needed, where pupils would be able to voice personal opinions, indicate likes and dislikes and give their judgment of pupils and teachers. The group of pupils identified as being the most deviant through the questionnaire would be named 'questionnaire group'.

Various questionnaires were consulted, and informal interview questions used in similar studies were taken into account (Gold, 1963; Rutter, 1979; Corrigan, 1979). The main principles determining the choice of questions were to:

(i)   serve the stated purpose of each section;
(ii)   avoid repetition using it only to test and verify consistency of pupil opinion;
(iii) opt for positive questions, avoiding negative ones;
(iv)   opt for closed questions, easier to answer and compare.

Sufficient choice of answers was provided in the first three sections, reserving open-ended questions for the last section in order to give pupils the opportunity to express their feelings (appendix 5). There was also a section providing home background information.

The school demanded parental consent for the questionnaire. In an effort to avoid unnecessary risks I temporarily withdrew the home background section expecting to use it later (appendix 12: home background questionnaire). Upon the school's insistence that parents should be informed, I distributed to fourth year pupils a letter (appendix 2) informing parents of the administration of the questionnaire and asking them to contact the fourth year tutor if they objected to their child filling it in.

Questionnaire — Pilot Study

With all negotiations concluded and no letters of objection received, I carried out a pilot study to test the questionnaire on twenty-three third and twenty-seven fifth year pupils during class time[9].

Sections A, B and C were graded using a 0–4 scale, grades increasing from pro-school to anti-school attitude[10]. For section D a more complicated procedure needed to be employed comparing the answers given with each other, grades ranging from 0–4 (appendix 4). Each section was marked separately receiving a total: for example, A12, B2, C3, D14. Section totals were finally added up to a pupil total, for example, T31. This whole procedure produced the total scores for years 3 and 5 giving me an opportunity to compare the two and establish that on the whole fifth years achieved higher scores than third years. More importantly though it gave me valuable experience on the distribution of the questionnaire, and the opportunity to rephrase unclear questions. The final draft of the questionnaire was then sent to the printer.

Questionnaire — Main Study

I administered the questionnaire (see appendix 5) to all fourth year classes during class time[11] within two weeks[12]. After registration I was introduced to the class, explained that I was doing research in 'pupils' attitude to school' and asked for the children's cooperation in filling in the questionnaire. I emphasized that information given would be kept confidential, and asked them to work individually and be as honest and as accurate as possible. I then read the questions and answers aloud, explaining what was required. I urged pupils to ask questions when in doubt, and to wait until the necessary explanations were given. Some did, but most appeared to be clear and confident enough to proceed alone. The pupils were finally asked to print their name, class and gender, and to leave their questionnaire on their desk for me to collect. I collected the questionnaires thanking them for their cooperation. The pupils were on the whole very cooperative, and expressed no objections to filling in the questionnaire.

Those absent were asked to fill the questionnaire at the end of the second week. Most pupils still missing were later found and asked to fill the questionnaire during break. In the end ten pupils who had not yet filled the questionnaire were left out, due to lack of time. The total number of questionnaires filled was 131 out of a total of 141[13]. The marking procedure followed was the same with that described in the pilot study.

Each class was treated separately and the total score indicated a fairly normal distribution of scores. Most children seemed to concentrate between 30 and 35 points. The mean was 36.50 and the standard deviation 12.93. The score of 50 was taken as a cut-off point to form the 'questionnaire group', because it was one standard deviation away from the mean (36.50 + 12.93 = 49.43). These were seventeen pupils, 12.05 per cent of the fourth year, ten boys and seven girls. Table 2 indicates these pupils' total scores:

Table 2: Questionnaire totals per pupil

4.1	4.2	4.3	4.4	4.5
M 7 : 65	M 5 : 54		M 2* : 51	M 1 : 79
M 9* : 64	F 7 : 54		M 3* : 54	M 2 : 56
	F 9* : 71			M 3* : 50
	F 10* : 66			M 4* : 69
	F 11 : 54			M 6* : 51
				F 6* : 54
				F 7 : 60
				F 11* : 58

Note: Marked with asterisk are pupils who were later found to qualify for the observation group (see analysis of the general observation data).

Table 3 indicates the pupils' distribution in classes:

Table 3: Distribution of questionnaire group members per class

Class	4.1	4.2	4.3	4.4	4.5
Boys	2	1	0	2	5
Girls	0	4	0	0	3
Total	**2**	**5**	**0**	**2**	**8**

The concentration of 'questionnaire group' members in classes 4.5 and 4.2, and their complete absence in 4.3 seems to indicate the existence of sub-cultural groupings[14].

Table 4 shows the distribution of the questionnaire section totals (see the section on questionnaire — pilot study) per class:

Table 4: Section totals per class

Class	A	B	C	D	N
4.1	15.00	5.7	3.6	11.9	27
4.2	13.00	6.8	5.0	10.8	28
4.3	12.50	4.4	3.4	11.0	24
4.4	13.50	5.9	3.9	13.5	25
4.5	15.00	6.8	5.3	14.8	26
M:	13.80	5.9	4.2	12.4	130

ABCD: sections N: number of pupils M: mean
Maximum score 28 for ABD, 25 for C.

'Questionnaire group' members belonging to class 4.5 have consistently scored higher in each individual section than any other group members. This suggests the existence of a sub-cultural grouping within 4.5. The results are not so consistent for 4.2.

Observation — General Information and Structure of the Observation Sheet

General observation, used alongside the questionnaire to help identify the most deviant pupils in the fourth year, was carried out during the first eight weeks of the fieldwork. At the end of this period, and after the Q (questionnaire) group had been formed in the way described above, the general observation data were examined. A description of the procedure followed during observation is first given below.

Observation timetables were first prepared with the help of the fourth year tutor, attempting to cover a variety of subjects, teachers and pupil groups, and give an overall picture of fourth year lessons. A structured observation sheet was used for greater efficiency. It was based on a simple 'teacher demand — pupil response' formula, wishing to concentrate on teacher-pupil interaction in the classroom, and the way individual pupils responded to teacher demands[15]. A4 size paper was used, divided in five columns of various sizes for different items. The date, period, subject and name of the teacher were noted in the left-hand column. The next column was used for comments which would help understand the incidents described. The name of the pupil interacting with the teacher was written in the third column. In the fourth column the teacher's request was noted in the exact words used, with remarks on his/her tone of voice and his/her actions. The last column was used to describe the pupil response, verbal or otherwise. The pupil's exact words were noted and also comments about the pupil's gestures, tone of voice or any other information that would help reconstruct the incident and draw conclusions. A short comment on the pupil's behaviour was also noted based on Turner's six categories of deviance (Turner, 1983). There was 'C' for compliance, 'DC' for distant compliance, 'DD' for disguised deviance, 'W' for withdrawal, 'S' for sabotage and 'R' for refusal. Hence, the incident was recorded in the most clear and accurate way possible to avoid misunderstandings or loss of data[16]. This was the last in a series of modifications of the original idea, following the first two weeks in school, concerned with the structure of the observation sheet rather than its content.

I had originally planned to use another observation sheet for interactions occurring outside classroom hours. This proved unnecessary, informal contact with pupils during break being considered more important. Information obtained during this time was consequently recorded in my diary[17] and used to give more insight into pupil actions.

Analysis of the General Observation Data

A simple demand-response formula was used for the analysis. A teacher's demand from a pupil followed by a recognizable response by that pupil constituted an **interaction**. If the teacher repeated his or her demand, this was considered a beginning of a new interaction to which the pupil was expected to give a new response. A lengthy and distinct series of interactions was taken to constitute an **incident**. An incident usually took place when there was a disagreement between a pupil and a teacher, and more than one interaction was needed to settle it. There were no incidents during observation that demanded a more sophisticated method of calculation, every interaction falling easily into this pattern. Interactions were also initiated by pupils, but this was less common.

Every interaction with a teacher was taken into account, including those concerned with lesson content rather than pupil behaviour. There were differences in teacher-pupil interactions between academic and practical lessons, and it was more difficult to record a private interaction during a practical lesson, but all public interactions were noted, and so were all private ones observed.

Cases of unclear identity were abandoned in the analysis. This resulted to some loss of information, but was considered necessary. Most abandoned interactions concerned pupils who were not interacting with teachers very often, hence the lack of familiarity with them.

For every child the total number of interactions with teachers was counted and so was the number of sessions when he/she had been observed. The two amounts were then divided: interactions with teachers/number of observation sessions giving an individual score, ranging from 0 to 5.07 interactions per session. A high score was taken to indicate a high degree of deviance showing that the classroom teacher had been obliged to devote large part of teaching time to this pupil. Average scores per class are listed in table 5:

Table 5:   Average observation score per class

Class	Score
4.1	0.39
4.2	0.57
4.3	0.24
4.4	0.56
4.5	0.87

The total average was 0.52. As table 5 indicates, in class 4.5 the average pupil had an interaction with a teacher in almost every lesson, while pupils in 4.3 were much less demanding of teacher time. The distance of a standard deviation from the mean was calculated to be 1.16, and so one (1.00) interaction per session was taken as the cut-off point for qualifying for the deviant group identified through observation. This group was called 'observation group' (O). Twenty-seven children qualified for the group according to this measure, a total of 19.14 per cent of the fourth year pupils[18]. Ten of them were already included in the 'questionnaire group'.

Table 6 shows the distribution of the members of the 'observation group' in classes:

Table 6:   Distribution of observation group members per class

Class	4.1	4.2	4.3	4.4	4.5
Boys	3	4	0	5	6
Girls	0	3	2	1	3
Total	**3**	**7**	**2**	**6**	**9**

It is evident from table 6 that most members of the 'observation group' came from class 4.5, phenomenon similar to that observed with the 'questionnaire group'. Class 4.3 on the other hand appears once more to have a very low number of deviant pupils.

Table 7 presents the detailed distribution of the twenty-seven individuals and their observation scores in classes:

Table 7: Average of pupil interactions with teachers per hour of observation

4.1	4.2	4.3	4.4	4.5
M 5 : 1.80	M 2 : 1.60	F 9 : 1.09	M 2* : 4.07	M 3* : 1.00
M 9* : 4.33	M 7 : 1.20	F10 : 1.00	M 3* : 2.57	M 4* : 1.90
M11 : 1.04	M 9 : 1.25		M 4 : 1.05	M 5 : 2.50
	M12 : 1.26		M10 : 1.71	M 6* : 5.07
	F 8 : 1.27		M13 : 1.11	M 9 : 1.60
	F 9* : 1.66		F 9 : 1.33	M13 : 1.16
	F 10* : 1.42			F 6* : 1.81
				F 11* : 2.00
				F 13* : 1.33

Clearly, members of the 'observation group' demanded constant attention from their teachers, some having more than one interactions per teaching hour. Class 4.5 appears to include the pupils with the highest scores, as well as the largest number of attention demanding pupils. Pupils of group O who also qualified for group Q are marked with an asterisk[19].

When the analysis of the questionnaire and the observation data was completed, and the two deviant groups identified, the study concentrated on the thirty-three pupils of the two deviant groups identified.

Main Study — Methodology

At the end of eleven weeks the thirty-three most deviant pupils of the year had been identified and the fieldwork was ready to enter a new phase. Information regarding the rest of the fourth year pupils was now irrelevant, and I concentrated on these thirty-three pupils. The object was to identify the decision-making behind the pupils' actions. Assessing their short and long-term goals in school was a useful technique for this. Two main approaches were used:

(i)   observation of the pupils in the classroom and the playground; and
(ii) interviews with the pupils.

Other techniques used were teacher interviews and examination of school records, registration books and subject timetables. All fourth year pupils were also requested to write an essay about an incident with a teacher, and had to fill in a questionnaire concerning home background information.

Observation

During the main study period the whole day was spent with the pupils. In the classroom during lesson time, in the dining hall at lunch time and in the fourth year area at break time. Informal contact was considered crucial for developing a relationship and gaining an insight into their behaviour and thinking. Classroom observation was intense constituting a major task of the school day.

Observation was of vital importance, as it gave the opportunity to directly witness pupil interactions with teachers and observe their decision-making 'in the making'. During classroom observation the pupils' short and long-term goals became apparent, and their accounts were both better understood and put to the test. Continuous contact with pupils, as well as their interviews, gave a clear insight into their classroom behaviour. The observation technique remained the same as before, and the same observation sheet was used, the focus of observation now being the pupils of groups Q and O. Other members of the class were largely ignored, observed only when influencing members of the groups under observation. Description of incidents was more elaborate given the smaller number of pupils involved. Following a classroom incident, I would quite often approach the child involved during break and ask his/her view about the incident.

Three new timetables were made ensuring that every individual belonging to groups Q and O was observed for at least two teaching sessions a week, in a variety of groups, subjects and teachers. The number of deviant pupils included in a class group influenced the choice of groups to be observed, and so did the wish to observe the same pupil in a variety of situations. There were, of course, limitations imposed by the school timetable, and relationships with teachers[20]. During the remaining ten weeks of the fieldwork eighteen different groups, thirteen different teachers and ten different subjects were observed. By the time the second period of observation started I had established a good relationship with the pupils and they were ready to accept my presence in the classroom, apparently not modifying their behaviour in any way[21]. During the interview the pupils stated that they often forgot about my presence in the classroom.

Interview

Interviewing the pupils was the other major task of the remaining study period. The purpose of the interview was to obtain the pupils' own explanations of their classroom behaviour, mainly through discovering their goals in school. The pupils were not made aware that the two were linked, and were expected to make this connection themselves. As we shall see in the next chapter some did, and some did not. The interviews were carried out in parallel with the main observation study over a period of eight weeks. Interviewing was one of the most interesting parts of the fieldwork.

Because I wanted to use a tape-recorder the school would not agree to interviewing without parental permission. It requested that I sent another letter to parents, giving more information about the research, and asking for their positive consent. The children were given such a letter (appendix 9), and were told to bring it back signed by one parent. Thirty-five letters were handed out (including pupils for pilot interviews), but only nineteen answers were received, a percentage of 55.88 per cent. This appeared from the pupils' comments to be a result of their failure to show the letter to their parents or to bring the answer back, rather than a sign of parental opposition. So after allowing a few more days I started interviewing.

Out of thirty-three children, (27 O + 17 Q – 11 common total) one refused to be interviewed, apparently under his parents instructions. He did not, however, avoid informal chats where he was asked most of the questions normally asked during the interview. Another boy felt uncomfortable with the tape-recorder, so written notes had to be taken instead in his case. All thirty-three pupils were thus interviewed, even those for whom formal parental permission had not been given. No further complication arose from this matter.

The interviews lasted twenty minutes on average, and were conducted mainly in the video room of the school, but also in various other rooms on five occasions when the video room happened to be occupied. They were all recorded, apart from the two cases mentioned already. Only one child was interviewed at a time except on two occasions where the interviewees had to be persuaded by a friend to come. In both these cases the friend was not present for the whole interview. Most interviews were conducted continuously from beginning to end, but on three or four occasions the time available was limited and the pupil had to return later in the same day to complete the interview[22]. Twelve pupils were interviewed during lesson time. Allowing for individual differences, the pupils were cooperative and friendly once in the interview room, and some were particularly lively and stimulating with their answers and comments.

The interviews were semi-structured and flexible enough to allow for individual contributions. After I had explained the purpose of my research, I asked pupils to give me their date of birth and used the questionnaire they had filled in to start the conversation. Each question was individually examined, and issues such as attitude towards school, respect for school rules, current and past reputation in school, friendships, incidents with teachers (real and hypothetical), and future plans were discussed. In the case of real incidents, the pupils were asked to recall them, describe what had happened as accurately as possible, explain their behaviour, justify their position, consider that of the teacher, and finally mention the consequences suffered and their feelings after the incident was over. Because I expected that some pupils would not have any incidents to refer to or would not be able to recall them sufficiently well to give a clear picture of what had happened, and also because a common ground for comparisons was needed, three hypothetical situations were given for consideration:

(i)   There is noise in the classroom. The teacher enters and says: 'Quiet everybody, we are starting the lesson now'. You are still talking to the person next to you, so the teacher comes to you and says: 'X I have asked you to be quiet but you are still talking; get out!'. What do you do?

(ii) The teacher had set some homework and you have not done it. He/she asks for the books to be handed in. What do you do?

(iii) At some point in the lesson the teacher says: 'Put your pens down and listen to me now'. You are still playing with your pen, so the teacher comes to your desk and without saying anything takes the pen from your fingers and puts it on your desk. What do you do?

Quite often an interesting discussion was stimulated by reference to these situations, about teacher and pupil rights, teacher judgment, etc. At the end of the interview I asked about my presence in the classroom and its influence on the pupil's behaviour. There were also questions about the pupil's family background, which all pupils but the two mentioned already answered without hesitation. Concluding the interview, the pupils were always invited to comment on what had been discussed, or touch upon points that had been omitted, and offer their views. Only two took this invitation up.

When the observation and the interviews were completed teacher opinion was also sought, in order to obtain more insight into pupil behaviour.

Teacher Cooperationw

Teachers were only interviewed at the end of the fieldwork when all work with pupils had been completed. One reason for 'ignoring' teacher views was that teachers in a secondary school experience only part of a pupil's behavioural repertoire, and they are often not in a position to give a complete picture of pupil behaviour and goals. This was initially a theoretical consideration (Werthman, 1963; Furlong, 1976), validated during fieldwork through the notion of established behaviour patterns which will be described in detail in the next chapter. Another reason for 'ignoring' teacher opinion was that pupils were considered the best source of information regarding their own behaviour and plans. External evidence was only considered necessary for assessing and verifying pupil accounts. It was in this context that teacher views were requested, their testimonies expected to offer valuable help in the assessment process by verifying past incidents.

First a letter was sent to all members of staff involved in fourth year teaching, explaining what the purpose of the research was, and asking them to give names of pupils they considered the most disruptive in the fourth year groups they taught (appendix 10). The purpose of this exercise was to establish how much teacher opinion coincided with my choice of pupils, and to make a step towards closer cooperation with teachers facilitating interviews with them[23]. Only twelve out of the thirty-nine letters sent were returned, a percentage of 30.79 per cent. Two of the teachers stated that they did not find anybody in their groups disruptive, and the others mentioned between one and six names each. Seventeen pupils were named altogether, three more than once. Three of them were girls and fourteen were boys[24]. Six of them were in group O and five in group Q. Six of them, all boys, were not included in the deviant groups; one mentioned by two teachers. One teacher said that she wanted to talk to me rather than commit herself on paper, and a couple of others requested clarification for the term 'disruptive'.

The last week of the fieldwork was devoted to teacher interviews. Fourteen teachers were interviewed altogether: the fourth year tutor; all five class tutors; and eight teachers who taught fourth year groups. Twelve interviews were recorded and two were not. Apart from the year and class tutors, who were considered necessary, the choice of the other teachers was based on the value of information considered likely to be achieved, as most of them had been observed teaching and could be asked questions about specific pupils.

I started the interview explaining my special interest. If I had received an answer to my letter from the teacher interviewed, the pupils mentioned there were discussed, with particular emphasis on pupils belonging to my deviant groups. Teachers usually gave a pupil profile and, more often than not, family background information. The discussion eventually led to Burleigh High, its area and its intake, information particularly welcome. All teachers interviewed were very helpful.

Other Techniques

As the fieldwork was coming to an end, new ways of obtaining more information about the pupils to help complete the picture were sought. All fourth year pupils were asked to write an essay entitled 'Trouble in the classroom', in which they were to describe an incident they had with a teacher. The class tutors volunteered to administer the task to the pupils, following a general announcement in the fourth year assembly by me[25]. Each class tutor was given an instruction sheet to read to his/her group during class time (appendix 11). This was a time saving measure — time was running short by then — which resulted in some loss of information as two of the five class tutors did not remember to ask the pupils for their essays, despite being reminded by the year tutor. The essays received were rather poor evidence, because most pupils did not follow the instructions given. Some described a true incident that had happened to somebody else, others — mainly pupils outside the deviant groups — stated that nothing of the kind had ever happened to them, nor could they ever envisage happening, and a few made up a very fictitious story. The standard of writing was generally low and the accounts of incidents rather poor[26]. Consequently the essays had only very limited value as a source of information.

A small home background questionnaire (appendix 12) was also prepared for all fourth year pupils. The school gave the new questionnaire severe scrutiny and eliminated two important questions concerning parental occupation and education. This information was later obtained from the pupils themselves during the interviews[27]. The class tutors volunteered to administer this questionnaire. This was the last stage of the fieldwork.

Relationships in the Field

Case studies in mainstream, as well as special schools, have traditionally been carried out by British males in this country. Female sociologists entered the scene later and for a foreigner to attempt such a study is even more rare. My gender and nationality is thus a factor that has to be mentioned — not because it was always negative; its novelty often excited interest — because it played a significant role in relationships with pupils and teachers alike[28].

Researchers in education do not always see and present themselves in context, and it is often through indirect evidence that their relationship with staff and pupils becomes apparent. These relationships present, in their overwhelming majority, a picture of perfect harmony. Willis (1977) and Corrigan (1979) appeared to be almost one of the 'lads' they studied, and Delamont (1976b) and Davies (1984) also appeared to have been very easily assimilated into the pupil groups they studied. This is perhaps because in all these cases the researcher was of the same gender as the pupils studied. However, Pollard (1984) does not describe any difficulties in studying female pupils although he was a much older male researcher. It is only very occasionally that researchers admit to having some problems in penetrating pupil groups (McRobbie and Garber, 1976)[29], or report pupil behaviour that indicates some kind of resistance towards the researcher (Turner, 1983)[30].

Fieldwork in Burleigh High was a very exciting and enjoyable experience but I did not find it smooth and easy. The combination of quantitative and qualitative methodology may well have contributed to that. The use of either of these approaches on its own does not present particular difficulties, as in the first case the pupil consent is rarely required, and in the second the researcher often only works with pupils who are willing to be part of the study. The fact that I first chose the pupils and then approached them on a more personal level, complicated matters. So most pupils — although friendly when approached — did not particularly seek my company[31], neither did they go out of their way to help me if doing so interfered with their enjoyment. I formed warm relationships with most fourth year pupils, and especially the ones I closely observed, but there were individuals who felt uneasy and incidents where boys or girls ganged together in an effort to sabotage my task. These were mostly well meaning jokes, but they could well present problems, when, for example, they put pressure on individual pupils to turn down an interview. Teacher and pupil attempts to read my notes[32] also had to be dealt with, but were not a serious problem as my argument of confidentiality being best protected if no one had access to my notes, appeared to be convincing enough. When the question of 'what am I writing' came up I usually provided oral information.

Some difficulties arose from the fact that I was addressing myself to both genders. To help approach the boys I was casually dressed in cords, jumpers and flat shoes. This image appears to have alienated the girls somewhat. The majority of fourth year girls celebrated their femininity in pencil skirts and stiletto shoes and wore a lot of make-up. Identifying with a woman dressed in a less feminine manner presented some difficulties[33]. On the other hand, the boys, not forgetting that I was a woman, never fully accepted me as 'one of them'. On one occasion I was asked out for a drink[34], on another a boy was teased about the time he had spent alone with me during the interview. In defense, he made a cartoon which provoked laughter but I was not allowed to see. Finally, having kisses blown to me in the classroom was not uncommon. The nickname 'Rupert' was attempted for me because of my check trousers, but in the end my surname was used mispronounced, appearing amusing enough in itself.

It is therefore clear that I had to constantly negotiate my way, the pupils not having surrendered their defenses to accept me in their groups. Nonetheless, relationships between us were the best possible given the limitations of age and role differences. The warmth of the relationship is perhaps most evident by the jokes exchanged which would never have been evoked by a formal relationship. I was not mistaken for a teacher, most probably because of my informal dress and conduct and also because of my clearly different role. This was evident from the views confided in me which, if reported, would have given the pupils serious problems[35]. Information like this was passed on easily as well as personal information about girlfriends or problems at home. Pupils often looked up to me for company or support, and occasionally offered advice about how to handle other pupils, or helped persuade their friends to come for an interview. Relationships improved steadily, and it was an advantage that the interviews were conducted during the last period of the fieldwork, when trust was well established between the two parties.

Relationships with teachers were also very friendly. Although two teachers indicated that they would not like to be observed on a permanent basis, even they consented to be observed for a short period of time. Most teachers showed an interest in the research topic, and some asked for the researcher's opinion and advice, because 'you follow them around and so you know a lot about them'. Some teachers made attempts to incorporate me in their lesson, for example by asking questions about life in Greece, but most allowed me to do as I pleased and felt at ease to leave the class when I was there. Teachers also confided in me about difficulties with particular pupils or future career plans, always respecting confidentiality and never forcing me into a difficult situation by seeking information I was not allowed to give.

Considering the diversity of daily tasks in a big comprehensive and the time pressures operating on everybody, it is impressive how well relationships were allowed to develop, and it comes as no surprise that life was not always smooth and easy.

Data Analysis and Groups Identified

Data analysis proved to be quite a surprise. By the end of the fieldwork, information had been collected on thirty-three pupils, in the form of tape-recordings, observation notes, diary recordings, teacher interviews, essays, questionnaires, and school documents. All this made up an immense amount of data to be mastered. The transcription process alone demanded a considerable amount of time, and then the transcripts, as well as the observation sheets had to be coded. The first reading of observation notes and interview transcripts revealed an unexpected wealth of information. It soon became apparent that if the study was to develop as planned, part of the material would have to be discarded and analysis would have to concentrate on a smaller number of pupils facilitating an in-depth study.

The choice of pupils to concentrate on for further analysis was facilitated by the methodology used. The combination of questionnaire and observation data was considered a safe approach as pupils identified by both methods, eleven in total, had to be the most deviant, and therefore the most suitable to compare with pupils of a special unit. So they were chosen for closer study. These are the mainstream pupils that will be the object of this book.

After this differentiation had taken place, all observation sheets were screened, and all information relevant to these pupils was identified and coded for ease of reference. At this stage, Glaser and Strauss' suggestions (1967) relating to analysis technique were of invaluable assistance. A second reading of observation sheets and transcripts produced conceptual categories that helped structure the analysis. There were thirty-one such categories, divided into four sections, concerned with:

(i)   the pupil in the institution;
(ii)   attitude to teachers;
(iii)   relationships with peers; and
(iv)   the pupil as a person.

Observation sheets were analyzed first. Each interaction was recorded in one or more conceptual categories and compared to all previous interactions in that category. During this process two deviant sub-groups began to clearly emerge as individuals were consistently coded in different conceptual categories, group A and group B. When the conceptual categories were 'saturated' (see Glaser and Strauss, 1967) with observation data, each interview was similarly examined and analyzed so that pupil profiles were completed. Having established very clear and detailed individual and group profiles, the analysis then attempted to describe the pupils' short and long-term goals, and to show the effect of these goals on pupil decision-making.

The next two chapters will examine in detail the deviant groups and their members in Burleigh High and will try to explain the decision-making behind the pupils' actions.

Postscript

I have made a conscious effort to reduce the chapter to the bare minimum so as not to make it tiresome. It is, however, difficult to reduce it any further and still retain all necessary information. If the details presented here are not wanted, proceed to the next chapter and use this only as a reference point. If on the other hand you require more information on the methodology used, you are advised to consult Phtiaka (1988). Trying to retain a balance between presentation of factual evidence, i.e. numbers, and warm presentation, i.e. words, is not easy. As a consequence chapter 2 is not exactly charming. I apologize for that.

Notes

1   The total of the fourth year pupils was 141 but ten of them were not screened because of practical difficulties.
2   Without, it appears, experiencing any major changes in the quality of its intake.
3   As a part of this agreement Burleigh High teachers had to provide these colleges with a few teaching hours a week.
4   The four groups were: (a) physics, biology, chemistry, human biology, general science, French, physical technology; (b) German, history, geography, commerce, social economics, typewriting; (c) geology, art, pottery, music, computer studies, physical education, textiles; (d) woodwork, metalwork, motor vehicle engineering, combined materials, technical drawing, home economics, child care.
5   Girls appeared to be affected particularly by these limitations, and often complained of having been refused a place in what was considered a traditionally 'male' subject that was very much in demand, for example, computer studies, because the boys were given priority. It is worth noting here that the number of boys taking computer studies was over three times the number of girls taking the subject, and that during the practical sessions when the pupils were making use of terminals, four girls were usually crammed around a single terminal, while most boys were allowed a terminal each, or had to share one between two. This seating arrangement, although not initiated by the teacher, was usually tolerated.
6   Due to shortage of space I shall avoid a detailed description. Those interested a more detailed description of the methodology used will find it in Phtiaka (1988).
7   This was taken as an indication that these pupils were considered 'closer to normal' (see Lloyd-Smith, 1984a, and Tattum, 1985).
8   Teachers' views on individual children were still regarded as a valuable source of information, and were obtained later, after the groups of deviant pupils had been formed, and all other information related to the pupils had been collected (see the section on teacher cooperation).
9   Class time was simply a class assembly in the teacher's room which gave the form teacher the opportunity to keep in touch with his/her pupils and deal with their problems. This time proved extremely useful during the fieldwork, for interviewing and for administering the questionnaire.
10   The way sections A, B, and C were marked in the pilot as well as the main study, is indicated in more detail in appendix 3.
11   Class time provided intimacy and flexibility not available during year assemblies.
12   Due to the existence of five classes and the availability of only three class time days a week.
13   Burleigh High hosted a visually impaired unit which three fourth year pupils attended. A special effort was made to accommodate the pupils of the unit by translating the questionnaire in Braille. However, for various reasons, only one of the three pupils finally succeeded in filling it in. These pupils are included in the class numbers given.
14   It would be interesting to speculate how these groupings were formed, since the distribution of pupils in classes was argued by the school to have been made on a random basis.
15   The idea was based on Turner (1983), and suggestions for the structure of the sheet were taken from Hinde (1973). See appendix 5 for its final structure.
16   See appendix 6 for an example of a completed observation sheet.

17　I kept a daily diary throughout my fieldwork in Burleigh High. See appendix 7 for an extract.

18　The overall number of boys in the 'observation group' was double the number of girls, eighteen boys versus nine girls. This was a bigger sex difference than the one observed in the 'questionnaire group'. It seems to indicate that although approximately equal number of boys and girls appeared to have equally negative school attitude when measured against a 'neutral' instrument such as a questionnaire, twice as many boys as girls demanded above average attention from teachers.

19　There is a total of eleven asterisks in this table. Ten of these pupils had already been chosen, through the procedure described, for group Q when this table was compiled. The eleventh pupil was first identified as a member of group O, as she filled in her questionnaire late. She had thus not been included in the statistical calculations of table 1 (this is why the total there is 10 instead of 11) but was treated the same as the other members of groups Q and O once identified.

20　The members of the school staff were in general helpful and cooperative, and no teacher refused to be observed during the general observation period. Two teachers were however less happy to accept me in their class on a permanent basis. This wish was subtly expressed, but could not be ignored. (Surprisingly these were not necessarily the teachers with the most serious problems of classroom discipline.) This was unfortunate, but the information collected during the general observation period gave a clear indication of the pupils' interactions with these teachers and compensated for the loss.

21　Occasionally pupils would put up a fight and demand that I should take notes about it, but this kind of playful behaviour was rather an indication of the friendly relationship between observer and observed and did not take place when the teacher was in the classroom.

22　The lunch time break was originally considered the best time for pupil interviews, because it lasted one hour allowing time for two interviews. This initially proved effective, but I very soon run out of volunteers as most pupils were unwilling to give up their break and some had to go home for lunch. The teacher's strike action, which began at the same time as the interviews, made things even more difficult, as more pupils than usual were sent home for lunch. So I started using class time, break time and even lesson time for interviewing. The latter was used as a last resort and mainly for those pupils who were unwilling to give up any break at all for a discussion.

23　I was by that time well aquainted with most fourth year teachers, but there were still three or four teachers who were less familiar to me.

24　Boys appeared to prevail in teacher opinion as they had done in the 'observation group'.

25　I took the opportunity during this assembly to formally thank all pupils for their help and cooperation.

26　It seems that pupils saw the exercise as an extra piece of work, and tried to do as little as possible.

27　The school allowed the administration of this questionnaire to take place without demanding parental permission, partly because the consent had been obtained earlier, but mainly because the questions left were considered 'safe'.

28　Gender (female) appearing to be more significant than nationality (Greek).

29　It is also McRobbie and Garber (1976) who point out the possible significance of the gender difference between researcher and pupils for past treatment of girls in the literature.

30　Turner reports that pupils used the nickname 'Mr Kalkitos' for him, borrowed from a TV series, which indicated that the pupils were themselves observing and categorizing him.

31 With the exception of group B boys who were isolated and lonely.

32 It was considered best to keep the notes secret from pupils and teachers in order to avoid influencing their behaviour in any way.

33 Girls' sensitivity to other women's appearance is widely documented in the literature, (Delamont, 1980; Davies, 1979; Llewellyn, 1980), although it usually refers to teachers or other pupils and not the researcher. Comments about the appearance of female staff and occasionally, in the form of a joke, about my own appearance were also made by girls during this study.

34 This kind of behaviour, exhibited only in public, was seen rather as a 'showing off' technique. See the section on chapter 3 'Showing off techniques and perfect balance'.

35 An example of this is the case of a girl who argued that she could not stand a teacher because 'she was scruffy and smelly', and of a boy who stated that he hated the year tutor but he had to put up with him.

Chapter 3

Showing Off:
Group A — The Fun-seekers of Burleigh
High

Introduction

The main task of the study outlined in this book was to evaluate the dividing line between mainstream and special school deviance. It has been pointed out that traditionally research has not crossed the boundaries between these two areas in a single study and as a result questions about the nature of the difference between the two populations have not been answered satisfactorily. It is apparent, to me at any rate, that a combination of disciplines, theories and methods is necessary, in order to bridge the gap in our understanding between mainstream and special education. The two areas have long been dominated by sociologists (Hargreaves, 1967; Lacey, 1970; Willis, 1977; Woods, 1979 and 1980a), and psychologists (Stott, 1956 and 1982; Rutter, 1975; Rutter *et al*, 1979; Laslett, 1977 and 1982) respectively. The combined strength of a sociological examination focusing on surrounding factors and a psychological emphasis on the individual, was in this case expected to produce the desired effect.

Concentrating on the individual has not been an established sociological method. Lacey (1975) attempts to give an explanation for this phenomenon stating that: 'Sociology as a discipline had to fight for space against established explanations of behaviour couched in terms of psychological determinants (mental attributes) genetic determinism (inherited characteristics) and, ironically, strongly established notions of unfettered free will and individual choice.' (p. 168). He goes on to dismiss the assumption that the individual merely transforms him/herself into the kind of person that a situation demands, as only a part of the process of socialization. He suggests that individuals are able, and should be encouraged, to analyze their problems and foresee future possibilities for themselves. In line with Lacey's 'reconsideration of the importance of the individual and notions of individual autonomy', this study has concentrated on the individual. Pupil decision-making has been the main focus of attention, although other factors (such as home and school background) are expected to influence the pupil's career in school.

This chapter will explore the thinking of the deviant pupils in the mainstream, trying to provide an understanding for their actions. It will be the task of chapter 5 to attempt a similar exploration on the thinking of the pupils in a special unit, and of the final chapter (chapter 7) to make the comparison between the two, and draw conclusions.

As stated in the methodology section, two main groups of pupils were identified for study in the mainstream school using questionnaires and observation. They were named group Q — seventeen pupils selected because of their high questionnaire score — and group O — twenty-seven pupils identified because of their high classroom profile during observation. The common total of these two groups, six boys and five girls, identified by both methods, were considered the most deviant in the fourth year. All eleven pupils were interviewed and closely observed, in an effort to discover their way of thinking, their short and long term goals regarding school, and the motivation behind their actions. Further analysis indicated that behaviour and attitude polarized them into two smaller groups, group A (the fun seekers) and group B (the troubled ones). This chapter and the next will concentrate on the two groups and demonstrate how different they were.

Group A

Group A consisted of three boys and three girls. Their distinguishing feature was their ability to define short and long-term school goals and their skill to achieve them. All six pupils possessed a coherent school philosophy and appeared able to relate their behaviour to their final aims and act accordingly. The clarity of their vision and the skill of their performance were truly remarkable.

Gender issues per se are not examined in this study, but they have been taken into account for it has been shown (Delamont, 1976 and 1980) that gender influences deviant behaviour. Because of similarities in school philosophy the boys and the girls of group A were grouped together, but because of their gender difference will be examined separately. As the argument develops each gender's particular characteristics will be outlined. This approach is expected to preserve the clarity of the argument, while doing justice to the particularities of both sexes. To avoid repetition, the main argument for group A will be presented in the first section which deals with the boys. The second section will concentrate on the special characteristics of the girls and their contribution to the group's profile.

I shall first introduce the fun-seeking boys indicating the scale of the problem they presented for their teachers. A presentation of their school philosophy will follow, outlining their academic ability and relating their behaviour to their goals. It will be shown that their short-term goal was to 'have fun in school', and two ways of achieving this goal will be described. The pupils' relationship with their peers will be examined next, and their dominant position in the pupil hierarchy will be established. Behaviour techniques aiming at retaining the group's dominant position will then be pointed out, and the differentiation between established behaviour patterns and active decision making in the classroom will be made clear. The purpose of the next section will be to explain why these pupils were interested in keeping a good balance between behaviour and attitude. A commitment to school qualifications will thus be revealed as a long-term goal, and the pupils will be seen to be interested in remaining within the school system, albeit without sacrificing their short-term goal of having fun. The interesting relationship of these pupils with their teachers will finally be described in an effort to strengthen the argument that these pupils sought and achieved a 'perfect balance' in school.

The Fun-seeking Boys

Getting to Know Them

The fun seekers were three: Michael, David and Richard. Although individually identified the pupils knew each other well as they were all in the same class. They would often sit together in common lessons and encourage and support each other's misbehaviour. When asked who their best friends in school were, they named each other. They all had a positive self image, and spoke confidently about school[1].

> **Michael:**   Fifteen years and three months old when interviewed, Michael was the most lively of the three, with the highest classroom profile. He always put himself forward in the class and was in constant interaction with teachers. For them his presence was a source of constant trouble and he used to be reported to the year tutor on a more or less regular basis. Nevertheless he was better known for the quantity rather than the quality of his misbehaviour.

> **David:**   Fifteen years and five months old when interviewed, David had the worst school record of all three, having been involved in fairly serious incidents with teachers and pupils alike. In the past he had hit a teacher and had repeatedly been excluded from lessons and from school. His classroom profile was also high, and teachers usually felt that they had to continually 'keep an eye' on him.

> **Richard:**   Fifteen years old when interviewed, Richard kept the lowest profile of the three boys. His misbehaviour was more covert, but he was particularly noticeable in the classroom during lessons common with the other two boys, who influenced him considerably. Richard was very critical of school and offered very strong views about how it should be run. He had also been involved in a number of fights with other pupils.

Relationships with the Establishment

The fun-seeking pupils by no means resembled the ideal pupil described by Woods (1975) and Keddie (1984). They were the least conformist group of the year and a main source of concern for their teachers. They criticized the school's academic orientation and general ethos which they considered dry and lacking in spirit and humour, and they were particularly critical of teachers[2].

HP:	Do you care about what teachers think . . .
David:	(interrupting me) No!
HP:	Why not? Is it because you don't respect them enough, or they don't matter much?
David:	Well, I don't really respect them . . .

And elsewhere:

David:	(describing an incident with a teacher) No teacher should hit any pupil!
HP:	Why not?
David:	Because they haven't got the authority to hit . . .
HP:	. . . So, what would you do if a teacher took your pen because you were writing while you were supposed to be listening?[3]
David:	I'd go and get it. They can't take the pen away! It's my pen! So . . . I'd go and get it . . .

HP:	You say that sometimes you like school and sometimes you don't. What does it depend on?
Richard:	What teachers treat you like and . . . things like that . . .

School rules carried no weight for group A pupils. They, like teachers, were open to judgment and criticism, and they did not always meet the pupils' criteria. Rules considered unnecessary or too strict or — even worse — silly or patronizing were not taken seriously, and were broken given the slightest opportunity.

Michael:	People without uniform is murder . . . And then, if you come to school without a tie and that . . . ten pence to hire a tie out! . . .
HP:	So, you would like them to be a bit looser . . .
Michael:	Yeah! About uniform . . .

HP:	Why do you smoke in school? Is it because you cannot go through the day without a cigarette?
Richard:	No, It's just a break really . . . When you have a break . . . I don't see why you can't smoke a fag . . .
HP:	. . . Is there anything you want to say that I haven't asked you about?
Richard:	Yeah! School ties! Why should we wear those? I don't like wearing a tie. I can't see the point. I just like to be casual. No smart ties and things like that . . .

As it is clear, no aspect of schooling was beyond question for the fun-seekers (see also Werthman, 1963). Questioning school staff and regulations was a matter of principle for them and their questionnaire score reflected their often unfavourable judgment. Implementation of these beliefs in everyday school life became apparent in the high classroom profile that helped identify them during observation. So we are dealing here with the most deviant, in attitude and behaviour, group of the fourth year, which appears to have a crystallized philosophy about school to base attitude and behaviour alike.

All three pupils had shown a considerable amount of misbehaviour in school which varied from lack of homework, to fights with pupils and arguments with teachers. The first led to detentions, and the latter two resulted in meetings with the year tutor, exclusions from lessons and suspensions from school. Confrontations with teachers were not uncommon, and the following incident, although rather atypical in its extremity, clearly illustrates the kind of misbehaviour these pupils were prone to.

HP: Tell me an incident . . . Something you can remember well . . .

David: Oh yes! A teacher called Mrs Levis . . . She hit me . . .
           She was a German teacher . . . She's not here now . . .

HP: How did it happen? Can you tell me from the beginning?

David: All right. I was messing about during the lesson, and she told us
           to go on with the work, and I was just talking and she came up
           to me and she slapped me on my face, so I hit her.

HP: She slapped you?

David: Yeah! So I hit her back and then just run out of the class, home.

HP: What were you thinking when you hit her? Did you have any-
           thing in mind?

David: Yeah! I was angry because she hit me! Any teacher who'd hit
           me, I'd hit him back. I was only talking about the work . . . Said
           what we had to do . . .

HP: And what happened?

David: When I got out of the door she followed me and tried to drag me
           back in. So I said 'f . . . off' and she just kept on pulling me
           about, so I hit her and just run out of the school . . . I was down
           by the road traffic lights when she got up to me and asked me
           to go back to school. I could see she was upset, so I came back
           into school. I went back and she said she was sorry . . .

HP: Did SHE apologize?

David: Yeah . . .

HP: YOU didn't apologize?

David: NO! (emphatically) I went back to her room and then she said:
           'I'm sorry about . . .'

HP: Ah! So you had a little chat . . .

David: Yeah . . . (smiling) We got on all right for a few weeks . . .

Of course not every argument with a teacher reached such a peak. Most of them never turned into a confrontation. But they were part of the pupils' everyday life, as indeed were other forms of misbehaviour.

HP:	Why were you outside the tutor's office the other day?
Michael:	Oh! I burned Jason's (group O) book in chemistry. It was a spastical little (intranscribable)
HP:	Who sent you out?
Michael:	Mr Hunt. It was risky, but I took the risk. He weren't there, but he came back and looked for it . . . See . . . most of the time I don't get caught.
HP:	What would you do if the teacher asked you to get out of the classroom because you were still talking when you were not supposed to? (*Hypothetical situatian number 1.*)
Richard:	Start moaning and groaning . . . Some of the times I say I was talking about the lesson . . .
Michael:	Start arguing . . . Always start arguing . . . I can't lose!
David:	I have an argument with him . . . So I show that I didn't notice him . . .
HP:	Why do you smoke in school?
Michael:	It's just, I don't know . . . Something like keeping in the back side and taking a drug! It's probably just the risk of it . . . I can give up if I want . . . But it's just the fun of it . . .
David:	I don't any more . . . I used to sometimes for fun . . . But it wasn't worth it! Teachers would come and we would have to throw it away and waste it . . .

The pupils' behaviour will become more understandable as their philosophy about school is explained.

School Philosophy

It has been mentioned that the fun-seekers were competent and skilful. This was not meant in academic terms. Their skill becomes apparent from the clever way they handled incidents with teachers. They were sensitive to teacher moods to the degree of anticipating their responses, and ingenious in the ways they modified their behaviour and manipulated every situation to their best advantage (Woods, 1980a). Keeping such a perfect balance was far from easy. Apart from insight into teachers' thoughts, it required ability to judge where the limits were, courage to push the situation up to there, and finally skill to control the incident so that it would not escalate any further. It can thus be argued that this was a very difficult task indeed. Yet, the fun seekers seemed to be perfectly able to meet the challenge and prove themselves successful. Intelligent thus the pupils were, but not in a strictly academic way[4].

None of the three pupils was academically minded, or had any plans for further education. In streamed classes they never qualified for the top groups. They mostly attended mixed CSE/'O' level courses, but were not particularly strong candidates for any significant number of 'O' levels[5]. Overall, the pupils' academic attitude and performance was inconsistent with their highly developed social abilities and skills, indicating that their academic potential was not fulfilled. So, while there was evidence to suggest that they were capable of performing better in school, they seemed to have accepted a 'second rate' academic part and to have opted for vocational subjects strongly linked with specific future plans[6].

HP: What do you want to do when you leave school?
David: Be a footballer I should think best!
HP: But it is very competitive. Isn't it? Are you good enough?
David: Yeah! I'm good. I'm in the school team . . .

Richard: I wanna work in a farm or be a bricklayer . . . 'Cause my father is a bricklayer and he took me to work with him a couple of times and I enjoyed it . . . And I used to work in a farm and I enjoyed that . . . Sitting in tractors . . .

The explanation for this 'underachievement' appears to lay with the pupils' home culture and the expectations developed there[7]. Whatever the reason for it, given the school's emphasis on academic achievement and the pupils' awareness and sensitivity to peer and teacher judgment, this 'failure' seemed to be a source of frustration for them (see Davies, 1979, about social pressure on boys to succeed academically). They refused to accept a second rate status, and they, like Werthman's gang (Werthman, 1963) wanted to make it clear to everybody that they were not second rate pupils. The academic field not being favourable for competition, a new field was required and found in the pupils' social world. The pupils exploited the existing social world for their own purposes, in the way suggested by Hargreaves (1967) and Lacey (1970). By emphasizing it in contrast to the official school world they appeared to be more successful than the academically able pupils, who were in effect excluded from it. In this way they created a culture with its own aims and rewards, detached from the school's academic culture. Pupil and school goals developed separately as Turner (1983) suggests. Within their culture the pupils were able to 'succeed', and prove that they were intelligent and competent[8].

Having fun in school by exploiting the system as much as possible was a genuine concern and the alternative this new culture offered to academic work[9]. Within this culture, success was judged on how much one could get away with, without becoming involved in serious trouble himself. The techniques used to achieve this purpose were useful for offering the pupils a genuinely enjoyable time and also very effective in proving that group A pupils were intelligent, because of the skill involved. Classroom behaviour shows how this was achieved:

First, fun was organized in a **social way**, through a group activity. *Communal eating* was a good example of that, attempting to fool a teacher by involving in the joke the whole class, teacher aside. This was implemented passing a packet of crisps or biscuits from one person to the other under the desks without the teacher noticing (see also Davies, 1979, and Mahony, 1985, for similar tricks used by pupils). Another example of communal fun was *asking for permission to go to the toilet*, one pupil after another, until a whole group was outside the classroom simultaneously. This game was not always successful, and often permission was granted to only one pupil at a time. An indication of it being a game and not a genuine need, is the fact that this activity was only attempted in lessons where the teacher was known for his/ her tolerance, or his/her inability to control the classroom effectively. What really happened once the pupils were outside the room is open to speculation, but Michael's response to my question after such an expedition is very enlightening.

> Michael asks for permission to go to the toilet, and he stays away for over ten minutes. My curiosity provoked by the time length, I go to ask him why he was away for so long. 'I was having a fag!' is Michael's calm answer.

A third method of communal fun was *taking advantage of a real classroom need to extend the limits of one's behaviour* — or misbehaviour. That was easily done in practical lessons because of the genuine need for pupil mobility in the classroom. In keyboarding lessons, for example, the pupils would often walk around pretending to be looking for the corrective fluid to correct their typing mistakes[10] or some other indispensable item.

Individual initiative could also function as a source of fun:

> In a History lesson with Mrs Kilby there is a knock on the door.
>
> *David:* (shouting from the back of the class) Come in!
> *Mrs Kilby:* David, will you please keep your comments to yourself?

Incidents where the effort to exploit the limits of the school rules and ridicule the system is evident, also occurred outside the classroom. Here is a good example.

> Michael has come to school in an unusual pair of jeans. According to school rules, jeans are not allowed, so his teacher sends him to see the year tutor. The year tutor, however, is faced with a problem about punishing Michael, because although his trousers are not of the acceptable material, they are not denim jeans either. The tutor is looking at Michael puzzled.
>
> *Mr Daff:* Why are you wearing these trousers Michael? Don't you know that they are not allowed?

Michael: Sir, I bought them because the advert said: 'If you don't want your son to wear jeans, buy these trousers!'
Mr Daff: They are not denim jeans. I'll grant you that . . .

While the tutor is looking confused and is wondering what to do with Michael, the latter is trying to look innocent and keep a straight face, but there is a laugh in his eyes. Finally the tutor says:

Mr Daff: Well, I'll let you off this time, but don't wear them again!

Michael leaves the tutor's office with a big smile on his face.

As it is evident, the pupils thoroughly enjoyed these incidents which gave them the opportunity to challenge teacher and school authority. This behaviour also won them other pupils' admiration. These were achievements that would not have been possible through the school's official culture and rendered this 'alternative' culture very rewarding indeed.

Status amongst Peers

Because of their success in challenging school authority, the fun-seekers appeared to hold a high position in the pupils' social hierarchy. This hierarchy could be assessed by observing pupil behaviour and attitude to each other, pupil fights, and victimization of certain individuals or groups. Group A being at the top, it appears that the majority of pupils identified through the questionnaire and the observation followed, with group B at the bottom, conformists and high fliers excluded (see Hargreaves, 1967, and McGrew and Phtiaka 1984, on social hierarchies). The high position of the fun-seekers was expressed in the way the pupils of the group were respected and occasionally feared by their peers. The following incidents which occurred during observation might help clarify the group's position in their peers' eyes.

Michael is having a quiet fight with Matthew (group O) in Biology. Matthew seems to be in pain but he doesn't dare call the teacher in assistance, probably because he is anxious about what Michael's revenge might be after that. So, the incident finishes without the teacher ever noticing, but it has been tough enough for Matthew to have tears in his eyes.

And:

Robin (group O) is talking to Michael across the classroom in Maths:

Robin: What did you do in the PE yesterday?
Michael: Basketball.

> *Robin:* Woody woofters go there!
> *Michael:* Shut up! It's better that football.
> *Robin:* (He quietens down and does not make any further comments.

It is clear here that Robin, a natural tease, has been intimidated by Michael to the extent of not daring to make any more comments challenging the status of basketball as a game.

> David is restless in English. First he throws a paper ball to the pupil sitting in front of him. The pupil does not respond. Then, he starts sticking pieces of sellotape on Martin's (group O) hair. Martin, who is sitting next to David, does not react and allows David to do as he pleases. A minute later, the teacher notices the paper on the floor and asks the class who has thrown it. Nobody says anything, except Martin who tries to tell the teacher about David. Before he has a chance to open his mouth, Dave twists his arm and holds it up. Martin does not say anything to the teacher.

The dominant position of this group was occasionally disputed, however, and challenged by other pupils. When this occurred, it provoked direct confrontation.

> *David:* I've been on report for beating this boy up . . .
> *HP:* Which one?
> *David:* The Italian boy. He was new, he was loud . . .
> *HP:* Why did you beat him up?
> *David:* He was claiming he was the he-man, he could beat everyone up. So he told Daniel, you know Daniel (group O), he told him, and we all went to see the Italian boy, and then he said that I was staring and that . . . and he started pushing me, so I hit him . . . I knocked him out . . .
> *HP:* And what happened?
> *David:* I knocked him out!
> *HP:* And what happened with Mr Daff after that?
> *David:* Nothing! He put me on report . . . I was excluded from school . . .
> *HP:* Oh! You call this nothing?
> *David:* Well, really, I've been excluded a couple of times . . .

Showing off Techniques and Perfect Balance

The high hierarchical position appeared to offer the satisfaction pursued, but it also created responsibilities for showing off, and this kept the pupils in constant struggle. Retaining a good reputation with one's peers may be important for all pupils, but it was absolutely essential for the fun seekers. A good deal of effort and thought was devoted therefore in devising showing off and face saving techniques. Six such techniques were identified, requiring various degrees of subtlety. Special attention has to be drawn to the way all of them were used to achieve maximum results with minimum danger. Being successful in showing off to other pupils without taking any major risks with the teachers was a phenomenon consistent throughout the pupils' classroom behaviour, indicating just how clever and skilful they were. These techniques are described below.

Creating and retaining a masculine image has been shown to be vital within sub-culture groups (Willis, 1977), and it was an important part of the showing off behaviour techniques used by group A, as the following example indicates.

> It is my first observation of the technical drawing lesson. Michael starts waving to me as soon as he gets into the classroom. He comes close and tries to see what I am writing. I hide my papers and he eventually goes away. From his seat he keeps waving to me. As I try to ignore him, he says something to David and they both laugh, looking at me. All three pupils, Michael, David and Richard, appear to be quite disturbed by my presence. They keep nodding and smiling and they sing the tune of the British Telecom television advertisement: 'It's for youhou!'. In the end, the teacher has to turn to them and say: 'Shut up!'. A little later, David — after making sure that the whole class is listening — asks me to go out with him for a drink.

This type of incident occurred mainly in the most 'masculine' classroom groups, constituted exclusively of boys attending a traditionally male topic, such as motor vehicle engineering, technical drawing or computer studies, where the teacher was also a man. Group A were always prominent in making these jokes in the classroom, behaviour contrasted to that maintained when alone with me. In the latter situation they were shy and reserved, never attempting similar jokes.

This phenomenon was far from being directed solely at me. Female pupils were not any safer. They too were considered legitimate targets for similar jokes or patronizing behaviour. Willis (1977) and Mahony (1985) give a very detailed picture of the girls' role in schoolboys' exhibition of masculinity. The next incident indicates this point:

> It is the last period on a Thursday and David starts getting restless in English. He begins to throw paper balls into a girl's handbag as if he were playing basket ball. The girl does not react and the teacher does not notice.

Another showing off technique was *to delay conforming with the teacher's demand*. Timing was very important here, because it was used to prove that the pupil was not afraid of the teacher or overtly conformist and obedient. On the other hand, too long a delay could cause friction with the teacher which was best avoided. An incident between Michael and Mr Harris in computer science will illustrate this technique:

Michael is playing with a roll of sellotape. He cuts strips from it and then sticks them on his lips, so that he is, in the end, unable to open his mouth.

Mr Harris:	(facing the blackboard) Do you want some more paper?
Michael:	Mmmm . . . (he can not talk).
Mr Harris:	(looks at him and notices what he has done) I didn't think it was possible for you to get more stupid that usual!
Michael:	Mmmm . . .
Mr Harris:	Stop messing around now and listen! Right?
Michael:	Mmmm . . .

The teacher ignores him and gets on with the lesson. Michael does not take the sellotape off right away. He takes his time and eventually does so a little later as if he became bored with his own game.

The delay in Michael's final reaction is important in this incident. Michael did, in effect, comply with the teacher's demand by removing the sellotape, so the teacher had no reason to punish him. Because of Michael's delay however, the teacher's command appeared to have been ignored.

A similar technique, based on time delay, required *compromise only after the teacher had repeated his/her command a few times.* It was very effective, because the pupil demonstrated to the whole classroom that he could trouble the teacher for as long as he chose to, before he paid any attention, but at the same time did not take any major risks, and kept a relatively low profile during the incident. This was a very popular technique because it offered plenty of opportunity for showing off being proud and daring and unwilling to compromise. So popular was it, that direct compliance occupied no part in the group's behaviour repertoire. Often the teacher gave up before the pupil did. Below is a small example of the way the technique was used.

Michael and Richard are talking in the keyboarding lesson.

Mrs Currell:	Gentlemen!
Michael and Richard:	(they smile and happily keep talking)
Mrs Currell:	Just do your work please . . .
Michael and Richard:	(keep ignoring her)

Having the last word could also be extremely useful even if the pupil did conform in the end, which was not always the case. The fun-seekers used every possible opportunity to have the last word.

In English Richard is talking to the pupil next to him.

Mrs Brown:	Get on with your work!
Richard:	(whispering) I am . . .

A minute later and while Richard is still talking.

Mrs Brown:	Shut up!
Richard:	(gives her a nasty look).

And a more successful attempt:

In a TD lesson Michael is shouting across the classroom ignoring the teacher who is asking him to get on. The teacher decides to move him in an effort to isolate and quieten him down.

Mr Hodder:	Move a bit please. (He moves Michael's desk himself).
Michael:	That's all right Sir! (and moves his desk a few inches back which brings him close to his previous position).

Misbehaving in some way while conforming overall was another popular method of keeping one's name clear of conformist accusations, while retaining a level of compliance that could satisfy the teacher[11].

During a Maths session with Mrs Manners the pupils are having a test. Michael appears to be concentrating on his exam while he is chewing gum (forbidden by the school rules). There is total silence in the classroom and the chewing noise is distinctly clear and audible.

Mrs Manners:	Shhh!
Michael:	(stops chewing for a moment and then starts again.)
Mrs Manners:	Shhh!
Michael:	(repeats his previous response and that takes him to the end of the test without more trouble).

And David in history with Mrs Kilby.

The pupils have recently come into the classroom. David still has his coat on, although he knows that this is against school regulations.

Mrs Kilby:	Take off your coat.
David:	(takes it off and starts ripping a piece of paper)
Mrs Kilby:	David!
David:	(ignores her and keeps ripping the paper; a little later he starts distributing crisps).

The teacher does not insist any more.

Finally Richard using a more subtle way to deviate in maths.

The teacher has just finished talking and he has set some exercises for the pupils to do.

Mr Murfet: Get on with your writing now.
Richard: (starts writing with a red pen)
Mr Murfet: Write in blue please, not in red normally.
Richard: (changes pen).

Using humour was finally one of the best ways of showing off and one of the most sophisticated techniques used.

Michael has come to school without a tie, which is against school regulations. His maths teacher observes that in the beginning of the lesson.

Mrs Manners: Michael where is your tie?
Michael: I forgot it Miss.
Mrs Manners: OK. You go and tell Mr Daff about that.
Michael: (gets up to go to the year tutor's office and takes his coat with him)
Mrs Manners: What do you want that for?
Michael: To keep me company!

With his last move and comment, Michael has turned the whole situation around. Until a minute ago he was a pupil being told off for disobeying the school rules. After his comment he appears to be in control of the situation. He is implying that he is going to take his time and enjoy this walk offered especially to him when everyone else in the class will be working. Instead of being in a difficult position, he appears to be enjoying himself.

Effective as all these techniques were for retaining a good reputation for group A when used in isolation for minor interactions, they became much more powerful used in combination during an incident with a teacher. It was in situations like this that the particular skill of the group became apparent. This fine art of perfect balance in exploiting every possible limit of school and teacher rules without getting in trouble was the epitomy of the group's achievements, encapsulating their whole school philosophy (for the distinction between the two see Pollard, 1979 and Bird, 1980). A perfect example of this method is given here by Michael. The techniques of masculine image and humour are employed for the particular situation.

The incident occurs in a computer studies lesson with Mr Harris. It is a theory session, and the subject is difficult and tiring. Michael is restless. Instead of concentrating on the lesson he keeps waving to me.

Mr Harris: (staring at him) If you can't behave yourself you'll have to come at the front.
Michael: (complains)
Mr Harris: (does not insist and ignores him for the time being.)

A minute later Michael is playing with the boy sitting next to him.

| *Mr Harris:* | Michael listen! |
| *Michael:* | (stops being noisy for a moment) |

Only a minute later he starts laughing. He and his friend are looking at me. Michael blows a kiss to me.

Mr Harris:	Shut up Michael.
Michael:	(stops being noisy but does not start working).
Mr Harris:	Come on, get on!
Michael:	(ignores the command).

A minute later the teacher notices that Michael is still not working.

Mr Harris:	What are you doing?
Michael:	(tries to find excuses).
Mr Harris:	(calmly) Come and sit with me at the front.
Michael:	(does not move) I have something to do . . .
Mr Harris:	(lets him off for a second time).

A little later. Michael has still not started working or behaving himself.

| *Mr Harris:* | Come on Michael! (tries to move him). |
| *Michael:* | (initially refuses to go, but eventually moves declaring that he is on strike). |

In his new place, Michael keeps a low profile for some time and eventually, when things appear to be back to normal, he starts misbehaving again.[12]

Michael kept switching on and off conformist behaviour responses here. Instead of being consistently negative, he occasionally conformed to the teacher's demands. This gave the impression that Michael did not wish to upset the teacher and, somehow, that he was not continuously misbehaving. Eventually the time came for him to decide if he was going to conform or not, when the teacher insisted on his command and seemed, for the first time, not to be prepared to take 'no' for an answer. At that crucial point, Michael took the decision to conform, for no other reason, it appears, than not wanting the incident to become serious. He appeared to believe that it was time to obey and 'give the teacher a break'. He could always start again later, which indeed he did, without taking any risks. So, it was the apparent wish to keep the teacher happy and the situation within limits that seems to have led Michael to a conformist approach.

It has been shown that these pupils possessed a number of techniques which helped them retain amongst their peers a reputation for being 'tough' and daring with teachers. This was achieved not only because they were successful in challenging teacher authority, but also because they succeeded in doing so without being punished, by remaining just within the limits. Before going on to investigate the reasons why the pupils were so concerned with retaining this balance, it is worth examining their decision making process.

The high level performance described was not continually kept up as there was no constant need for it. Pupil behaviour was generally governed by patterns established for each lesson and teacher. This became apparent by the subtle differentiation of pupil behaviour in different lessons. Furlong (1976) clearly demonstrates this differentiation in the behaviour of the pupils he studied. Using techniques similar to those described by Woods (1975), Gannaway (1976), Ball (1980) and Measor and Woods (1984) during their first time with a new teacher, the pupils 'tested the ground' and discovered how much they could 'get away with'. They then used this information in their daily decision making.

This use of established behaviour patterns was very economical and saved both time and effort while deciding about everyday matters[13]. By familiarizing them with the limits of teacher behaviour tolerance, it helped prevent unnecessary risks. Describing a similar situation of established behaviour patterns between pupils and teachers, Pollard (1984) argues that this is the result of a 'common consensus' or a 'truce'. This did not seem to be the case here. These patterns seemed to be the result of a clearly competitive process (see also Delamont, 1976; Denscombe, 1980). The more powerful party, be it the teacher or the pupils, appeared to be imposing its own terms on the relationship, not always to the satisfaction of the other party. The result, rather than being a 'truce', was a 'status quo' after a struggle. Ideal balance between the parties was very rarely achieved. Depending on a variety of reasons[14], there were lessons where the teacher had virtually no control over the pupils[15], and yet others where he/she was in complete control, and the pupils could use only very subtle ways of deviating.

The majority of interactions for classroom survival were apparently carried out using established behaviour patterns. However, decision making was still important when things went beyond the normal and a 'crisis' situation arose. The pupil had to be quick at recognizing it as such and realizing that established behaviour patterns would be of no use. New decision making was needed. It was not always easy for a pupil to pick up in the teacher's behaviour the clues that warned him/her about the change of situation[16]. The fun-seekers were very successful in achieving that, an important skill indicating yet again their awareness and sensitivity.

Becoming aware of this change was a necessary but not sufficient condition for modifying one's behaviour. Factors like self-judgment, teacher judgment, pupil-teacher relationship and last, but not least, status amongst peers[17] necessarily influenced the pupil's decision. The skill of these pupils lay in being able to adapt quickly their behaviour to fit the new circumstances and find responses that would provide maximum gain with minimum loss. In the incidents that follow their ability to adapt their behaviour according to the circumstances will be confirmed, and the motivation behind their willingness to do so will be examined.

How Deviant is Deviant?

We have established so far that although the fun-seekers invested an enormous amount of effort in challenging school and teacher authority, they also took great care in remaining within the limits of acceptable behaviour. It has been argued that this attracted their peers' respect and helped them maintain their reputation for being skilful as well as daring. But this was not the main reason for the pursuit of a perfect balance. The pupils of this group had reasons connected with their long-term school goals to want to remain within acceptable limits. This section will explore these reasons.

Having examined the lengths these pupils went to in order to retain their peers' respect, it is time to examine two incidents where their decision making does not appear to be addressed to their peers. (It is essential to know the important role of peers for group A, in order to appreciate the sacrifice made in the incidents described below.) Both incidents occurred in the technical drawing lesson[18], in a day when the lesson had been particularly noisy and the pupils particularly restless. The teacher was Mr Hodder.

> Michael and Jason (group O), who is sitting next to him, are fighting with their rulers and their desks.

> | *Mr Hodder:* | Leave the tables alone and get on! |
> |---|---|
> | *Michael* | |
> | *(and Jason):* | (ignore him) |
> | *Mr Hodder:* | Both of you will have to stay later if you go on. |
> | *Michael* | |
> | *(and Jason):* | (stop fighting) |

> A minute later Michael is walking in the class.

> | *Mr Hodder:* | Go to your seat. |
> |---|---|
> | *Michael:* | (annoyed) Oh! Kiss my . . . (he doesn't finish his sentence) |
> | *Mr Hodder:* | Right! You better stay late! |
> | *Michael:* | Oh! Sorry Sir! |

Michael's humble response to the teacher's threat was very surprising. The level of behaviour tolerance shown by this teacher was such as to result in a very low respect response from the pupils[19]. The pupils were very frequently beyond his reach, and rarely addressed him as 'sir'. Established behaviour patterns therefore allowed for a great degree of deviance on Michael's part. Consequently Michael's behaviour was very unusual and uncharacteristic. His reaction, however, had apparently been appropriate and his timing evidently good. The teacher allowed him to leave as soon as the bell rang without any further punishment. Nevertheless, the image damage had been done. Michael had been obliged to humiliate himself in front of his friends in order to avoid detention. Importantly, he had willingly chosen to do so.

It was in the same lesson that a more extensive and dramatic incident between Mr Hodder and David occurred.

> David is talking during the lesson.

> | *Mr Hodder:* | Come on please! |
> |---|---|
> | *David:* | (quiets down) |

A little later he is walking in the classroom.

Mr Hodder:	David! David come back!
David:	All right! (annoyed)
Mr Hodder:	Any more of this and you are out!
David:	(comes back and sits in his seat)

A few minutes later he becomes restless again and lights a match under his desk.

Mr Hodder:	Get out!
David:	(in a low tone) What for?
Mr Hodder:	For this . . . (shows the box of matches)
David:	(gets up and walks out without another word).

David stays outside the class for the rest of the lesson. A little later I can see him, through the door window, lighting another match when the teacher is turned with his back to the door. (The teacher has not taken the matches away from him.) When the bell rings David comes in and asks for permission to go:

David:	Can I go sir?
Mr Hodder:	No, sit down.
David:	(whispers f . . . but comes in and sits down)

The teacher keeps David in for about five minutes of the lunch break. The pupil is flushed, looks desperate to go and very annoyed. His friends are watching him through the door window and are making silly faces to him. David looks very humiliated but he does not make a move or whisper a thing until the teacher lets him go.

There was a small effort to save face on David's part, when he initially tried to answer back to the teacher: *'What for?'*, and again when he lit another match outside the classroom. However, he was not taking any major risks with either of these actions. In the first case he kept his tone carefully low, so as not to cause an argument with the teacher. In the second, he took care to light his match when the teacher was placed in such a position that he was unable to see or smell the match. Both of these actions were clearly directed to his friends in the classroom. Finally, his swearing was between his teeth, not for anyone to hear, indicating frustration rather than resistance. However not even these efforts could significantly reduce the impression David's final compromise created on his friends.

The peer pressure under which both pupils were operating during these incidents would appear to be considerable, and should not be underestimated[20]. It is for this reason that their compromise was all the more important. When one considers the lengths to which the fun-seekers usually went in order to retain their reputation in front of their classroom 'mates', one can not but appreciate the sacrifice made by allowing the teacher to have a 'victory' over them in the above incidents. One cannot but disagree again with Pollard's statement (Pollard, 1984), about pupils preferring to maintain their image when other interests are threatened. This possibly occurs in extreme situations where the pupil publicly humiliated is given no alternative. In these cases the pupil has to protect his/her image at any cost. A good example of this is the incident where David hit Mrs Levis. In other cases, stepping back seems to be a preferred technique by deviant pupils within the mainstream. Considering that this was the most deviant group of the year priding themselves on lack of fear and manipulating abilities, the wish to avoid further trouble seems to be the only possible motive for compromise. The question thus arises what were the reasons for the group's wish to avoid any further trouble. Why would such pupils be interested in not going too far? Why the need for maintaining a balance at all?

The answer would seem to be, because the pupils were not as disinterested in school as they hitherto appeared to be. Some of their views might indeed be very surprising in the conservative attitude they reflect.

HP: Would you like to have a pupil smoking room?

Michael: It wouldn't be too bad, but it would start a lot of people smoking . . . (implying this wouldn't be a good thing)

David: School ain't too bad . . . It's not too bad . . . It's all right . . . . . . I don't wanna be told off, I don't wanna get in trouble . . .

HP: You say that teachers punish pupils because they don't want them to do bad things.

David: Yeah . . .

HP: That means that you actually accept punishment.

David: Yeah.

HP: You believe in keeping the rules . . .

David: Yeah . . .

HP: You say that you care very much what teachers think of you. Why do you care?

Richard: 'Cause I don't want them to think I'm a dosser or something like that . . .

HP: Why? Does it matter if they do?

Richard: Yeah! 'Cause I'm not! It's reputation and things like that . . .

HP: . . . Why do you stick on the rules?

Richard: 'Cause it's not worth breaking them! You know . . . Don't wanna get in trouble . . . It's not worth it . . .

So, it appears that the fun-seekers did not completely reject the school system. They accepted some of its goals, and were not indifferent about their school reputation. A validation of the pupil statements came from classroom observation.

David's effort to keep in touch with the development of the lesson, while engaging in quite disruptive behaviour in the following incident, gave a proof of the truth of his statement about keeping the rules.

> It is a history lesson with Mrs Kilby. David likes both the teacher and the lesson, but this is not enough to stop him at the back of the class from continually talking and encouraging others to do the same. The noise is enough to often prevent me from hearing what the teacher has said. David, however, seems to be keeping in touch with everything in the lesson that interests him, and not only for the opportunity of making a joke. The lesson is about Germany in the period before the Second World War, when the Nazi party was becoming stronger.
>
> > *Mrs Kilby:* Lots of bully boy acts in Germany . . .
> > *David:* (loud) Lovely!
>
> A minute later, the teacher asks him a question about the lesson and he is in a position to confidently give the right answer.

David's behaviour did not seem to isolate him from the lesson or interfere with his learning in a major way. In this instance he managed to have fun without failing to learn. This is because he entertained some respect for learning partly extending to some teachers. This respect was apparent in a wide range of pupils activities outside the classroom, an example of which is given here:

> On 15 October the school's youth club had organized a disco for the pupils and their friends. During that night a group of people caused a big fight which had resulted in damage to school property. The next day, Michael, along with other pupils having been at the disco the previous night, was called out of the classroom to give evidence to the head of the pastoral care on what had happened. Not only did he appear to adopt a serious attitude and help as much as he could with the inquiry, but he came back to the lesson looking concerned and he gave no cause for attention for the rest of the lesson, a form of behaviour unusual for him.

It seems that despite exploiting all possible limits in pursuit of fun in school, these pupils knew very well what serious trouble was and where its limits were, and were very concerned not to cross those limits. This explains the pupils' determination to compromise in critical moments and to avoid major risks. It also suggests that there was clearly a point where these pupils drew the line[21], and this will prove to be of major importance in the group's comparison with the other deviant groups, because it indicates that the main reason keeping this group of deviant pupils within the mainstream school was their own wish not to cross this line.

Deviant as their behaviour was, the pupils of group A appeared to subscribe to some school values, and to believe that they needed the qualifications the school had to offer, if they were to make progress in later life[22]. This ultimate commitment to education as a useful tool for the future was apparent in the interviews:

HP: What lessons do you like?

Michael: I like drawing, English I've got to like 'cause I've got to do it, maths I've got to do it, so I've got to like it, and general science is all right . . . And I've got to do motor vehicle engineering 'cause I'm trying to work in a garage . . .

           . . . You need MVE and that, and you need English and maths to be all right. I'll probably take some lessons . . . I shall go to a further education course . . . 'Cause all these people are trying to get jobs . . . I bet I won't stand a chance . . .

David: . . . I don't want to be on the dole! (strongly)

HP: What do you want to do then?

David: Anything!

So, their future career was an issue these pupils had considered, and school qualifications were apparently regarded as necessary for it. This did not result in unquestionable keeping of school regulations, but prepared them to compromise and ensured that they remained in school and made use of the opportunities offered[23], feature that separates them from other deviant groups. Their philosophy could be summarized as 'making the best of school'. If their behaviour is seen in this light, its apparent contradictions can be understood and explained.

The explanation[24] for the pupils' ultimate conformism therefore, one can only speculate, seems to lie in the job opportunities arising from qualifications gained in school. These kept their hope alive and did not allow them to become disillusioned with school. The pupils possibly believed school could help them in their future quest for a job because in West Town, and Westershire in general, unemployment rates were amongst the lowest in the country. It seems that for such an area, where competition remains high but the hope is not lost, schools can still be seen to offer important services, and can be considered worthy places to attend. High unemployment has been seen to have an immediate effect on pupil school views (Willis, 1977; Corrigan, 1979). It is not surprising that low unemployment should also be reflected in pupil attitude towards school. Parental belief in school value should also be taken into account. Although the school was firmly located in a working class area and the people there were mainly relying on manual labour to make a living, the majority of parents were employed, and appeared to keep a close eye on their children's school progress. School had not lost its value with the parents either[25] as the following interview extracts indicate.

HP: How do you get on with your homework? Do you do it?

Michael: Yes, most of the time . . . not most of the time, sometimes . . . Well . . . if my Mum finds out, I've got to do it on the night and hand it in next day!

HP: You said you smoke in school . . .

Richard: Yeah, not a lot . . . I'm trying not to get caught because if that goes home . . . I'm in trouble . . .

Relationships with Teachers

I have so far shown that group A consisted of the most deviant pupils in the fourth year who had in their record a number of detentions and suspensions for arguing with teachers and fighting with pupils. I have also indicated how their underlying commitment to education ultimately led them to compromise, and how this created a conflict with the image they were trying hard to portray in school. Evidently, being critical of school without rejecting it is not impossible. Having a good time is not incompatible with retaining fairly good relationships with the establishment. A closer examination of these pupils' relationships with their teachers will verify this.

An initial examination of the incidents described so far between pupils and teachers gives perhaps the impression that these pupils were in constant war with their teachers. This was not true[26]. Despite the fact that there was constant interaction between the two parts, the incidents — as we have seen — very rarely went out of control. In spite of the strong language sometimes used, there were no apparent hostile feelings on either side. The pupils, although very critical of the teachers, generally liked them on a personal level. The majority of the teachers felt the same way about the pupils. There appeared to be an adult-to-adult relationship which often turned what looked like a battle into a game. This was evident in the way pupils and teachers interacted, each party giving the other breathing space between and during incidents. It was also apparent in the light-hearted comments exchanged between pupils and teachers in daily classroom interaction. Often the comments developed into a game that seemed to be enjoyed by both parties as is apparent here:

> In Maths with Mrs Manners, Michael is eating a lollipop offered to him by Sean (group O), who is sitting next to him.
>
> | *Mrs Manners:* | (going close to him) Open up! |
> | *Michael:* | (opens his mouth and the teacher takes the lollipop and throws it in the bin despite Michael's protests). |
>
> Sean gives Michael new sweets. They both start eating, and they throw the wrapping papers on the floor. The teacher sees the papers and says:
>
> | *Mrs Manners:* | Will you please not throw rubbish on my floor? |
> | *Michael*: | (he stops throwing papers but does not collect the ones that are down already) |
>
> A little later Sean offers Michael another lollipop. Michael puts it in his mouth. The teacher approaches him and pulls the end of the lollipop stick.
>
> | *Mrs Manners:* | Get it out! |
> | *Michael:* | (keeps playing around and won't open his mouth and let go of the lollipop) |
>
> The stick comes off, and the teacher throws it away allowing Michael to chew the lollipop. The atmosphere is light and relaxed throughout the whole incident.[27]

The point of this section is not to undermine the argument developed so far, but to highlight the reality of the situation. There is no doubt that these pupils demanded extra effort and thus created extra work for their teachers. There is no doubt that life in school would have been much easier for the teachers, but for these pupils. There is finally no doubt that some teachers suffered enormous stress from the presence of these pupils in their classroom[28]. Nevertheless, a general feeling of good will came across from both teachers and pupils, indicating a lack of any fundamentally hostile feelings on either side. This is going to be another important point in the comparison of this group with group B.

At first glance it seems strange that such a relationship should exist, but there is an explanation. Respect for education can lead to respect for, or at least tolerance of, teachers, because they are the people who own and transmit the respected knowledge. This seems to have happened here. Even if it was not respect these pupils felt for their teachers, it is not surprising that skilful and shrewd as they were they should know the value of good working relationships. If they believed that school had something to offer them, then they probably realized that the teachers were the key to accessing it. And so they tried to be on reasonably good terms with them[29].

Finally, it seemed to be understood on both sides, and somehow agreed upon, that the pupils' misbehaviour was only a way of making their time in school more enjoyable, and rarely developed into a serious challenge of teacher authority. As a consequence, the teachers on the whole did not appear to feel threatened, and did not attempt to humiliate or control the pupils as long as they did not step out of the 'agreed' limits. Woods (1975) and Hargreaves *et al*, (1975) also mention this phenomenon.

HP: Have you ever had an argument with a teacher?

Michael: Nothing really bad . . . Talking . . . That's all . . . I don't know why . . . Always start arguing . . . I can't lose! I suppose I have to lose sometimes . . . 'Cause if they start getting too high, you might have to back out, say sorry and all that . . . and give up . . .

HP: So, you don't argue back in a nasty way . . . You don't get angry . . .

Michael: I don't get angry, no. When they start . . . say I've got a detention . . . If I haven't done it by a certain time, I have to do it . . .

It would not be an exaggeration to argue that some teachers even enjoyed the company and the challenge of the fun-seekers, who often offered them a 'laugh' in a dull school day (also see Pollard, 1979 and 1984).

Conclusion

Summarizing, I have to point out that the fun-seekers, who presented teachers with the most challenges and possessed a coherent anti-school philosophy to back their behaviour up, appeared, when examined more closely, to believe that school was of some relevance to their lives. As a result, they developed two apparent sets of aims for their school life. Their **short-term aim** was to have as much fun as possible taking advantage of what the pupil social world had to offer. Their **long-term aim**, taking advantage of what the school as an establishment had to offer, appeared to be far more important, and forced the pupils to make a number of compromises, even at the expense of their short term satisfaction, in order to remain in school. The behaviour of the group appears thus to be ruled by coherent reasoning and premeditated thinking of a profound level. This was also true for the girls of the group whose views will now be presented.

The Fun-seeking Girls

Getting to Know Them

As indicated above, the two genders are discussed separately, so that the similarity of their thinking and motivation will not be overshadowed by differences in their behaviour owing to gender differences (noted in Delamont, 1976)[30]. In order to avoid repetition, only the pupils' differences are described here. As a consequence the pupils in this section appear to deviate from some forms of behaviour described above. For the same reason, this section is smaller in size. Nevertheless it should be seen as an extension and a compliment to the previous one. Before concentrating on the fun seeking girls, some information about the position and behaviour of fourth year girls in general is necessary. It will also help clarify the differences described later.

The girls and the boys of each group, Q, O, Q-O A and Q-O B, exhibited broadly the same school attitude, their views not being very different. The differences observed were mainly located in classroom behaviour apparent during the extensive observation carried out in Burleigh High. Inside the classroom the boys seemed to monopolize teacher attention, a point also made by Davies (1979) and Mahony (1985). The majority of girls' misbehaviour was confined mainly to minor 'sins'[31]. These were forms of misbehaviour that did not necessarily demand interaction with the teacher, and did not cause any noise which would threaten the 'quiet orderliness of the classroom' (Denscombe, 1980), such as whispering, eating, combing one's hair, wearing a coat inside the classroom (strictly forbidden by the school rules), etc. While teachers were constantly kept busy by the boys, the girls took every opportunity to do as little work and as much talking as possible without giving much cause for attention (Measor, 1983, reports a similar phenomenon in the behaviour of the pupils she studied). Direct challenge of teachers by girls was rare, and the most serious incidents they became involved in, were — not surprisingly — related to other girls[32]. On the whole, it was fighting with other pupils that brought some of these girls to school attention, and not arguing with teachers.

The hierarchy, so clearly defined and fought for in the boys' case, was not a major issue with the girls. The only clear hierarchical division was that girls came after boys[33]. This status was expressed in a multitude of ways spreading from boys' priority to favourite classroom seats, to girls been told off by boys in class for misbehaving or not acting lady-like, (also reported by Measor, 1983). As will be shown later, group B, the troubled boys, were at the bottom of the pupil social hierarchy. It seems, however, that even that group was higher up than girls. An example of this is given here from observation notes:

> The pupils have been told to wash their hands after an experiment in general science. There is a queue for the washbasin and Mark (group B) and Zoe (group B) are the last to wash. Mark is fighting with Zoe about who is going to wash first and he wins.

Mark, as it will later become clear, was the most timid of pupils who carefully avoided confrontation with peers. He was often bullied by other boys, especially group A boys, and as a rule he gave in very easily. It seems however that even Mark was not prepared to be beaten by a girl[34].

Although the relationship between the two sexes was generally very friendly, some of boys' comments to girls could be particularly harsh, and often touched the boundaries of sexual harassment, as the example here indicates[35].

> In Mr Harris' Maths lesson, a girl makes a loud comment to her friend about losing her pussy. The boys hear it and start laughing and teasing her. Martin (group O) goes over the top with his comment. He shouts across the classroom:
>
> *Martin:* Ask your boyfriend! He might have it . . . Is it a male or a female? What colour is it? Black?
>
> The girl blushes and does not respond. The teacher does not interfere.

Incidents of that type were not uncommon, and teacher interference — when observed — was not always in support of the weaker party, which was most frequently the girls[36].

This being the girls' position in general, group A girls seemed to be at the top of the girls' social hierarchy[37]. They like the boys of their group — were far from the 'ideal pupil' model. They criticised school, its rules and its teachers, and though more subtle, they made their objection quite clear. The three fun seeking girls were:

Fiona: Fifteen years and four months old when interviewed, Fiona had already been involved in a serious fight with a girlfriend from Burleigh High, which had brought her to court. She had been punished with twelve months conditional discharge and she was after that trying to be more careful. It seems that occasional outbursts in temper were (according to her own account verified by the year tutor) largely due to a very unhappy home situation, and her school record was not as bad as this incident suggests. Fiona was very lively and talkative, and found it difficult to be quiet in the class. As a result, she attracted a lot of attention but she never became involved in a serious confrontation with a teacher.

Jackie: Fifteen years and one month old, Jackie had the worst school record of all three girls. She had been expelled from one school already for a fight with an older girl, which had been considered serious enough to be taken to court. She had been charged with Actual Bodily Harm, had been fined £25 and ordered to stay out of trouble. After being expelled she remained out of school for a few months before being accepted by Burleigh High. Jackie was quick to respond to harsh language or rough treatment from teachers, but she could be cooperative and hard working when treated with respect.

Clare: Fifteen years and five months old, Clare was new in West Town (and Burleigh High). She was highly critical of school in general, and of Burleigh High in particular, and argued that it did not teach her anything. Her presence in the classroom, although not as obvious as Jackie's, was always felt, and she was often a focus of teacher attention without ever being involved in a serious argument with any teachers. She had also very quickly acquired a reputation in school for playing truant in her early days there.

Bad as their record was, none of the three girls had had a serious incident with a teacher, and they reported relationships with them as being reasonably good. They all made clear that they expected to be treated with respect and that their own response to teachers depended on teacher behaviour towards them[38]. They felt as well placed in school, as boys did. However, their criticism of school ethos and regulations was sharp, and covered all aspects of school life:

Fiona: I don't like the rules of uniform! I never wear collars . . . I don't like them . . . I don't mind blue. It's all right . . . But I prefer black, you see . . . So that's why I wear black on the top . . .[39]

HP: And you smoke a lot . . . Why?

Fiona: Just a habit I think . . . I could stop if I wanted to . . . I've got the power to do it, but I just do it for something to do really . . .

HP: What about homework?

Jackie: I do my English . . . Sometimes my maths . . . It's a waste of time . . . I think you come to school to work . . . Then you take it at home . . . I was sitting there three hours trying to do my maths homework last night. He gave us a sheet. It was really hard. My dad wasn't able to do it.

Clare: In this school I don't learn nothing! This school is not worth coming to . . . Teachers are getting worse every term. I have learned nothing in this . . . Since coming from my last school to this one[40].

> ... We do lots of sissy work in geography ... Geography and commerce ... We are not doing nothing like we were doing in my last school. Lessons get so boring ...

They were also very critical of teachers, although each girl had her own reasons for that:

Fiona: I think they are nosey, because they get into your family business ... you know ...

Jackie: I don't like teachers ... Some of them are all right ... They sort of listen to you in the lessons and that ... But ... like Mr Harris ... you know ... the maths teacher ... he is soft! He does nothing to ... he doesn't sort of ... shout at you ...[41]

Clare: They are not very nice ... Because when I first came here, I had the whole class picking on me, and they don't do nothing! Just sit there laughing at you ... Teachers can not control pupils now ... Can they?

So far it seems that girls were as critical of teachers and school as boys were. But these three girls, probably because they had all come to school at different times and belonged to different classes, did not form a 'gang' the way the fun seeking boys did. They did not sit together in lessons or spend time with each other at break times. And they did not name each other as friends. Instead, they each named one or two other girls from a variety of pupil groups. Because of lack of sub-cultural grouping and because of girls' low position in the pupil social hierarchy, as well as behaviour expectations arising from sex role stereotyping, 'showing off' appeared to be less important for girls than it was for boys. 'Having fun' was therefore not influenced by an effort to show off in class. It remained a primary interest, but it was a private affair to be enjoyed with one's neighbour, and not for the whole class to see (Measor, 1983, also reports a similar phenomenon). These factors significantly minimized the need for overt misbehaviour and arguments with teachers[42]. This is possibly why only a few of the classroom techniques popular with the boys (see previous section 'Showing off techniques and perfect balance') were used by the girls, usually the ones offering the enjoyment required, without involving any major risks (the same observation is made by Llewellyn, 1980). For instance, 'conforming in one's own time' and 'conforming only after a repetition of the teacher's command' were very popular methods with the girls:

In the commerce lesson Clare is busy talking:

Mr Rowell: Turn around!
Clare: (half turns but keeps talking)
Mr Rowell: Can I go on please?
Clare: (she stops talking for a minute)

And another example:

> In biology Fiona is noisy.
>
> | | |
> |---|---|
> | *Mrs Hoover:* | Just behave yourself! |
> | *Fiona:* | (ignores the teacher's command) |
> | *Mrs Hoover:* | Be quiet! |
> | *Fiona:* | (keeps tapping on the desk still ignoring the teacher) |
> | *Mrs Hoover:* | I've asked you to be quiet and listen! |
> | *Fiona:* | (this time she stops tapping) |

Occasionally, 'having the last word' was also used by the girls:

> Jackie and Carmel (group O) are giggling in commerce.
>
> | | |
> |---|---|
> | *Mr Rowell:* | Jackie! |
> | *Jackie:* | (keeps talking quite happily) |
> | *Mr Rowell:* | Shut up please! |
> | *Jackie:* | (keeps giggling and protests) We didn't do anything! |

And another example:

> | | |
> |---|---|
> | *Fiona:* | (is singing to herself in biology) |
> | *Mrs Hoover:* | Stop making that noise! |
> | *Fiona:* | It wasn't me! (but stops it) |

Occasionally, unlike the fun-seeking boys, girls responded to teacher commands with straightforward compliance.

> It is a maths lesson and Jackie is walking in the classroom.
>
> | | |
> |---|---|
> | *Mr Harris:* | Go and sit down. (softly) |
> | *Jackie:* | (goes without a word) |

And another one:

> In commerce Jackie is sitting near the window. There is noise in the courtyard which is distructing the pupils' attention.
>
> | | |
> |---|---|
> | *Mr Rowell:* | Shut the window please. |
> | *Jackie:* | (does so right away) |

Nevertheless, their compliance was not always complete, as it often only lasted while the teacher's attention was directed to them. As soon as the teacher became distracted by someone or something else, the girl would return to her previous mis-behaviour. This method was very effective with teachers, and it affected them as profoundly as boys' direct confrontations did. Davies (1979) reports similar techniques used by the girls she studied.

The fine act of balancing was not used by the girls as often as it was by the boys. Due to the rarity of confrontation with teachers, there was not the same need for it. However, the girls could use it very successfully and could also take serious risks, if necessary, as Fiona demonstrates here.

Fiona has been restless in biology and the teacher is growing impatient:

Mrs Hoover:	(after a previous interaction with Fiona) You can go away! I'm not taking this sort of behaviour! (she does not look as if she means it)
Fiona:	(does not stop giggling)
Mrs Hoover:	I don't know what's funny, but you are beginning to irritate me beyond measure, and I think you'll be staying in!
Fiona:	(still giggling)
Mrs Hoover:	Fiona, will you please listen to me?
Fiona:	(conforms at last)
Mrs Hoover:	Thank you!

Underlying Philosophy

We have so far seen that the fun-seeking girls had very similar attitude towards school to the boys of their group, but were expressing them somewhat differently owing to their 'different social and personal realities' (Llewellyn, 1980). As a result, they appeared to use forms of deviance that were more subtle and less likely to cause a confrontation. We have also noted that these girls did not operate as a gang, a fact which appeared to relieve them from the pressure of having to prove themselves in front of the classroom in the way the boys did. We can now go on to see how the girls' philosophy about school was manifested, by showing that they, as well as the boys, knew where to draw the line. Their self-control was also dictated by ultimate respect for education based on the belief that school had something to offer in terms of qualifications relating to their future life.

It is clear once again that despite their severe criticisms and their far from perfect behaviour in school, the fun-seeking girls had not altogether lost faith in school. Their overall attitude appeared to be quite positive. School was after all the place where they met their friends, and it offered them a variety of opportunities.

HP:	You don't enjoy coming to school in the morning very much, do you?
Fiona:	No! I can't get up! (laughs)
HP:	Is this the only reason or is it something to do with school?
Fiona:	I don't mind . . . I like school actually . . . It's something to do really . . . In holidays I get really bored! It's never nothing to do . . . Except the weekends, 'cause then you have time . . . you know . . .

HP: Do you get on with teachers?

Fiona: Yeah. Most of them . . .

HP: Don't you have trouble with anyone?

Fiona: Don't think so, no . . . I don't think I've ever had an argument with a teacher . . .

Jackie: (talking about shouting at teachers) You know . . . I sort of feel guilty after I've done it . . . 'Cause I'm doing wrong to shout back at teachers . . . 'Cause they got . . . I come to school for them to tell me what to do, not to tell them what to do . . . So I feel guilty afterwards . . .

. . . I like school, 'cause there is something to do, cause if you didn't have school, like summer holidays and that . . . They are so boring! Nothing to do all the time. I can't stand it for another day. I'd rather come to school and do something . . .

HP: So you like working?

Jackie: Yeah!

Just like the boys, they were all careful not to go to extremes with their behaviour, and to back down when they considered they had gone too far. They also tended to distance themselves from pupil actions they disapproved of, and to emphasize that some sort of order was necessary if school was to function properly. Their comments showed a sensible and mature attitude.

HP: Why do you keep the rules? Do you believe in keeping the rules of the school?

Fiona: If you don't do this, you get in trouble all the time. I don't like being in trouble all the time! Some people feel that . . . you know . . . they don't like coming to school and all that, and they destroy it . . . They just don't like it I suppose . . . But I don't know, 'cause I don't agree with them . . .

HP: How about homework? Do you do your homework?

Fiona: Most of the time . . . Unless I forget . . . I usually do it.

HP: And what happens if you don't do it?

Fiona: It depends what teacher it is really . . . I usually do my home-work. If I don't hand it in for maths or something, Miss Sinker keeps us in and she just gives us like a life . . . you know . . . next time you do it.

HP: . . . How are things in this school?

Jackie: They are more strict. At my previous school I used to come to school in my jeans and they didn't say nothing. Here, I got eh . . . excluded I think they call it here . . . So I wear my jeans in the week, and my other trousers to school.

HP: Did you come in your jeans more that once?

Jackie:	No.
HP:	Only once.
Jackie:	Yeah!
HP:	And you haven't done it again ...
Jackie:	Well, I've worn my light blue jumper the first day back after Christmas holidays and I got sent home to wear a dark one. It was blue, but light blue, so. ... they are stricter with school uniform. (Jackie like Fiona, was experimenting with school uniform.)

Jackie's experimental attitude towards school rules is clear in this conversation as she tries to explore the limits and discover how much she can get away with. Nonetheless, her eagerness to compromise is equally clear, as she only tries everything once and then, knowing where she stands, starts conforming. The same attitude is apparent in Clare's answers:

HP:	Do you like coming to school in the morning?
Clare:	Yeah, if you HAVE to ... (laughs)

Clare, like Michael earlier, does not challenge the basic assumption of having to go to school.

HP:	Do you ever have arguments with teachers?
Clare:	Not really ... There's no point in arguing with them. They always think they are right ... Like all adults ... If they think they are right there is no point arguing against them. You always end up being wrong ...
HP:	Do you think that teachers should punish pupils when they do things wrong?
Clare:	Yup! Otherwise nothing is going to be there ...
HP:	What sort of things should they be punished for?
Clare:	Just messing around ... Because if one person is messing around, the whole class starts messing around and then pupils wanna mess, and then nothing ...

Given the girls' record in school and constant friction with authority, their conformist comments and eventual compromise appear to be a result of careful thinking about school. The next section will attempt to confirm this interpretation.

Future Plans

The suggestion that these girls, as well as the boys of their group, were driven by a coherent philosophy about school and were following well thought through short and long-term plans, became more apparent than ever when the pupils talked about their future plans.

HP: What are you thinking of doing after school?

Jackie: I want to work in a nursery. So I've put my name down for next year for community service . . .[43] I couldn't do it this year, 'cause I came late and all the places were filled up . . . But I'd rather do it next year anyway, 'cause if I do it well, they'd probably say . . . come!

. . . I was gonna stay on until I was 17 . . . But all my friends said: 'No, don't'.

HP: Why not?

Jackie: Well, 'cause they're not . . . But I don't care what they do . . . I said to my Mum I want to stay on, and she said: 'It's up to you'[44]. None of my brothers, my two older brothers and sisters stayed on. They left before the exams. But the more CSEs you've got, you got a chance to get a job!

HP: Are you going to take any exams?

Clare: Yeah.

HP: What are you taking?

Clare: Probably . . . You have to take English and maths . . . Geography, typing, cooking . . . If I want to take exams I got to come back, so the proper time I'll be leaving is about next summer . . .

HP: What do you want to do after school?

Clare: Secretarial work or something . . .

HP: . . . Why do you care what teachers think of you?

Clare: 'Cause I don't wanna leave school with reports saying that I was cheating and things like that . . . Cause I've got no chance of getting a job then . . . Have I?[45]

HP: Why will you be glad when you leave school? What are you looking forward to?

Fiona: Going out to work . . . Looking after children. Cause I've been wanting to do that all my life . . .[46]

The pupils' ultimate faith in school and what it had to offer is clear from these quotes. It becomes apparent that even the most deviant girls of the year ultimately subscribed to school aims. Their compromises appear therefore to be the result of conscious decision making aiming towards their long-term goals regarding school.

Conclusion

We have now concluded the examination of group A girls and identified their attitude and behaviour in school as well as their thinking and decision making. We have seen that, by challenging major school rules, this group of girls presented problems for their teachers. A closer examination of their behaviour has however revealed that their criticism and challenge of the school system did not go so far as to prevent them from making the compromises necessary to keep them just within the accepted limits and help them remain in school.

Conclusion

This chapter examined the behaviour of the fun-seeking group which was identified as one of the two deviant pupil groups in the mainstream school. The two genders were examined separately, but it has been shown that they shared similar views and operated with a double set of goals in mind. First, they were concerned with the quality of their daily life in school and aspired to an enjoyable time with their friends. To this end they devised techniques which offered credibility amongst their peers. Second, the pupils were seen to be interested in making use of school facilities for future employment and obtaining qualifications for the occupations they wanted. The pupils' deviant behaviour was argued to be designed to achieve their short term aims in school without jeopardizing their long term goals, and the pupils of group A were seen to be successful in achieving the desired balance. It is now time to concentrate on a very different kind of pupil, that of group B.

Postscript

Pupil comments retain their freshness and relevance after all these years indicating the never ending pupil effort to create space in school and to brighten up a dull school day. The ultimate conformism of these most deviant pupils of the fourth year, now young men and women, never ceases to amaze me.

Notes

1 Unlike group B pupils whose self image was very negative and whose comments were hesitant and lacking in confidence.
2 The dialogue extracts are taken from pupil interviews. To avoid repetition my question is only reported once.
3 Hypothetical situation number three. The hypothetical situations are described in the methodology section.
4 Keddie (1984) also differentiates between intelligence and academic motivation, and so does Hargreaves (1967).
5 This is of course a 'relative' academic failure, because none of the pupils were at the bottom groups either. But as Lacey has shown, (1970) relative failure can be very frustrating indeed.
6 Woods (1976) gives a very detailed account of how pupils come to choose the subjects they do, and how they are influenced by low expectations from working class homes, and academic labels attached to them by teachers.

7 Davies (1979) refers to a similar phenomenon of 'underachievement' observed in girls. The problem of performing below one's potential has also been explained in terms of underlying psychological problems and frustrations (Galloway, 1976).

8 It appears that this process began here as an individual effort. The fact that the three pupils ended up in a friendly group, was due as much to their being part of the same class, as to their all being successful in their balancing effort and recognizing each other as 'comrades'. Friendship patterns did not develop in the same way in group B.

9 Werthman (1963) also describes behaviour techniques aimed at communicating rejection of authority while at the same time glamorizing pupil culture.

10 Boys in general, and the fun seekers in particular, were especially restless in keyboarding. This behaviour, uncharacteristic of practical lessons in general, seemed to be the result of the pupils' perception of the subject as 'feminine' and an effort to prove their masculinity by detaching themselves as much as possible from it (for gender stereotyping of school subjects see Measor, 1983).

11 Turner (1983) bases his categorization of deviance on behaviour techniques very similar to the ones described here.

12 The use of humour in a situation like this serves at least three purposes. Firstly, Michael showed to the whole class that his compromise was not an act of fear. Had it been so he would not have dared making a joke at such a crucial moment. Secondly he checked the teacher's mood, a move that provided useful information about how to behave in the immediate future (a strong reaction from the teacher would have required a long period of low profile keeping from Michael). Finally, the joke functioned as a catalyst to diffuse the tension that might have been created between the teacher and Michael. The sophistication of the technique is remarkable and gives another strong indication of the skill involved (see Woods (1976) for use of humour in the classroom).

13 Werthman (1963) describes a similar form of teacher-pupil relationships, established after the process of recognition is over.

14 Ball (1980) stresses the importance of the personality of the teacher and the techniques he/she uses to assert his/her authority.

15 Pupils' wish for a teacher who can keep firm control of the classroom is well documented in the literature (Nash, 1976; Gannaway, 1976; Ball, 1980).

16 See Ball (1980) on 'cues and information' between teachers and pupils; also Pollard (1979).

17 Werthman (1963) shows how this influence usually manifests itself.

18 This particular lesson had a tradition of misbehaviour. It was a very challenging all male low set, (TD was streamed) the subject gave the opportunity for talking and walking about, and the teacher appeared unable to control the class and was often absent on the day he used to teach this group.

19 See Woods (1975) for ways in which the teachers can lose the respect of their pupils.

20 See Hargreaves (1967), Lacey (1970), Pollard (1984) for the significance of peer pressure.

21 As a Maths teacher has put it elsewhere (Ball, 1980), 'They know exactly where the red line is and what will happen if they step over it . . .'.

22 The pupils described by Werthman (1963) and Furlong (1984) showed a similar commitment to school, which also led to a fine balance between reputation for style within school, and job aspirations demanding exam passes. It is interesting that in those cases, unlike this one, the pupils were black.

23 Werthman's pupil (Werthman, 1963) must have felt very much this way when he said: 'I say to myself, I can't get suspended no more. If I get suspended again, I f . . . I never will pass.'

24 Similar behaviour patterns where pupils were not subscribing to the 'ideal pupil' model, but were nevertheless prepared to make compromises in pursuit of a better future, have been reported in the past, (Fuller, 1975; Rex and Tomlinson, 1979; Furlong, 1984). It is interesting to note however that all theses case have been related to pupils of West Indian origin. Cultural resistance explanations for commitment to school are inappropriate here, as no pupil was of West Indian origin.

25 See Woods (1976) for the importance of parents' opinion of school and its relevance.

26 There were, of course, teachers who were liked less than others, and not only by this group. The teachers who were popular usually liked children and were able to create good relationships with them. They had a good sense of humour and were eager to participate in the children's jokes. They were fair towards pupils and had the sensitivity not to humiliate them in the class, unlike the teachers Woods (1976) describes. The teachers at the other end of this continuum were facing problems like those described by Werthman (1963) and Gannaway (1976). For descriptions of the 'ideal teacher' see Nash (1976).

27 When asked later the teacher said: 'They don't have breakfast you see, and they get very hungry as soon as they start working. They need sugar.'

28 One or two teachers were observed to be frequently absent on a day they were teaching an especially difficult group. An observation also noted by Kyriacou (1980).

29 As Michael put it: 'Ehh! Teachers ain't too bad I suppose . . . I GOT to get on with them . . .' (his emphasis).

30 I am very aware that my way of dealing with the girls can be criticized as 'locating girls by indicating a presence or absence of them in the male sub-culture' (Meyenn, 1980). It can also be argued that I examine the girls separately because they 'mess up the model' (Davies, 1979). Valid as these criticisms may appear to be, I wish to argue that I examine the girls separately exactly because I do not want them to be sucked into a model of male sub-culture, and because I judge that despite the similarities in philosophy, there are differences in behaviour that cannot be grouped together and need to be treated separately. It is true that the division between the genders could be explored in further detail, but that would be a major disadvantage in a study with so many groups to compare. And so I wish to argue that this way of handling the material is of service to the study as a whole.

31 What Llewellyn (1980) calls 'individualized and personalized resistence'; also described in Meyenn (1980).

32 See Davies (1979) and Meyenn (1980) for similar evidence about girls' fights.

33 McRobbie and Garber (1976) argue that it is quite possible to note both the relative shift in the visibility of girls in relation to the sub-cultural trends, and the fact that no matter how visible and active a small group of girls become, the relative subordination of girls in the sub-culture remains.

34 See Shaw (1980) for similar observation of boys who are not prepared to even compare themselves to girls.

35 For sexual harassment of girls by boys in school see Shaw (1980) and Mahony (1985).

36 Woods (1975) and Mahony (1985) show how teacher interference can sometimes be even damaging for the girls.

37 The dominance order mentioned here was of course relative. Individual girls were occasionally above individual boys. The order described was generally observed with relation to groups.

38 Werthman (1963) also mentions similar reciprocal action to teachers.

39 Pupils were asked to wear navy tops. Sensitivity about appearance was very high with

girls however. Personalizing their uniform was not at all uncommon as is also mentioned by Davies (1979), Meyenn (1980) and Measor (1983).

40 For similar comments from pupils and the importance they place on being able to learn from a teacher, see Delamont (1976b), Gannaway (1976), Nash (1976) and Davies (1979).

41 Gannaway (1976), Nash (1976), and Ball (1981) also report that pupils have clear expectations that their teachers should be strict and competent and able to keep order.

42 The boys' need for masculine solidarity within a relatively large group is argued in detail by McRobbie and Garber (1976) and Willis (1977). Occasionally the girls did go as far as to openly argue with teachers in the class, as the girls studied by Davies (1979) did, but this was the exception rather than the rule.

43 The school curriculum included an alternative to physical education called community service. This was only available in the last two years of schooling and it was a form of work placement supervised by a teacher. Among the placements available was a children's group, to which Jackie is referring here.

44 See Woods (1976) for parents' opinion about school, and its influence on pupil decision making.

45 Compare with Richard's statement in the previous section: 'How deviant is deviant'; also see Werthman (1963) for similar sensible statements from pupils.

46 Willis (1977) also argues that the desire to leave school and get a job was a main priority with his 'lads'.

Chapter 4

Problems, Problems . . .
Group B — The Troubled Ones of
Burleigh High

Group B

We have now become acquainted with the fun-seeking group in Burleigh High. It has been argued that they had a well thought out theory about school, and their actions were the means for translating this theory into practice. It has been established that there were two dimensions to their thinking about school, and that they were operating on the basis of long and short-term plans. Their short-term goals were concerned with making life in school easy and enjoyable amongst a multitude of friends who respected and admired them. Their long-term goals were decided on a more individual level, and were closely related to their future career plans. The effort to balance and to satisfy both sets of goals was seen to absorb a great deal of their time and effort. The same balancing effort was seen to be the clearest indicator of their ability and skill, and to attract the respect of their peers and the occasional friendly attention of teachers. We have thus achieved a better understanding of those pupils' deviant behaviour in school. It is time to examine the behaviour of group B, the troubled group, and show what the motivation behind their actions was.

The second sub-group of Q-O, group B, was a very different group, both in attitude and behaviour. In contrast to the fun-seekers, this group's main characteristic appeared to be a remarkable lack of planning and thinking in school. Its five pupils, three boys and two girls, appeared to lack long-term goals, and act entirely on impulse. They appeared to be unable to relate the part to the whole, and an isolated incident and its consequences to their position and career in school. They also appeared unable to take decisions about their own future, and seemed resigned to outside forces and influences. As with group A, the two sexes will be examined separately here, so that gender differences do not interfere with the structure of the main argument.

The Boys

Introducing the 'Troubled Boys'

The three boys of the group were:

Garry: Fourteen years and six months old when interviewed, Garry was a rather lonely pupil preoccupied with his work problems. His school record covered a variety of misbehaviours, from being disruptive in the classroom to stealing a computer printer from school. He could be an 'awful nuisance' in the classroom and present teachers with a serious problem, but, along with the other members of group B, Garry avoided openly challenging teachers.

Wayne: Fifteen years old when interviewed, Wayne was the most representative member of the group, encapsulating with his contradictory statements and his profoundly immature attitude and behaviour the characteristics of the group. He too, was an 'awful nuisance' in the classroom, and he usually succeeded in aggravating teachers and pupils alike with his behaviour. Although never caught doing anything very serious, Wayne was continually in trouble for minor incidents. He was generally unpopular with teachers and pupils, and under the constant supervision of the year tutor.

Mark: Fourteen years and seven months old when interviewed, Mark was the most unhappy member of the troubled group. He had tremendous problems with his work, and relationships with his peers had reached the level of complete rejection. School had very few joys for Mark, so it is not surprising that he had come to hate it. His classroom behaviour could vary from cooperative to bizarre, and most of his teachers had despaired of him as far as work progress and behaviour changes were concerned. He had by the middle of the fourth year, reached such a degree of disillusion, that he ended up leaving Burleigh High for a special unit before the end of that academic year.

Unlike the fun-seekers, the pupils of this group were not happy in school. They appeared dissatisfied and lonely and their problems seemed to overshadow their joys there. They lacked the confidence and self-assurance of the previous group, and appeared generally timid and frightened.

In this chapter, the position of these pupils within the school establishment will be presented first, in order to facilitate an understanding of their position. An account of their feelings towards school will follow, which will make clear a conflict between their attitude and behaviour, and will show contradictions in their disposition towards school. The pupils' academic performance will then be examined, in a first effort to resolve these contradictions. It will become apparent that the troubled pupils, having experienced a disheartening academic failure, had turned, like group A before them, to the pupils' social world as a possible alternative. Relationships with their peers will be described at that point, and as their isolation becomes clear, the pupils' failure in this field too will be confirmed. This double, academic and social, failure will then be questioned in order to try to understand the reasons behind it. A description of the pupils' relationships with their teachers will conclude the examination of the various aspects of their school life and confirm the pupils' isolation in school. A final conclusion will summarise the main points of

this section, point out to the group's differences from group A, and also examine the reasons for the group B's continuing attendance of a mainstream school.

Relationships with School

It has already been indicated in the pupil profiles that the three boys were not very successful or happy in school, and in this aspect they were very different from the fun-seekers. There was, however, one similarity with Burleigh High group A, and this was that both groups of pupils presented their teachers with difficult to handle forms of behaviour. We can start by examining this similarity.

Garry: I just start arguments, then they chuck me out of the lessons and I have to sit outside the lessons and that . . .

HP: . . . What do you do if a teacher asks you to get out of the classroom for not quietening down when asked?

Garry: If I didn't hear him say 'calm down' and he says 'get out' I'd just give him a loud lip and that . . . I'd just answer back all the time, and be cheeky and that . . .

HP: Do you do your homework?

Garry: Sometimes . . . I don't . . . I don't like doing homework . . .

HP: What do you say when the teacher asks you where is your book and you haven't done it?

Garry: I just say I haven't done it . . . just tell that I haven't done it . . .

HP: And what happens usually?

Garry: They probably set you more . . . or . . . I just don't know what they'd do . . . yeah . . . give you lines or something . . . I don't know . . .

It is interesting to note Garry's hesitant style and his inability to give a satisfactory answer, despite the fact that this was a situation that he had repeatedly experienced. This hesitation comes in striking contrast to the fun-seekers' assertiveness.

HP: What do you really think when you have an argument with a teacher? What do you have in mind?

Garry: Nothing really . . . depending on the teacher . . .

HP: What say if you have an argument with Mrs Haw?

Garry: She'd probably argue back and I would argue back and she'd send me out . . .

HP: What if the teacher says: 'Put your pen down and listen to me'. And you still have your pen and you are playing with it . . . So the teacher comes along and takes it and puts it on the desk . . . (Hypothetical situation number 3)

Garry: I'd go along and take the pen . . .

HP: Would you? And what would happen then? After that anything

could happen . . . The teacher might say 'get out' or he might
say . . .

Garry: (interrupting me) Yes . . . that's what they probably would do . . .

HP: And what would you do then?

Garry: I just get out . . . Depends on the lesson again . . .

HP: But would you still take the pen?

Garry: (nods yes)

HP: Why? (surprised) Do you want to prove something to him?

Garry: I don't know . . .[1]

Mark appears to be equally uncooperative in the classroom:

HP: What about homework? Do you always do it?

Mark: No!

HP: What happens when you don't? What do you say?

Mark: I don't say nothing! They just say 'You haven't done your homework' and I say 'Yeah, I couldn't be bothered to do it.'

HP: And don't they punish you for that?

Mark: They used to . . . but they don't now . . .[2]

HP: What would you do if a teacher took your pen from your hands
because you were still writing while you were supposed to be
listening?

Mark: Just sit there . . . Just pick it back up . . .

HP: And what if the teacher gets angry?

Mark: Why should he get angry?

HP: Because you're disobeying his orders . . .

Mark: I ain't doing no harm in that . . .[3]

HP: Yes, but you might make him more angry and get a more severe
punishment . . . be sent out of the class or whatever . . .

Mark: It don't bother me . . .

HP: You don't care at all about school. Do you?

Mark: No.

HP: Why?

Mark: Just don't bother me . . .

It is evident from these quotes that the pupils of this group exhibited a kind of
behaviour that was difficult to deal with. They did not prepare their homework and
they also misbehaved in the classroom, and by doing so presented teachers with a
variety of problems.

Feelings and Attitudes towards School

Evidently there were some similarities between the classroom behaviour of groups
A and B. However there were deep differences in the thinking — or lack of it —

that lay behind it. Group B pupils did not appear to have any coherent philosophy about school, or even a major attitude orientation. Their accounts and behaviour were full of contradictions that can only be compared to those of the Emery Centre group D, as we shall see later. Wayne encapsulated this indecision in one statement.

> *Wayne:* I like school because it helps you to learn before you get older . . . And sometimes I don't like it because teachers get on your back and they are always harassing you and the things you can do at home you can't do at school . . . And . . . school is all right sometimes . . .

When interviewed, these pupils tried very hard to give the impression of a good pupil who tried to keep out of trouble.

> *HP:* So, you don't always carry a pen, pencil and ruler. Why not? Don't you like to conform with the rules of the school?
> *Mark:* Sometimes I bring them but they either get pinched or get lost . . .
> *HP:* So you try . . . You try to do your best in school. Do you?
> *Mark:* Yeah . . .
> *HP:* And not get in trouble . . .
> *Mark:* Not really . . . No . . . I don't get in trouble . . .
> *HP:* So you think you have average trouble as every pupil would . . .
> *Mark:* (nods yes)

Garry also suggested that he tried to distance himself from any serious kind of misbehaviour:

> *HP:* You say that pupils destroy school property because it is a laugh. Do you do it yourself?
> *Garry:* No. I'm not doing it. It's not worth doing it. You'll only get in trouble for it at the end of the day really . . . So, I am not bothered doing it . . . But other kids do it for laugh . . . They think it's funny . . . And at the end of the day he is the one who's given a detention . . .
> *HP:* So, you try to avoid trouble as much as you can . . . Do you?
> *Garry:* Yeah.
> *HP:* And you say that teachers do well to punish pupils because they should be punished. Do you think so?
> *Garry:* (nods yes)
> *HP:* What should they be punished for?
> *Garry:* Like . . . swearing and . . . I don't know really . . .
> *HP:* Not working?
> *Garry:* Yes, but when we don't work they don't really punish us all that much . . .

And so did Wayne:

> *Wayne:* It's not worth teachers wasting their time on me, because I am a kid who's misbehaving . . .

Their views on school and teachers showed very negative feelings without, however, including any convincing arguments. Their criticism seemed to be superficial, based on frustration rather than reasoning. They also appeared unable to grasp the importance of the situations they were commenting on, and unaware of (or indifferent to) the reasoning behind basic school rules, and the significance of teachers' opinions of them.

> *Garry:* School is just a bit boring . . .
> *HP:* You don't do interesting things . . .
> *Garry:* No, not really . . . We don't. It's just boring . . .
> *HP:* What would you do if you were not coming to school?
> *Garry:* Just stay home and go down town . . .
> *HP:* Wouldn't that be more boring?
> *Garry:* No, not really . . .
> *HP:* And you don't care about teachers . . .
> *Garry:* No . . .
> *HP:* You don't care what they think of you . . . Why not?
> *Garry:* 'Cause it's their opinion, and they've got as much opinion as they want, as we've got about them. I don't think they care so much about us, so why should we care about them?
> *HP:* Do you think they are fair? Teachers . . .
> *Garry:* No, not really . . .
> *HP:* Why?
> *Garry:* Because you're asked to do what they want you to do . . .
> *HP:* You mean they personally, or they as a school?
> *Garry:* They as a school . . . You have to do what they want . . .
> *HP:* How about the school rules? You don't break them too much. Do you?
> *Garry:* No, not too much . . . but I don't rather stick to them too much neither . . . 'Cause they are stupid rules most of them . . . Not allowing you to bring tape-recorders into the lessons . . .

Wayne was equally negative:

> *Wayne:* I don't really care what teachers think . . .
> *HP:* Is that because they don't matter to you?
> *Wayne:* No! They are only here to help us and teach us things . . . so we get older . . .

And so was Mark:

> *HP:* You say that you don't care what teachers think of you. Why do you not care?

Mark: Just don't bother me . . .
HP: You don't respect them enough or they don't matter?
Mark: They don't matter . . .

A major contradiction as well as a very particular attitude is revealed here. Group A pupils appeared to be faced with a conflict between a negative attitude, based on genuine reservations about school, and a relatively conformist behaviour, resulting from their belief that despite its faults, school was not worthless. The conflict of group B appeared to be quite the reverse. They appeared to have a mild attitude towards school, and made an effort to show how they conformed, as well behaved pupils are expected to. But they ended up contradicting their own statements in attitude and behaviour. Unlike group A's conflict, which was between two principles, group B's conflict appeared to be owing to lack of principle. Unlike group A's final compromise, which appeared to result from an understanding of the necessities surrounding them, group B misbehaved in defiance of the picture they wanted to present, and despite the destructive consequences this behaviour entailed.[4]

This unexpected behaviour can only be understood and explained as a result of spontaneous reaction to a situation at hand rather than a product of thinking. Group A pupils appeared to make constructive criticism based on reflections about school, and examination of their life and position there. They made valid and interesting points, which appeared to be related to an underlying theory. Group B pupils did not seem to have a coherent theory about school. Their views regarding school constantly changed, apparently depending on the outcome of the most recent incident. It seems that this was the cause for their inability to reason. Led by impulse, they appeared unable to grasp the complexity of their school interactions, and to examine and foresee the consequences of their actions. The pupils' comments remained impulsive and superficial, as will soon become apparent, to fit any given situation. Each incident was judged on its merits and was never related to past lessons or future consequences.

Furthermore, in group A's behaviour, there was a visible 'clear cut' line within which the pupils were prepared to operate. This line was well thought out and drawn at a point that gave the pupils a perfect balance between 'having fun in school' and 'been acceptable in its premises'. There was no such line in group B's behaviour. There were no limits to how far their behaviour could go. External punishment was the only means of putting an end to it, and there was no sign of internal discipline. Group A pupils appeared to live their school lives according to a sophisticated plan that catered both for short-term satisfaction and long-term achievement. Group B appeared to have no such plan; no initial consistent and coherent philosophy about school to live by, and not even an acquired feeling for boundaries. Group A's conflict led to the implementation of a careful balance that clearly indicated their intelligence and skills. Group B's conflicts led to contradictory and often bizarre behaviour that brought them more trouble and illustrated, for everyone to see, their lack of judgment and inability to cope in school. The position of group B and its differences from group A will become more evident as the various aspects of their school life are examined in more detail.

Academic Record

Academic performance appears to be a good starting point. The pupils of group B had very serious problems with work[5]. Mark in particular had been unable to follow the flow of his classes, and had been taught English and maths by the remedial teacher up to his third year, the last year remedial help was available in the school. His difficulty in coping without this extra help became very obvious during his fourth year, and had major influence on his final withdrawal from the mainstream system. The other two pupils had very similar, if not as extreme, problems. All three were in the lowest maths and English sets, and they were bottom of the class in the mixed groups they attended. They needed constant teacher attention in the classroom because their abilities were very limited, their concentration span very short and they were very easily distracted[6]. Their academic failure was evident, and the pupils themselves were aware of their limitations in this sphere, not least because of teacher comments in the classroom[7].

> *HP:* Why do you say that teachers think of you as daft? Did they tell you that?
>
> *Garry:* No, they just . . . it's when they start putting you in lower groups and things like that . . . you can tell they think you're daft . . . They put you in lower groups like . . . lower maths groups and lower English groups, and things like that . . .

Their anxiety about work came up repeatedly during the interviews.

> *Garry:* I don't like work very much . . . I don't know why . . .
>
> *HP:* You do some work in the class, don't you?
>
> *Garry:* Yeah, not much, I don't bother doing much. I don't like work. I just keep having arguments with the teachers. I don't like their lessons . . .
>
> *HP:* Why will you be happy when you leave school?
>
> *Garry:* I don't know why . . . I won't have to do all this writing . . . all this work . . .

Mark appeared to be equally anxious:

> *HP:* Why didn't you like Mrs Kroner?
>
> *Mark:* She used to always make me work . . . Most of them (teachers) do . . . She . . . When we used to get up and there was one thing, she used to pile them all on top of that . . .
>
> *HP:* Did you have arguments with her?
>
> *Mark:* Most of the time . . . yeah . . . She kept giving us a lot of work and wouldn't help us . . . She used to tell us if we couldn't get it . . . she'd just say go and sit down and work it out, and she used to sit there and didn't do anything . . .

HP: Why did you have problems with Mrs Haw?
Mark: You got to do a lot of work . . .[8]

School had evidently been an academic failure for the troubled pupils. Work was the sphere in which they performed worst, and they were well aware of it. Having failed academically, they too turned to school social life for comfort and a new means of success. They appeared to be very interested in 'having a good time with the boys'. Wayne seemed especially enthusiastic with this prospect.

Wayne: Well, I find that . . . when I was in the junior school, I used to be quite lonely, cause I didn't use to have any friends you see, and all the boys in here, in the school now, will come around and make friends and that . . . and when we get in the class, (gets excited) we want to doss . . . you know . . . throwing things about and talking and shouting and that . . . It's great!

Relationships with Peers

Before success could be achieved in this field however, earning peer recognition and respect — as group A had done — was absolutely necessary. The way to earn this recognition was for pupils to prove that they were 'one of the boys'. Joining in with general classroom misbehaviour was one way of doing that.

It is a Careers lesson with Mr Rowell. There is a video show. The classroom atmosphere is very relaxed. Everyone is talking or giggling in a low tone. Garry also starts playing around, but it is not long before his misbehaviour begins to stand out. The teacher has to keep reprimanding him[9].
Garry's hand is visible on the screen.

Mr Rowell: Do you want to go to the loo, or are you making butterflies on the screen?
Garry: No! (complains he was doing nothing like that).

A minute later Garry interrupts the teacher with a loud sneeze.

Mr Rowell: (looks at him)
Garry: Sorry!

The teacher goes on and Garry keeps talking.

Mr Rowell: You are displeasing me today! It's three times I've talked to you today (the teacher is still smiling).
Garry: . . .

A minute later Garry is having a minor fight with the boy next to him. He ends up on the classroom floor laughing.

Mr Rowell:	Oi! Get off! (the teacher is angry by now)
Garry:	Sir . . .
Mr Rowell:	Sir nothing!
Garry:	(complains that it wasn't his fault, he was pushed.)

It would seem here that Garry simply followed the general classroom mood when he started being noisy. It was not long, however, before he surpassed everything everybody else was doing, and started to stand out with his behaviour. Despite the repeated warnings given in a friendly manner, Garry failed to judge correctly when it was time to stop misbehaving, and ended up provoking the teacher's anger. In a class where no one was behaving perfectly, he alone was the one to be reprimanded by the teacher. Nobody else in the class was told off for their behaviour.

In English Mrs Brown has just reprimanded Richard (of group A) for talking and not working. She can be quite sarcastic, and the pupils are very aware of the risk of humiliation involved if they displease her. Her reprimand is followed by complete silence in the classroom. Everybody is quiet, except Wayne who is still talking. The teacher has to address him separately. Instead of shutting up, Wayne complains that he is not doing anything. The teacher has to use stronger language to put her message across.

| *Mrs Brown:* | Shut up Wayne! I don't wanna know! You are here to work. |

This time, Wayne quietens down.

Both incidents indicated an effort to participate in classroom activities. Both times the situation was misjudged and the timing was bad enough to draw teacher attention and provoke a comment. Both times the pupils failed, in effect, to take part in the classroom way of 'having fun' without going over the limit.

Complaining, or trying to find excuses, was a very common method group B used as a last resort when in trouble. This was another indication of impulsive acting, lacking in technique and advanced thinking on their part. Having failed to pick up the clues that indicated when it was time to stop, and having become very involved in a troublesome situation, all they could do when faced with the teacher's anger, was complain. However, this reaction seldom helped, either to defuse the tension with the teacher, or to project a positive image with other pupils. In a strange way, the pupils of Group B appeared to be very timid, scared even, of teachers. Punishment succeeded with them where reasoning had failed, and external discipline proved more effective than any form of self-discipline, as fear appeared to be the main motive behind any behaviour changes. Hence Garry's humble replies to the teacher in the example quoted above, but actual failure to control his own behaviour.

Challenging teachers — a popular pastime for group A because of the risks it involved and the excitement it offered — was not a conscious choice for group B. Group B pupils often appeared to provoke the teachers' anger to a far greater extent than group A pupils did, but this did not appear to be done intentionally. It seems that it was more frequently the result of their not knowing when to stop when they tried to show off. The pupils' surprise when faced with the teachers' harsh comments or punishments, was clear evidence of that. So were their last minute attempts to excuse themselves, which also harmed their dignity in the eyes of their peers.

Making jokes against the teacher, in an effort to initiate classroom laughter at the teacher's expense and in the hope that the rest of the pupils would join in, was another technique tried by group B in their effort to show that they were 'one of the lads'.

It is a nice sunny day. Mark is having a maths lesson. He discovers that his metal watch strap can reflect the sunlight, and he starts playing with it. It is not long before he starts directing the light reflection onto the teacher's eyes. Mrs Kroner starts shouting at him to take his watch off. Mark tries to do so but, for some reason, he can not take his watch off.

Mark: I can't take it off miss!

The teacher does not believe him. She becomes very angry and rushes down from her desk. She tries to pull the watch of Mark's wrist, but she is also unable to do it. She pushes and pulls Mark in a rough manner, and in the end, realizing that there is nothing she can do about it, she shouts at him:

Mrs Kroner: You'd better not use it again!

Mark looks surprised and puzzled with the teacher's behaviour. It is probably one of the few times that he appreciates how strong the teacher's anger against him is. The rest of the class, instead of joining in, have remained silent during the incident, probably shocked by the teacher's overreaction.[10]

Mark follows a similar pattern in the next incident.

In the general science lesson the pupils have just used carbon dust for an experiment.

Mrs Froster: You can blow the dust off now.

Everybody blows the dust gently. Mark blows heavily on his desk and causes a cloud of dust in the room.

Mrs Froster: You'll be out! I think I've tolerated your stupidity
long enough!
Mark: (looks at her surprised and stops blowing.)

Again, Mark's efforts to make the class laugh and join in failed quite dramatically. Both times Mark misjudged his peers' attitude, and ended up on his own against the teacher.

Finally, a proportion of group B jokes were not directed at the teacher, but concentrated on making the class laugh. To achieve this the pupil often acted like a buffoon and made a fool of himself. This type of joke indicated the group's immature approach, in their effort to win peer support[11].

> In a maths lesson Mark is sitting on his desk pretending to be working. It is unusually quiet in the class. Mark takes the opportunity to loudly pass wind. He then bends over his desk, hides his face in his arms, and starts laughing. Both teacher and pupils ignore him and nobody laughs with him.

> In English the teacher is called outside the classroom for a minute. Wayne takes the opportunity to rub his hair until he makes a complete mess of it. He then tries to attract everybody's attention to it. One or two children laugh. The teacher comes back, looks at him and says:
>
> *Mrs Brown:*   Wayne stop being an exhibitionist!
>
> Pleased to have been noticed by everyone, Wayne starts tidying up his hair.

Evidently, the troubled pupils were making a painful effort to become accepted by their peers. The intensity of their struggle and the risks they took indicated how important it was for them to be recognized as members of the pupil community. But this hard fought for recognition was apparently never granted them. Instead they were rejected by their peers and the group's social failure was even more marked than their academic one. The next incident clearly indicates the degree of peer rejection these pupils were faced with.

> In general science Mark has been quite restless. He is sitting next to Peter, who does not miss a chance to push Mark into doing something silly so that he can have a good laugh[12]. The teacher says that she feels really tired because she had had a hard day. Mark starts laughing and dropping hints about what the teacher might possibly have done. He openly implies that the reason for her tiredness is that she had sex in the morning, and he expects the other pupils to join in the joke. The response of the class is astonishing. Not only does no one join in, (unlike a similar incident described in Measor, 1983) but the other pupils openly distance themselves from this joke, and turn against Mark.
>
> | | |
> |---|---|
> | *Jenny:* | You grow up a bit! |
> | *Lesley:* | (to the teacher) Slap him on the face miss! |
> | *Mrs Froster:* | Come on Mark, move! (in an effort to separate him from Peter, whom she suspects of having a bad influence on Mark). |
> | *Mark:* | (does not respond right away) |
> | *Jason:* | (shouts at Mark) Move! |

Mark looks surprised and puzzled. He does not seem to understand where he went wrong.

In this incident Mark found himself completely isolated. This isolation, brought about by his own joke, appeared to be aiming at protecting the teacher from Mark's remarks, and showed quite clearly whose side the pupils were on. Considering that pupils as a rule support each other against teachers, this incident illustrates in the most clear way the denial of Mark's classmates to accept him as one of them.

Rejection from peers often took the form of harassment. Mark in particular was very often the victim of harsh practical jokes:

> In the careers lesson the teacher is taking small groups of pupils to the next room to show them the employers' catalogue. While Mark is away two pupils search the pockets of his coat and find a brand new bag of sweets. They take it and pass it around. By the time Mark comes back there are very few sweets left. As soon as he walks into the classroom there is laughter. Mark checks his pockets and realises that his sweets are missing. He withdraws in a corner. The teacher remains unaware of the incident.

Rejection from peers was so overt that even group B pupils themselves could not fail to see it. Their own statements indicated their awareness of being rejected.

HP: How do you get on with the other pupils?
Mark: I get on all right with most of them . . .
HP: But there are some that you don't like?
Mark: Yeah . . . Some people in computer studies would pick on me . . . I want to move back to my old group. Because these kids keep picking on me but the teacher won't do anything . . .[13]

Garry also felt rejected:

HP: Who are your friends?
Garry: There's not many friends in the lessons really . . .
HP: Don't you have any friends around in school?
Garry: Not really . . .

Garry's isolation was particularly evident in his behaviour towards me at break times. He used to seek my company and try to make friends with me as he was usually on his own. This was very unlike other pupils' behaviour who were too preoccupied with their own activities to pursue informal contacts.

Wayne was the only one of the pupils in group B who presented himself as being happy with his social connections, (see his comment in the section 'Academic record' above). The truth of the matter, however, was that, far from having many friends, Wayne was very unpopular with the pupils of his own year. As a consequence he tended to 'hang around the juniors' area and show off to the first year girls' (from the interview with the year tutor). His unpopularity is also evident in teachers' comments (see the section 'Relationships with teachers' below).

Repeated rejection made the troubled pupils try harder to make friends, exposing themselves to risks and becoming involved in more and more trouble. The result was increasing isolation from teachers and pupils alike.

It is crucial to examine the reasons for this new and important failure. The success of the fun-seekers will assist us in this task. The reason why the pupils of group A were so well respected by their peers seems to be the fact that they were very successful in challenging and defying school rules and handling difficult incidents with teachers. The pupils of group B on the other hand were not able to control their behaviour. Consequently, most of their incidents with teachers inevitably escalated. This phenomenon had two consequences. First it lost them the tolerance of teachers, who became impatient with them and whose punishment became harsher as their language became stronger. Second, it brought them to the attention of their peers, who were amused by their unsuccessful efforts. It would have been wise at this stage for the pupils to modify their behaviour and put an end to the constant humiliation they suffered in front of the class. But they did not. They continued trying, making teachers increasingly angry, and losing completely, at last, the respect of their peers. This happened because the behaviour of group B pupils appeared irrational and unnecessarily risky. Much as their peers respected daring, they disapproved of pointless risks. Moreover, the group's failure rate could not but generate disrespect. It was thus not surprising that group B had completely lost the recognition and respect of their peers.

Lower Intelligence?

The reasons for the pupils' unusually high failure rate in manipulating situations and teachers during incidents, have not been discussed hitherto. Yet it must by now be apparent that the pupils of group B were inferior in perception and skill to their colleagues of group A.

This was evident in: (i) the group's serious academic failure; (ii) their apparent lack of judgment before and during classroom incidents; (iii) their inability to appreciate their position during or after an incident; and (iv) their inability to learn from past mistakes.

The group's poor academic performance has already been mentioned (see 'Academic record' above). It has been argued that problems with work were a recurring theme during discussions with pupils. It has also been suggested that implicit and explicit pupil statements indicated a very low overall ability. This low level of ability and performance was consistent in every form of interaction the pupils attempted, and evident in every aspect of their school life, not limited to the academic field.

Close examination of the incidents described so far reveals a wealth of warning signals directed at the pupil[14]. These were given through the teachers' body language, their gestures and facial expressions, the tone of their voice, and even through straightforward commands explicitly indicating that the teacher was growing increasingly impatient and angry with the pupil's behaviour. But as we have already seen, the pupils frequently failed to see and recognize these signals[15].

The incidents described in the previous sections were not in any way exceptional. They were typical of the group's general behaviour patterns and reactions. As shown, the pupils were so preoccupied with their effort to show off, that usually failed to see the crisis coming. When faced with contempt or punishment at the end of an incident they were often taken by surprise as if they had not expected it and could not explain it. Punishment, as shown, was the only successful way of putting an end to their misbehaviour. There was no sensitivity, sophisticated strategies or internal discipline. Fear of punishment after the consequences of the pupils' actions had started becoming clear appeared to be the main reason for most behaviour modifications observed.

What was even more striking, however, was the pupils' inability to learn from previous mistakes. These pupils had been involved in so much trouble that one would expect them to have developed a method of seeing it coming, even if they were not initially equipped with one. Alternatively they could have developed a kind of reflexive reaction that would intuitively stop them from misbehaving before a confrontation escalated. Finally, given their experience, they might at least be expected to have developed a sophisticated technique of dealing with trouble when it was already there[16].

None of these occurred. The pupils appeared to have learned very little from previous experience. They repeatedly made the same mistakes and were as surprised every time they were faced with punishment as they had been the first time. Equally, they stopped misbehaving when faced directly with punishment, but not earlier[17]. All this could be interpreted as evidence of a naive and immature way of thinking, or inability to exercise their judgment effectively. Observation and interview data however point convincingly to a very low overall ability and indicate a certain dullness[18]. A new incident might be helpful in clarifying these points even further.

> In maths Mark makes a comment about the school holidays approaching. He has been particularly restless today and Mrs Kroner tells him to shut up. But Mark repeats his comment. This repetition provokes the same command from the teacher, only this time it is said in a more explicitly intolerant tone. Mark still does not shut up but repeats his question for a third time. This time the teacher sends him out of the classroom.

Mrs Kroner had in the past tolerated quite extreme forms of behaviour from Mark, and so the established pattern of relationships between them was such as to allow Mark to take a number of liberties. However, the situation became critical when the teacher repeated her command. At that point it became obvious that new decision making was needed. Mark failed to see the clues that would warn him of that. He also failed to make the distinction between situations which can be dealt using the established behaviour patterns, and those where new decision making is needed. The incident did not end there.

> Mark reluctantly gets up to leave the room. As he reaches the door he turns to the rest of the class and shouts in a jolly tone waving his arms:

> *Mark:* Hi lads! I am the most crappy boy!

The children laugh and the teacher becomes furious. She gets up and phys-ically pushes Mark out of the classroom. The children are still laughing.

It seems that Mark was trying to save face by making the class laugh. However his timing was extremely bad because it provoked even more anger from the teacher. The deliverance was also unsuccessful in that it showed no subtlety or effort to test the ground or to defuse the tension. Mark appeared to have embarked on this com-ment in an effort to capitalize on his punishment by becoming a hero, and without considering the cost. But the cost was very dear indeed, because his reaction, with-out bringing him any closer to the teacher, alienated him further from his peers. Their laughter was not *with* Mark, but *at* him. A more subtle and less risky way of saving face would have been appreciated more.

The pupils' comments only confirmed what their academic record and class-room behaviour showed about their rather superficial way of thinking.

> *Wayne:* I tried to sleep in this morning without mum knowing. I made kind of a little (intransc.) and I hid underneath my bed, I put lots of pillows and clothes in, to make it look as if I was still in bed . . . I wanted to skive off, but my dad found me, so I had to come to school.
>
> *HP:* Why will you be glad when you leave school?
> *Wayne:* Well, I won't be getting up early . . . (laughs)
>
> *Mark:* I don't know . . . I'll be glad 'cause I won't have to get up early in the morning . . .

Wayne finally demonstrates in the following extract a remarkably naive view of relationships in school:

> *Wayne:* . . . Most kids just sit there . . . They don't care what the teachers do to them . . .
> *HP:* So, why do they sit there and listen to the teachers?
> *Wayne:* Don't really know . . . That's quite a funny thing . . . All my friends say things like . . . If they get told off, they always say: 'Why do I have to go out there?' They try to get some sarcasm in there . . . say . . . 'I don't want to go out there, It's cold out there, I haven't done nothing wrong, It's your fault . . .' you know . . . things like that . . . 'He threw something at me' or 'He said a naughty word at me' and that . . . they don't like it . . .
> *HP:* Do you not find that it irritates the teachers when you answer back?
> *Wayne:* Yeah . . .

HP: And maybe things get worse a bit . . .
Wayne: Yeah . . .
HP: So, maybe that's why everybody else doesn't do it . . .
Wayne: Yeah . . .
HP: But you still do it; do you?
Wayne: No! Not now I don't! That's babyish I think . . . I do as I'm told for once . . .

Wayne started his account trying to impress with his daring behaviour. He appeared to find it very difficult to understand why some pupils 'just sit there' and conform. But he ended his story contradicting himself, stating that he also behaved this way. This internal contradiction appears to be due to a last minute change of mind. It appears that my questions — intended to make him think about the issue — influenced his answer. This is another indication of the high suggestibility of this group. Wayne's statement, however, reveals more than that. It implies that he had thought very little about this phenomenon, and indicates the difficulty he had understanding why pupils conform. The major problem here was not one of principle. Wayne simply mentioned face saving techniques widely used by group A when he described 'his friends' reactions when reprimanded by a teacher. The problem was that he appeared unable to distinguish between different circumstances and act accordingly. He did not seem at all aware that there were occasions where compromising was wiser than showing off. As a result he did not seem to possess alternative techniques, but appeared to always uncritically apply the same form of behaviour[19]. This apparent lack of judgment, characteristic in all three boys, clearly demonstrates the problem.

Relationships with Teachers

So far we have witnessed and explained group Bs' failure in the academic and social sphere of school life. It is now time to examine their relationships with teachers and the latter's opinion of them.

As a rule, there were no teachers friendly with the troubled pupils. Even those who accepted and enjoyed the challenge of the fun-seekers, did not tolerate the pupils of group B. They considered them tiring and a nuisance. No rewarding relationships were expected from these pupils, and the teachers' feelings towards them varied from annoyance to rejection. The pupils' academic difficulties and their constant need for attention and supervision appeared to be the main reason for this. Their uncontrolled and unpredictable behaviour, and their supposed bad influence on their classmates seemed to be another reason[20].

Teachers who taught group B pupils tried to ignore them and minimize their misbehaviour by not making on them the demands they made on every other pupil[21]. Failing that, they simply tried — and often succeeded — to have them removed from their class. The way teachers treated the pupils of this group in the classroom, the language they used addressing them and the words they used to describe them in their interviews and informal conversations, left no doubt about their feelings. The teachers' comments are quoted here from their replies to a letter I sent them asking their opinion of these pupils.

> **Garry:** He is unable to sustain a consistent effort and to be sensible without full time supervision.
> - Babyish, requires attention.
> - Not normal. Talks too much!
> - Doesn't really know what is expected of him.

> **Wayne:** He is seeking attention continually and finds it difficult to get on with his peers.
> - He constantly irritates other pupils, slow to be quiet and settle, lazy.
> - Persistent attempts to cause distraction by name-calling etc. to other pupils. Immature.

> **Mark:** Time consuming due to lack of motivation.
> - Finds it difficult to concentrate for any length of time.
> - Disturbed behaviour, very easily distracted.

Teacher opinion therefore confirmed the suggestions made regarding the pupils' problems and their need for extra help and attention. The eagerness with which most teachers asked for, and the relief with which they greeted the pupils' transfer to a different group indicated how insecure these pupils' position in Burleigh High was and how isolated and lonely they were.

Conclusion

It has been indicated that group B boys had a very difficult time in school, mainly because of social and work problems. It has also been shown that these pupils enjoyed very limited success in school and their failure in all aspects of school life — work, relationships with pupils and relationships with teachers — was severe. It is therefore interesting to speculate why and how these pupils had remained in the mainstream, in view of their evident unhappiness and the problems they caused there.

Staying in school was not a conscious choice for group B the way it was for group A. The motivation that kept fun-seekers in a constant struggle for balance was non-existent for the troubled pupils. Remaining in Burleigh High was rather a result of the school's high tolerance level and restrained exclusion policy.[22]

Group B pupils appeared to have never thought that they had any choice at all whether to stay in school or not. Unlike other groups who turned academic failure into a celebration of their own sub-culture (Willis' 'lads' being the best known), Group B were defeated, because of lack of peer support. Academic failure alone would have been tolerable, but social failure made the pupils depressed and passive[23]. They developed a fatalistic approach to school, and appeared to be unable to take any decisions for themselves[24] and even unaware that they had the choice of doing so. They appeared to feel powerless, were often defensive, and rarely initiated any positive action. Each new failure appeared to make them more unhappy, but did not seem to motivate them to act in either a positive or a negative way. They became more frightened and withdrew further into their own unhappiness. As a consequence they drifted along, apparently only waiting to be freed from school by age. Misbehaviour as a route to freedom did not seem to occur to them, either because of the state of apathy they were in, or because they were too frightened of school authority to attempt anything so bold[25]. It is also possible that very small rewards in school made life there just bearable, and did not allow them to realize just how isolated they were[26].

The pupils themselves, therefore, never took positive action towards being expelled. Given the school's tolerance and protective policy, there was indeed no reason for them to be expelled as long as they remained within reasonable limits. And so there were only two possible avenues out of the mainstream. Either to be involved — always unintentionally — in a major incident which would give them a final blow[27]; or to become so unhappy and withdrawn that the school would have to intervene and take action. This is what happened with Mark. It has to be stressed, however, that neither method would be used as an active form of reaction and a means towards the final aim of been expelled, because the pupils were too subdued to take any such action[28]. If any of these phenomena occurred, it would either be as a result of the pupils' inability to control their behaviour, or as a genuine response to lack of friendship and support.

And so it would appear that group B's career in school was not decided by them, but by factors beyond them. That was a very important difference between them and their deviant colleagues in the mainstream, the fun-seekers.

The Girls

Introducing the 'Troubled Girls'

The two girls of group B[29] presented many of the same characteristics as the boys of their group. They had serious problems with work, and school appeared largely irrelevant to their lives. They were tiring and time consuming as they misbehaved constantly and were unable to concentrate for any length of time. They were not as disruptive, however, and they did not present a threat because the kinds of misbehaviour they chose, similar to those of group A girls, did not greatly interfere with classroom order and peace. The two girls were:

Lisa: Fourteen years and nine months old when interviewed, Lisa was probably the most disaffected girl of the fourth year in Burleigh High. She neither acquired knowledge nor derived pleasure from school and her main preoccupation was that of avoiding work[30]. She had a high classroom profile, not for arguing with teachers, but for being constantly in trouble never doing any home-work. Lying was her favourite technique for coping with teacher demands and she used to miss classes frequently. She was constantly given detentions and lines, and for a period of time she was asked to see the year tutor on a daily basis at lunch break, to show that she was present in school. However, Lisa had never been involved in a major incident, and she was considered a nuisance rather than a threat. She appeared to have gained nothing from school through-out the seven months of the fieldwork period.

Zoe: Fourteen years and seven months old when interviewed, Zoe was also apparently untouched by the school process, and — like Lisa — she appeared to be simply waiting to be set free of school. She was constantly talking and giggling in the classroom and required a lot of attention from the teacher but she never answered back, and conformed immediately with the teachers' com-mands — only to start misbehaving again a few minutes later. Her misbehavi-our, like Lisa's, consisted of doing as little work as possible at school and at home. She used to miss lessons occasionally but was never involved in any-thing more serious and had never received any severe punishments. Zoe initially appeared quite harmless and rather sweet, and it was only after a close exami-nation of the observation data that it became clear that she was in fact a major target for reprimands in the classroom.

Relationships with School

The girls of group B presented — if one allows for gender differences — a very similar picture with that of the boys of their group. Their behaviour too gave teachers considerable problems.

> *Zoe:*   Once he chucked me out of the lesson cause I didn't do my home-work . . . (laughs)

> *Lisa:*   I had an argument with Mrs Hughes. She tells me to move 'cause I talk, so I stand there and she gets angry and she takes my coat . . .
> *HP:*   To make you change place?
> *Lisa:*   Yeah . . .
> *HP:*   And what did you do?
> *Lisa:*   I got it back . . .
> *HP:*   And stayed where you were?
> *Lisa:*   Mmm . . . (nods yes)
> *HP:*   And what happened after that?
> *Lisa:*   She just sat down . . .
> *HP:*   (consulting the questionnaire) Sometimes you break the school rules . . . Do you?

Lisa: Mmm . . . (nods yes)
HP: Why do you do it? Say, when you don't wear the proper uniform?
Lisa: I've always got different reasons . . .
HP: Like what?
Lisa: Like washing . . .
HP: Is that true though or just an excuse?
Lisa: Most of it is excuses . . .
HP: So, why do you do it?
Lisa: 'Cause I'm bored with school uniform . . .

But their feelings about school were contradictory and not based on a coherent theory. Internal conflicts, contradictions and uncertainties were a constant feature of their interviews, as were with group B boys. Their only coping technique appeared to be a tendency to take everything as it came.

HP: So, if you think that teachers should punish pupils for smoking, why do you smoke?
Zoe: I don't know . . . (laughs) It's bad I suppose . . . But I just take the risk 'cause I haven't been caught before, so, you know . . . I don't really care about . . . Well, I do . . . but . . . I don't know . . . I can't really explain it . . .

Direct threats and punishment seemed here again to be the only means of stopping the pupils from misbehaving.

Zoe: Oh! I think I've had a little argument with Mrs Manners, the old one . . . She said: 'Take your coat off!' and I ignored her . . . And after I sat there she said: 'Take it off!' and I ignored her again, and she said something like 'If you don't take it off now, you'll get lines!' so I just took it off. (laughs)
HP: Have you ever got in trouble with Mr Daff? (Year tutor.)
Zoe: I have sometimes for skiving off . . . but it was Friday afternoon last two lessons . . . It was in Maths and the teacher checked up on me . . .
HP: So, you had to see Mr Daff after that . . .
Zoe: Mmm . . . (nods yes)
HP: And did he punish you for it?
Zoe: Detention and lines and told my Dad . . .
HP: So you haven't skived again . . .
Zoe: No . . .

Both girls appear here to respond to threat or punishment and modify their behaviour only when this threat has been made.

Their criticism also appeared to be an impulsive reaction rather than a product of consideration, and lacked the reasoning and depth of criticism offered by the fun seeking girls.

HP: Which teachers don't you like?

Lisa: Mrs Hughes, Mrs Manners, Mrs Bowers . . .

HP: Why is that? Is it because you don't like the subjects hat they teach or is there something about them you don't like?

Lisa: Something about them that I don't like . . .

HP: What is it?

Lisa: Ehm . . . I don't know . . .

HP: You don't like school very much . . .

Zoe: It's all right . . . (laughs)

HP: What is wrong with it?

Zoe: I don't know really . . .

HP: Is it that you don't like some teachers or that you don't like some subjects or what?

Zoe: Some of the teachers . . . Like Mr Michell.

HP: What is wrong with him? Do you not get on?

Zoe: Yes, but he is too strict. He's all right but . . . I don't know, we don't get on . . . (laughs)

Like the boys of their group, the girls appeared unable to reason and explain why they disliked school, even when given some assistance as to what the possible reasons could be for their dislike.

Academic Record

As far as academic performance was concerned, the girls' problems were as acute as the boys'. Both girls were in low academic groups, and had constant trouble with lessons and homework. The girls themselves knew how limited they were in this field and freely admitted that they were 'thick'[31]. This conviction was the product of what they thought the teachers' opinion of them was (see also Woods, 1975, for a similar effect of teacher opinion on pupils).

HP: Why don't you like school?

Lisa: I don't know, I just hate it . . .

HP: You do . . . What do you hate?

Lisa: The lessons . . .

HP: . . . Why don't you like Maths or English?

Lisa: It's boring . . .

HP: Do you find it difficult sometimes?

Lisa: No, it's just boring . . .

HP: Are there any lessons you like?

Lisa: Art . . .[32]

Lisa denies here that she found lessons difficult and tries to stress that they were simply boring[33]. It must be noted however that the word 'boring' is a favourite with this group, and it has a variety of meanings for them.

HP: What about the teachers? You say that they think of you as stupid. How do you know?

Lisa: I don't know . . . They think I'm thick . . .

HP: Why? How do you know what they think?

Lisa: I don't know . . .

HP: Do they tell you?

Lisa: Yeah! (laughs)

HP: How? What do they say?

Lisa: They'd probably be laughing and say . . . 'Lisa's a stupid girl . . .' or something like that . . .

HP: Do they mean it though or is it a joke?

Lisa: They mean it . . .

Zoe appears to entertain a similar idea about her abilities.

HP: You say that 'most teachers think of me as a wally'. What do you mean?

Zoe: (laughs) Yeah . . . silly, stupid, something like that . . .

HP: How do you know? Do they tell you?

Zoe: No, but I got to know what they think and that . . . The teachers say: 'You're silly' you know . . . in a funny way, but . . . they smile as well . . . but . . .

HP: And you don't think yourself you're a wally. Do you?

Zoe: A bit . . . (giggles)

Evidently both girls, Zoe in particular, had a very low opinion of themselves. This phenomenon was identified in the boys of the group, and comes to startling contrast with the self confidence of group A pupils.

Relationships with Peers

Much though the girls had in common with the boys, they seemed to differ in one respect. Relationships with their peers were better and they were not as isolated as the boys (unlike Samantha's group in Pollard, 1984). The reason was the gender difference in expectations for classroom behaviour. Girls' friendships did not depend on proving themselves in class. Because of the girls' low position in the social hierarchy, the fight boys had to put on to become publicly accepted was unknown to the girls. Showing off was far less important for them. As a consequence, confrontation with teachers was avoided, saving the girls the humiliation group B boys suffered in front of their peers. As a result, the social failure of the girls of group B was much less severe than that of the boys.

Instead of arguing with teachers or answering back to them, the girls had developed different techniques to save them working. First, they used to *lie*[34].

HP: How about homework? Do you ever get in trouble . . .
Lisa: (interrupting me) I never do it . . .
HP: And how do you get away with it?
Lisa: I don't know . . . (laughs) I just say I forgot it . . .
HP: And what do the teachers do?
Lisa: They say bring it next time.
HP: And?
Lisa: I don't bring it in . . .
HP: I see . . . So you keep saying next time and next time and they keep forgetting. Right?
Lisa: Mmm . . . (nods yes)
HP: Do they never make you do it in the class or keep you in detention or something like that?
Lisa: Mrs Hughes does.
HP: She keeps you in detention?
Lisa: Yeah, but I've never been to her detentions.
HP: And what did she do after that?
Lisa: I said I had detention with Mr Daff instead . . . She used to say: 'Next time you better come to detention' and that . . . and she believed me. But I don't do my homework for most of them . . . We do enough work at school.

The girls attempted to cover their actions by lying, while the boys freely admitted to not having completed their homework. (Zoe volunteered to be interviewed at a time when she was supposed to be doing PE).

HP: Why aren't you in games now? Do you have a note excusing you from taking games?
Zoe: No . . . I just . . . I can't be bothered to get the stuff out of the cupboard . . . The clothes . . .
HP: And does Miss Lovers let you get away with it?
Zoe: Yeah . . . (laughs) I've been doing it for about two, three months now . . .
HP: And what is your excuse? Does she accept it without an excuse?
Zoe: Yeah! She don't say nothing! She just looks at me . . . She asked me a couple of times. I said I'd forgotten . . . And my mum does write a note sometimes . . .

It seems very unlikely that teachers were fooled by these sorts of excuses, as the girls appeared to believe. It is more probable that they made similar allowances for the girls as they made for the boys and were prepared to put up with their behaviour because it did not cause a major disruption in the lesson[35]. Regarding homework, it seems that teachers, knowing the pupils' low ability, recognized the difficulties involved in their preparing work at home. As long as their classroom behaviour did not disrupt the flow of the lesson, they turned a blind eye and just tried to ensure that the pupils made at least good use of time spent in class. Keeping a low profile paid off saving effort for the girls and protecting them from public embarrassment[36]. As Lisa mentioned in her quote, 'telling off' was in such cases mostly private, held in an empty classroom after class, and the girls' reputation — or indeed the teachers' — was never at stake. This quiet way of deviating was accepted by the class as a perfectly appropriate form of behaviour for a girl[37] while overt misbehaviour was both disapproved of and punished by the boys as the following incident indicates:

> It is a geography lesson and the class has been relaxed and noisy during a working session. A group of four boys has been particularly noisy, but girls have also been talking and laughing. The teacher calls for quiet in order to give new instructions. The four boys eventually quieten down. Zoe, however, is still giggling with her friend. The teacher starts talking, ignoring her, but one of the four boys hits her on the head with a book and shouts: 'Quiet!' The teacher does not intervene.

Another popular technique used by the girls was *skiving*[38]. This presented more serious problems for the school than lying did, but it was popular because it offered pupils a relief from school. If caught, the girl was usually dealt with in private consultation with the teacher or the year tutor, so there was no danger of being shown up. The advantages of this method seem to have been known to the troubled girls from a very young age.

HP: So, you have lots of detentions. Haven't you? And you've been on report and everything . . .
Lisa: Mmm . . . (nods yes)
HP: How do you manage to do all that if you keep quiet?
Lisa: Skiving mostly . . .
HP: Skiving! That's what you get caught for . . .
Lisa: Yeah, and smoking . . .
HP: How do your friends like school?
Lisa: They hate it! (laughs) I don't know . . . We used to skive a lot from the primary school . . .
HP: Did you? All the little ones . . .
Lisa: Yeah . . . (laughs)

Thanks to these 'low profile' techniques, the girls' misbehaviour, although noted by the school and punished, caused them considerably less embarrassment than that of the boys. For this reason, the girls of group B were not as isolated from their peers as the boys of the group were.

Remaining in School. A Matter of Choice?

Relationships with peers was the only aspect of school life where the two genders differed. In every other aspect they seemed to be remarkably similar. School seemed equally irrelevant to their lives, and a source of frustration and contradictory feelings. Attending school was therefore not a conscious choice aiming at acquiring skills or qualifications, but simply a mechanical action. This was partly evident from the fact that the girls' future plans did not appear to be at all related to school qualifications.

> *Lisa:* I've got animals . . . A horse . . . I'd rather stay with him than come to this place . . . I went to see him this morning . . .
> *HP:* What are you going to do when you leave school?
> *Lisa:* I don't know . . .
> *HP:* Something with horses?
> *Lisa:* (laughs)
> *HP:* What can you do with horses that is clean[39]?
> *Lisa:* Nothing!
> *HP:* So?
> *Lisa:* I don't know . . .

And again . . .

> *HP:* Why will you be glad when you leave school?
> *Lisa:* I don't know . . . I will have more time . . .
> *HP:* And what are you going to do when you have time?
> *Lisa:* I don't know yet . . . (laughs)

Zoe did not seem to have any specific plans either[40].

> *HP:* So, will you be glad when you leave school?
> *Zoe:* Mmm . . . (laughs) I don't know. I just want to get out of school cause it's a bit boring . . . (laughs) It's all right, I like it sometimes, but not much . . .
> *HP:* So, are you looking forward to getting a job or something?
> *Zoe:* No, not really . . .
> *HP:* You don't have anything in mind?
> *Zoe:* (laughs and shakes head)
> *HP:* Nothing at all?
> *Zoe:* No . . . no.

This attitude, of attending school without thinking about it and without making any decisions relating to it, is very clear in the following statement:

HP:	And you don't care what teachers think of you . . .
Zoe:	Mmm . . . not really . . . (laughs)
HP:	Why not?
Zoe:	I don't know . . . (laughs)
HP:	Is it because you don't respect them or you think they don't matter? Do you think their opinion doesn't matter?
Zoe:	Doesn't matter! (laughs) The next lesson I sort of get on with them again and then it is as before. They are nice and that . . . and then I get again on report . . . (laughs)[41]

The girls, like the boys, drifted along, not through choice, but because of obligation and lack of alternatives. However, there is here an indication of what the external factors influencing the pupils' career in school could have been.

HP:	How do you get on with the year tutor?
Lisa:	I don't know . . . Sometimes I do and sometimes I don't . . .
HP:	So would you say that you like him overall or you don't?
Lisa:	I hate him . . . (laughs)
HP:	So you hate him but sometimes you get on with him for some reason . . .
Lisa:	Yeah . . .
HP:	What happens when you don't get on? Do you shout at each other?
Lisa:	I don't know . . . He shouts at me . . . I don't shout at him back . . .
HP:	Why? What would happen if you did?
Lisa:	I don't know . . . I'd get expelled from school or something like that . . .
HP:	And you don't want that . . .
Lisa:	(shakes head)
HP:	Why not? You could get rid of school altogether . . .
Lisa:	No, my mum would kill me . . . (laughs)
HP:	Ah! Does your mum want you to do well in school?
Lisa:	I don't know. I never ask . . .
HP:	Does she ask you about your homework and tells you to do your best?
Lisa:	No, she knows I don't do my homework . . . (laughs)
HP:	And what does she do?
Lisa:	She does nothing much . . . She just leaves it up to me . . .

It was argued earlier that school policy was a crucial factor in the development of the pupils' school career, and that the level of behaviour tolerance exhibited by the school was decisive in influencing the pupils' exclusion from the mainstream. Here the possible effects of the home factors can also be seen. There seems to be some parental pressure that has prevented Lisa from crossing the dividing line to a special unit. This pressure appears to be only very small, because Lisa's mother does not attempt to force Lisa to work hard and get the most out of school, as Michael's mother did (see section 'How deviant is deviant?'). She only appears to want her daughter to remain in school[42]. However, it must be stressed that this sort of external pressure — when present — did not appear to provide the pupils with a structured way of thinking and a coherent theory about school[43]. Because of the lack of such a structure, group B girls as well as group B boys remained vulnerable. External pressures appeared to confuse even further pupils who were already feeling very confused about school.

Conclusion and Comparison between Group A and Group B

We have now concluded the examination of the second deviant group of pupils in Burleigh High, group B. It has been seen that this group showed some similarities to group A, in that its pupils also presented teachers with a number of problems being motivated by a desire to have an enjoyable time in school. The pupils of group B however appeared to lack long-term goals in connection with school, and to be aiming solely for immediate gratification. They sought enjoyment and easy satisfaction, showing indifference for any other functions the school could fulfil. Lack of long-term planning may mot have been a problem if the pupils had been successful in satisfying their short-term aims, but this was not the case. For they seemed to lack the skill necessary to support their misbehaviour. They appeared to be unable to manipulate their behaviour to the desired effect, and unaware of the consequences of their actions. As a result their misbehaviour was immediately noted and suppressed by teachers. This deprived them of the satisfaction they looked for, and humiliated them in the eyes of their peers. It also placed them in a very vulnerable position regarding mainstream school, although the pupils seemed to be unaware of that.

A comparison between group A and group B would have to point out that arguments supporting the view that misbehaviour in school is an expression of pupil culture appear here to bear some validity. It is important nevertheless to stress that there are a number of pupils who seem to be unable to set their aims and proceed to fulfil them, because they appear to lack a certain degree of control over their own behaviour.

The pupils of group A seem to have two sets of goals. Their misbehaviour appears to result from an effort to satisfy their short-term goal of having enjoyment in school. Their long-term goal of obtaining certain qualifications from school, which would allow them to aim for a chosen career, seems to counteract their misbehaviour and produce a balance which keeps them within the accepted limits. These pupils appear to be in control of their actions and operate according to a premeditated plan based on the values of the pupils' sub-culture, as well as the official values of the school. Consequently, the pupils of group A appear to remain in the mainstream through their own choice.

The pupils of group B, on the other hand, appear to have no long-term goals. Their misbehaviour is a product of their desire to have an enjoyable time in school, which is not counteracted by any other aims. They seem to lack a sense of balance that would allow them to manipulate their behaviour in such a way as to offer them satisfaction without involving risks. Their misbehaviour therefore undermines their position in the mainstream school. Their remaining in the mainstream appears to be a result of the school's protective policy rather than a conscious product of their own will.

Having established the motivation behind the misbehaviour of groups A and B and the reasons that have helped them remain within the mainstream despite their deviant behaviour, it is now time to examine the motivation behind the deviant pupils of the special unit and the reasons for their transfer. The next part, Part III, will be devoted to the pupils of the Emery Centre in an effort to answer these questions.

Postscript

It would be fascinating, but is impossible, to trace the pupils up and find out exactly where their behaviour and lack of planning has taken them. All five pupils of this group had such serious problems with school, spilling off onto their self perception and self esteem, so their life after school cannot have been easy.

Notes

1 It is very interesting here that Garry is unable to explain his own behaviour in any way. He appears to simply give way to his impulse without questioning it.

2 A clear sign that teachers had given up with Mark by that time.

3 Mark appears here to impose his own judgment on this situation and to be unable to see the teachers' point of view.

4 Interestingly, their criticism of teachers seemed to concentrate on how helpful and understanding they were, in contrast to Group A who were more concerned with the teachers' ability to keep order and teach new and useful things. Concentration on these aspects of teacher behaviour seemed to indicate learning difficulties which will become more apparent in the next section. Nash (1976) summarises very well such pupil expectations of teachers.

5 The pupils' preoccupation with schoolwork is apparent in most of their comments regardless of the question asked.

6 See the teachers' comments in the section 'Relationships with teachers' below.

7 Werthman (1963) and Woods (1976) describe how pupils come to be aware of their ability in school.

8 It is interesting to note Mark's emphasis on lack of help from teachers, which appears to reflect a genuine need for more attention and help in the class.

9 The teacher's comments start in a light humorous manner and they slowly change as Garry fails to respond positively to them.

10 Teachers appeared to use a particularly harsh language with this group. This phenomenon will be examined when dealing with the relationships between pupils and teachers in the section 'Relationships with teachers' below.

11   This kind of attention seeking, as well as attention seeking directed to teachers, has often been used in the literature as an example of immature behaviour, (Galloway, 1976; Laslett, 1977 and 1982).

12   Mark considered Peter to be his friend, and he named him as such in the interview. Although Peter also named Mark as a friend, his behaviour when in the same class with him indicated a manipulation that led Mark to continuous trouble and let Peter enjoy himself laughing untouched by teacher punishment. Relationships like this were quite common for members of group B. It seems that even people they considered friends used them in order to have fun. As a consequence group B pupils were in reality even more isolated than they imagined.

13   Mark was originally in Mrs Haw's computer studies group. But the teacher could not, as she said, 'cope both with computers and Mark'. So she asked for him to be transferred to Mr Harris' computer group. Mark was having great difficulty being accepted there, as it was an all boys group and the atmosphere was very competitive, and also because the other boys gave him a hard time by bullying him. Characteristic of this bullying was the fact that they refused to call him by his name and they called him 'cabbage' instead. Sadly, but not surprisingly, Mark responded to this nick-name as if it were his real name.

14   Ball (1980) examines in detail the interaction between pupils and teachers and the communication signals used.

15   Pollard (1979) argues that failure to recognize these signals can be a result of conscious rejection, or a product of 'social incompetence'. It seems — because of the pupils' surprise with the results of their own actions — that the latter was the case with the group B pupils.

16   Their only technique available being complaints and excuses as shown in the section 'Relationships with peers'.

17   This lack of modification in the pupils' behaviour would have been interpreted as a lack of interest on their part, if the pupils had appeared to ignore the consequences of their actions, and had not shown genuine concern when reprimanded.

18   This is not meant as an easy excuse for labelling the pupils, but rather as a cause for genuine concern and a reason for providing them with extra attention and assistance. Werthman (1963) also makes a distinction between bright and dull pupils within his gang.

19   The same lack of flexibility in reactions will be seen to be a characteristic of the Emery Centre group D.

20   The teachers' difficulty in relating to these pupils often resulted in their seeking my advice. I, 'having followed the pupils around', was considered to know them well enough to be able to help.

21   Werthman's (1963) pupils characterized similar behaviour by teachers as 'bribery'. These pupils simply accepted it without questioning. See Mark's statement in the section 'Relationships with school' above.

22   Burleigh High was very conscious of its social role in the area and very protective of its pupils.

23   Woods (1975) describes how 'showing ups' might produce neuroses if they are kept up over a period of time, and especially if they are reinforced by peers.

24   Even their future plans were non-existent (Garry), unrealistic (Wayne) or thought out for them by someone else (Mark). Wayne stated that after his graduation he would go to art school. His art teacher however, when interviewed, appeared to consider this plan totally unrealistic. Mark on the other hand did not appear to have any preferences himself, but said that his mother wanted him to go to a further education college. This

plan also appeared to be totally without any realistic foundation, given Mark's general attitude towards school and low academic ability. Finally, Garry had no plans of any kind for the future. Not surprisingly there was no direct relationship between the pupils' choice of subject options and these plans.

25　It must be remembered that these pupils never challenged teachers deliberately.

26　This false picture of relationships in school has been indicated by Wayne's comments about friends, and by Mark's belief that Peter was a friend of his. A stronger picture of a similar false reality will become more evident in the accounts of the Emery Centre group D pupils.

27　This will be seen to be the case with Emery Centre group D pupils.

28　Even when he came to hate school, Mark appeared to never have thought of doing something to get out of it. Instead, he was frustrated and unhappy, and used the strongest words he could think of to describe how he disliked not only Burleigh High, but any school.

29　The reasons for the separate treatment of the two genders are the same here as in the previous chapter: to give the girls the opportunity to show their own classroom techniques, and to minimize the disruptive effect which gender differences might have on the main argument if there were presented together. This section should be seen as compliment-ary to the previous one.

30　Pollard (1984) describes how low academic girls saw the lessons as a 'waste of time' and spent the time 'doing nothing'.

31　Meyenn (1980) mentions that 'being thick' was the main characteristic of one of the girls' groups in the class he studied. Pollard (1984) describes a similar phenomenon in the class he observed.

32　Art was mentioned as a favourite subject by all members of group B without exception. Considering that none of them was particularly good at it, it appears that they liked it because of the lack of pressure and the relaxed class atmosphere where they could get away with doing only very little work.

33　Philip of Emery Centre group D attempts to do exactly the same.

34　A similar girls' technique is reported by Davies (1979).

35　Denscombe (1980) and Measor (1983) point out that disorderly behaviour that does not directly interfere with classroom activities is not given priority. They also document that most often these quiet deviants are girls.

36　Keeping a low profile was not a conscious decision made by the girls. This would indic-ate a kind of sensitivity and social awareness unknown to the pupils of this group. It was simply a type of spontaneous behaviour generally adopted by girls in the school, indicating their submission to a sex role stereotype rather than any deliberate action. Fortunately for the girls of this group, as well as the girls of group A, this kind of behaviour proved to be to their advantage.

37　Measor (1983) also points out the difference between types of misbehaviour appropriate for males and females.

38　Llewellyn (1980) describes skiving as a typically female form of resistance.

39　Lisa had fiercely argued during a group discussion in an English lesson, that girls should not do dirty jobs (see Clarricoates, 1980, for similar feminine stereotypes, held by girls across the behaviour spectrum). That was in fact the only lesson during the whole observation period which Lisa actively participated in. She was usually disinterested in what was going on in the classroom, and never showed the least interest in the lesson.

40　It is interesting to point out that none of the girls mentioned marriage as a possible future prospect.

41   It is interesting to note the pattern of getting in and out of trouble without worrying about consequences, and without believing that this behaviour is going to affect her school career.

42   It is interesting to speculate why this was, since Lisa did not appear to receive any benefit from school. It is a possibility that the mother suspected that being expelled from school would have grave consequences for her daughter's future. But it is also likely that she simply did not know of any alternatives, or was unwilling to challenge the school's authority (see Jackie's case in Emery Centre group D for parental fear of school). Hargreaves (1967) also shows that working class parents are often scared to challenge school authority because they have no knowledge of the way it operates and so they feel powerless.

43   And consequently the existence of this factor does not contradict the arguments that have been put forward regarding this group.

Part III

Emery Centre

This part deals with the work undertaken in the special unit. Chapter 5 presents the methodology used which will be seen to be similar to the one used in the mainstream slightly modified as identification of deviant pupils was not necessary here. Chapter 6 presents the pupils' memories of the mainstream and their views on their previous schools, and attempts a retrospective interpretation of the pupils' behaviour while in the mainstream in an effort to uncover the motivation and the thinking behind their actions.

Chapter 5

How Did I Do It? II:
Methodology Used at the Emery Centre

Emery Centre

Fieldwork in the special unit lasted five weeks. Although considerably less than the amount of time spent in the mainstream, this length of time was sufficient for the needs of the study, given the smaller size of the unit, which facilitated contact, the limited number of pupils, which encouraged familiarity, and the lack of need for an identification stage. The methodological approaches used to study the pupils in the special unit were very similar to those used in the mainstream school. Questionnaires, observation and interviews with pupils and teachers were also used here, adapted to the demands of the centre.

The most serious methodological problem arose from the fact that information had to be collected in retrospect, and there was no easy way of validating pupil accounts. Memory loss as well as personal interest in justifying one's behaviour, had to be overcome by observation, consultation of the unit records, interviews with the unit staff and scrutiny of the internal structure of pupil accounts. These could not compensate completely for lack of direct observation in the mainstream, but since pupils in units cannot be studied before they are placed there, these were the only methods available[1]. The methods used are described below, after a description of the unit and its character.

The Centre

Background

Emery Centre was established in 1973[2], and it operated in West Town for nine years, under the same headteacher and the same full-time teacher with only minor structural changes. During that time the number of pupils had been very small and its role insignificant. The year before the fieldwork started the old headteacher retired, and the Centre was due to close, functioning with only one member of staff and one or two pupils. However, in the beginning of 1986 a new headteacher was appointed and significant organizational changes took place. At the time of the fieldwork, the Centre operated with three full-time members of staff: the headteacher, who was also in charge of some subjects, a full-time teacher who bore the main teaching responsibility, and a secretary who also taught cookery and typing. The number of pupils had also been increased to nine.

Admission Procedure

The Centre was independent catering for a number of schools in the area. Its role was to provide 'a part time programme of alternative education for pupils in their final compulsory year', and it admitted pupils who presented a variety of problems in the mainstream. Some of them were disruptive during lessons, others exhibited anti-social behaviour towards staff and/or pupils, yet others were consistent truants. Pupils were referred for one or more of the above reasons. Once the decision to transfer had been taken, a member of staff from the Centre was allocated as a tutor to the case and visited the child's home. If the pupil and/or his/her parents objected, further consideration was given to the case. If they agreed to the planned admission, a visit to the unit was arranged and the pupil had the opportunity to examine the Centre before taking his/her final decision. If there was no further objection, a written agreement was signed between the unit, the pupil and the family. An admission date was agreed upon, and the pupil was obliged to attend under the terms of the agreement.

Description of the Premises

The Centre consisted of a one storey building situated in a wide courtyard near a primary school[3]. It was comfortably big, and although old, very warm and welcoming inside. There was a reception room (also used as a common room), three classrooms, a sports hall, a staff room and a big kitchen. There were also other small rooms used for various purposes; for example, a darkroom, store-room, etc. The registers and the telephone were kept in the staff room which was rarely used while pupils were in the premises. The staffroom door was kept unlocked, pupils having access to it at any time. The atmosphere was warm and relaxed, and although there was a constant effort to enforce basic discipline, the place never lost the relaxed and informal air that made it so different from a school. The creation of a 'homely' atmosphere was a primary aim of the staff in an effort to attract the pupils and help them make use of the facilities. This aim was obviously achieved. The children had a good record of attendance, and were unwilling to leave the building before closing time.

Timetable

The Centre was open Monday to Friday from 9.00 a.m. to 3.30 p.m. This included two working sessions a day, one from 10.00 a.m. to 12.00 noon, and one from 1.00 p.m. to 3.00 p.m. There was a small break during each session, whose time and length varied according to teacher judgment. Two parallel lessons, taught by different members of staff in separate rooms, took place during each session. There was no bell marking the beginning and the end of each session. The member of staff teaching the session would usually lead the children to the room and dismiss them when the lesson was over.

Between 12.00 noon and 1.00 p.m. there was a lunch break. The pupils were free to stay in the Centre or go home, their only obligation being to return punctually for their afternoon session. Most children chose to stay in the Centre, irrespective of the distance between it and their house. They usually had a snack, brought from home or bought from a shop near by, and played games or socialized. At 3.00 p.m. they were free to leave, but they quite often 'hung around' until 3.30 p.m. when the Centre closed.

Curriculum

As is apparent from the timetable (see appendix 14), there were no academic lessons in the Centre. A wide variety of thirteen practical subjects was on offer instead[4]. It was obligatory for pupils to choose at least four of the activities offered, and to attend the meetings held on Wednesday morning and Friday afternoon. That meant that each pupil had to be in the Centre twelve hours a week, sessions lasting two hours each[5].

With the exception of computer studies, which was a new subject for most pupils and required detailed explanation, there was no conventional teaching. Pupils would choose a project and work on it under staff supervision. The project choice was left to the pupil limited only by existing facilities. Once the pupil had chosen a project, s/he was normally expected to complete it. In the sports sessions a member of staff would accompany the pupil/s to the game court or the swimming pool outside the Centre. The only sport played within the premises was table tennis.

Wednesday's meeting was called the 'pre-employment' session, and it was the equivalent of a careers lesson. Its purpose was to prepare pupils for school leaving, teaching them how to apply for jobs and how to fill in forms for various benefits, including supplementary benefit. During this session the children were split into two groups, one under the teacher and one under the head of the unit. This session with its tight structure and emphasis on reading and writing was the closest to a school lesson and therefore the least popular. The Friday meeting was a form of weekly work assessment and an occasion for announcements concerning the following week. Everybody was welcome to contribute to the discussion, but it was usually the headteacher or the teacher who did most of the talking. The pupils would listen making a comment every now and then.

Ethos

The friendly atmosphere was achieved through a good balance of discipline and caring, evident in staff attitude and underlying the system of rewards and punishments.

Punishments

There were very few specific rules in the unit. Those which did exist could be summarized as:

> (i)   attending regularly the sessions one had opted for, and the compulsory meetings;
> (ii) being punctual for the beginning of sessions and meetings;
> (iii) no smoking inside the building[6];
> (iv) behaving in an adult and sensible manner[7].

When rules were broken, the problem was in the first instance dealt with by talking directly to the pupil concerned. This 'talk' usually took the form of a discussion rather than lecture. 'Telling off' was strictly avoided. The member of staff tried to be positive, emphasizing the pupil's past achievements and indicating the danger of failure arising from unruly behaviour. The problem was usually solved at that level. If there was a case of recurring misbehaviour, for example, repeated absenteeism, the pupil's tutor would make a point of seeing the pupil and his or her family at home to discuss the matter. An effort would then be made to influence the parents and the pupil reminding them — if necessary — of the agreement signed before admission. Some parents were uncooperative, and some children could not be persuaded[8]. If the outcome was negative the matter would be dealt with by the Education Welfare Officer, or not at all if the pupil was very close to school leaving age.[9]

Rewards

There were two kinds of rewards. One was the continuous encouragement and praise offered by members of staff during their everyday interaction with pupils. The other was an official system of points given mainly for punctuality during sessions. Pupils received ten points for every punctual arrival. The rewards earnt were as follows:

40 points:	a packet of potato crisps
80 points:	a chocolate bar
250 points:	£1 voucher
500 points:	£2 voucher
750 points:	£3 voucher
1000 points:	£4 voucher

The distribution of points was announced during Friday meetings, when pupils were given feedback about their performance during the week. During these meetings the staff made a special effort to give rewards, and criticisms were kept for private sessions between the pupil and his/her tutor. The choice of reward was left with the pupil.

The Fieldwork

Methods Used

Observation

During the first week of the fieldwork a lot of time was devoted to becoming familiar with the place and the people and I was in the unit from 9.30 a.m. until 3.30 p.m. every day. Because the working sessions did not start until 10.00 a.m., there was time to talk to staff and see the pupils arrive. The headteacher introduced me to each individual child on our first meeting, and I was then free to talk to them. I followed one group of pupils for the first session of the day, or observed both groups moving between classrooms, if the lesson allowed it. I usually spent lunch break with the pupils, and from 1.00 p.m. until 3.00 p.m. observed the second session of the day. Contact with pupils was therefore constant. The observation was informal and participant. I focused on the interaction between pupils and teacher, and paid special attention to interactions between peers. Because of lack of pressure, the possibilities for an incident[10] between a teacher and a pupil were limited, and confined to a possible challenge of basic Centre rules, such as not working or indeed continuing to work when the session was over (a phenomenon common with the boys when working on the computer).

I attempted using the observation sheet used in the mainstream but it did not prove efficient because of the different setting and the small size of the class. First, the pace of interaction was very fast. I attempted selective note-keeping of the incidents involving a clash of interest between the teacher and the pupil, but even then there was need for continuous writing, inhibiting the observation itself. Furthermore, note-taking in such a small place gave the pupils an awkward feeling of being watched. This observation style appeared to disturb the pupils[11], and distance me. I therefore felt that I had to discontinue it. It needs to be noted that after the first two weeks I also modified my observation schedule, following the headteacher's request. In the interest of pupil comfort I was asked to discontinue any form of classroom observation, and limit the fieldwork to informal contact during break time. The reason offered was that he had been the headteacher for only a few weeks and interference from outsiders could prove very distracting for the pupils. I did not agree with this estimate, my relationships with pupils being already excellent, but I had no choice but to follow this course of action. Fortunately, the opportunities to observe the pupils remained ample, as I continued to spend a considerable amount of time with them for the remaining three weeks of the fieldwork. The interviews were completed without further problems.

Questionnaire and interview

During the first week, and as a part of an effort to become familiar with the pupils, I held informal conversations with them about their experiences in school and the reasons for their transfer to the Centre. The pupils were cooperative and friendly, and there was never any difficulty in getting any answers from them. Our discussions were by no means one-sided, as they were curious to know more about me and my work and I was happy to answer their questions. Informal discussions like these continued to take place throughout the five-week period and were useful as well as pleasant.

During the second week I began interviewing. The interviews were semi-structured, conducted in a spare room during lunch break. Each pupil was formally interviewed once, each interview lasting between thirty and forty-five minutes. They were all recorded, no pupil having any objection to that. At the beginning of the interview I explained the purpose of my study telling them that I was interested in pupil attitude to school, and requested some personal information. I then presented them the questionnaire used in Burleigh High slightly altered to fit the new situation (see appendix 13), and asked them to fill it in. The children were asked to make direct comparisons between their mainstream schools and the unit. Discrepancies between answers regarding mainstream schools and those regarding the unit were common, and the reasons for them were always asked for. The issues arising were immediately dealt with, and the pupils were requested to justify their answers. The pupils were finally asked the following questions, which bore a special relevance to the Centre:

(i)   Do you think you could have stayed in the mainstream?
(ii) Would you have liked to?
(iii) What would have been necessary for the school to do in order to accommodate you?
(iv) How do you see yourself being different from the other pupils left behind?
(v)   Do you think you are losing out by being outside the mainstream?
(vi) Do you think the unit is of any use to you? If so, what is that?

Close daily contact with staff made formal interviews with them unnecessary. I had instant feedback on the pupils' everyday behaviour, as well as a wealth of information about the pupils' contact in the mainstream and the conditions under which they had arrived at the Centre. The pupils' files, including school records, were also at my disposal for further information.

The Pupils and their Relationship with me

During the period of the fieldwork in the unit nine pupils were registered there; five boys and four girls. They were: Colin, Darren, Philip, Sam, Terry, Louise, Jackie, Nichola and Teresa. Two of the boys never appeared in the unit during the fieldwork: Darren because he was convicted for theft during the first week of the fieldwork and sent to a detention centre; and Sam because he was constantly playing truant, despite the efforts of the Centre staff to bring him back. Of the seven remaining children, six came to the unit on a full-time schedule, and one boy, Terry, came only for one session a week, as he was working part-time[12]. Six out of the seven children who attended regularly were formally interviewed[13], all four girls and two of the three boys.

The pupils were initially shy and hesitant to volunteer for a formal interview, but cooperative and relaxed once the interview had started. They appeared trusting and uninhibited in their answers, girls more comfortable than boys. The boys appeared less eloquent, often resorting to monosyllabic answers. All pupils responded with confidence, and talked freely, describing incidents and offering details and opinions even before asked. It is to their credit that they all tried to be cooperative and helpful, and I am grateful for that.

Despite the relatively short time spent in the Emery Centre relationships between the pupils and me developed easily and reached a good level of understanding in a very short time. I was easily incorporated into what was in effect a family structure, and took part in all activities, including helping with projects and giving advice about computer problems or sewing tasks, or simply playing table tennis with the pupils during lunch break. The pupils, used to visitors and volunteer workers much older than them, treated me very much as an equal, and confided in me details about their personal life, or asked questions about mine.

The end of the fieldwork coincided with Easter break. Easter lunch prepared and hosted by staff in the unit, gave me the opportunity to thank teachers and pupils for their help. After the completion of the fieldwork I occasionally visited the Centre, and kept in touch with the pupils until their graduation day, two months later. On graduation day I was introduced to the parents present and posed with the pupils for pictures in the unit courtyard. Finally I retained correspondence with one pupil after graduation, keeping in touch with others pupils' news too.

The next chapter will tell the story of the Emery Centre pupils.

Postscript

Evidently fieldwork was, once again, far from smooth and easy, as fieldwork generally is. Interestingly the same pattern was followed here as in Burleigh High, with pupils being relaxed and friendly and more than happy to cooperate, and staff trying to 'protect pupils' from me. Who are they really trying to protect when pupils need and require no protection? This is the question.

Notes

1   Retrospective interviewing of mainstream school teachers would be another way of validating the information given by the pupils. This method would demand validation of teacher accounts and time and resources not available in this study.

2   The seventies were a time of rapid growth for special units throughout the country (see the Introduction in chapter 1).

3   The Centre was independent catering for a number of schools and its physical proximity to a particular school was coincidental.

4   The extent of the academic emphasis of the curriculum in special units before the establishment of the National Curriculum depended heavily on the head and/or the staff of the unit, with occasional limitations imposed by the LEA concerned. This emphasis was usually strongly connected with the philosophy and ultimate aims of each unit (Emerson, 1984; Leavold, 1984).

5   This was the minimum requirement. The pupils were free to opt for a longer than twelve-hour week.

6   There was a special 'smoker's area' in the courtyard for staff and pupils.

7   This rule was the least explicit, but the pupils were fully aware that sensible behaviour was expected of them.

8   There was one pupil, Sam, who was never in the Centre during the fieldwork, choosing to truant instead.

9   One of the pupils, Terry, stopped coming to the unit three weeks before he was officially due to leave, but no action was taken to bring him back. The reason for this was probably the fact that Terry had left to start a full-time job.

10 See the section 'Analysis of the general observation data' (chapter 2) for a definition of the word.

11 There were never any complaints from pupils, but this was the headteacher's view.

12 His working hours counted as a work placement and were included in his twelve hour attendance of the Centre excusing him from full-time attendance.

13 Terry refused to be formally interviewed. As he attended the Centre for one session a week he did not consider himself very much part of the establishment and remained rather distant from pupils and teachers alike. This seems to be the main reason for his refusal. Because of his limited attendance, an opportunity for a second attempt did not arise. His sudden departure from the Centre three weeks earlier than scheduled did not facilitate matters. Terry's views will not be reported as contact with him was not considered sufficient for drawing conclusions on his decision making in school.

Chapter 6

In Exile

Introduction

Rejection of the school system is not exhausted in the creation of deviant sub-cultures within school like the ones identified in previous chapters. It occasionally climaxes to an open confrontation which leads to departure from the mainstream. In these cases, as Galloway (1976) and Rosser and Harre (1976) indicate, what is perceived as an inexplicably extreme form of behaviour, often rests on a coherent anti-school philosophy and careful forward planning. It follows a rational decision 'to get out of school' based on objection to a school ethos which leads to failure at work and relationships with teachers and peers. When failure becomes unbearable, school dislike becomes a conviction, and leads to an 'escape' plan. Consequently, sociological explanations of deliberate use of deviant behaviour as a form of school resistance are needed to help us understand such cases.

Nevertheless, exit from the mainstream is not always the product of conscious choice. There are pupils whose failure to remain in school is apparently due to lack of good judgment and self-control. For them a moderately negative school attitude is accompanied by extremely negative behaviour resulting from an effort to copy shrewder peers. Because they lack a coherent philosophy, these pupils are equally likely to drift along in the mainstream or deteriorate and be excluded. Their school careers are largely determined by school ethos and tolerance. Transfer outside the mainstream is for them an initially traumatic experience, albeit without lasting effects, mainly because of their ability to rationalize. For them attendance of a special unit may be of significant help in providing much needed attention and assistance with academic work and social skills training. They thus justify traditional psychological explanations of 'problem' behaviour in school resulting from lack of control.

Emery Centre is an off-site special unit for pupils with behaviour problems which hosts nine attendants. This chapter will take us through the school life of the six pupils who attend more regularly. It will soon become clear that, once again, we are faced with two distinct deviant groups whose behaviour requires different interpretation.

Memories of the Mainstream

In an effort to retrace their steps leading outside mainstream schooling, all pupils in the unit were first asked to recall their old schools. In response to this the Emery

Centre pupils, like those described by Lloyd-Smith in a similar unit (1984b), were unanimous in their emotive replies. First they all stated that they had disliked school (pupil statements come from individual interviews).

Teresa: I didn't like school. Just didn't like it. Didn't get on well there . . .
HP: Who with?
Teresa: Teachers . . . they just pick on you and that . . . you know . . .

Jackie: I hated it . . . I hated the people.
(laughs)

Nicola: I hated it!
It's just the general attitude of the teachers . . . the people there . . . it's hard to explain . . .
(smiles).

HP: What didn't you like about school?
Colin: Everything . . .

When asked about their transition from the mainstream to the unit, they stated that, in retrospect, they were glad to have left. Teresa's answer is characteristic:

Teresa: I wouldn't want to stay there . . .
It's all right here, (Emery Centre) because they're more under-standing and that . . . They make you feel welcome.

Evidence of extreme unhappiness in school multiplied as the pupils talked about their everyday methods of coping.

Skiving appeared to be the most popular coping method, especially with girls, and had been used frequently, for various purposes:

HP: Tell me about that (skiving) . . . Where did you go?
Louise: Toilets.
HP: And smoked or something?
Louise: Yeah . . .

Philip: Home.

Colin: Down town.

Nicola: Ehm . . . it depends when it was . . . If it was in the morning I'd probably go home . . . If it was say in the afternoon, then I'd go and do something else . . . It depended . . .
HP: What could you do though? That they would not see you?
Nicola: Sit in the library . . . and they didn't take any notice of me . . .

Rule breaking was another way of expressing unhappiness and opposition to the school system, although not as popular as skiving. Arriving late for lessons, not wearing uniform, taking a radio to school, or smoking were some of the ways the pupils chose to show their dissatisfaction.

HP:	Did you carry a pen, pencil and ruler with you?
Colin:	Hardly ever . . .
HP:	Was that not a rule of the school?
Colin:	Yeah . . .
HP:	But you didn't care about it . . .
Colin:	. . . (shakes head: no)

This behaviour, regardless of its aims, could not go unnoticed. It inevitably drew staff attention and the children acquired the reputation of troublemakers. Their relationship with school authorities started to become truly problematic.

HP:	Would you remember the number of detentions you got in the last term?
Colin:	Yeah . . . Hundred . . .
HP:	Oh come on Colin!
Colin:	Honestly! I used to get one every week . . .
HP:	And were you ever excluded from lessons?
Teresa:	Yeah . . . I got excluded from games 'cause I wouldn't do it . . .
HP:	Why wouldn't you do it? You didn't have any medical reasons . . .
Teresa:	No . . . just, you know, I didn't wanna do their games and that . . . It was boring . . .

As a result, all pupils had been utterly frustrated in school and retained only bad memories from it. It was easier for them to remember things they had disliked than anything they had liked:

Jackie:	Nothing. I didn't like anything . . . and I mean nothing. Hometime! (laughs) That was the best thing about it . . . leaving it! I hated that school . . .

Not everyone was as negative as Jackie, but they all freely agreed that school had been a very unhappy experience. Nevertheless, there were important differences in the way individual pupils perceived this unhappiness and dealt with it. The differences are striking enough to divide the pupils into two groups of three. For comparison purposes, these groups will be called group C (the determined ones) and Group D (the drifters), and will be examined separately. A distinct picture of each group will finally emerge.

GROUP C — The Determined

Meeting the Pupils

Each one of the three pupils in this group had experienced different problems in school, and had his/her own reasons to want to leave. What united them, and at the same time differentiated them from the drifters (group D), was the fact that they all saw their life in school as a failure, and provoked their own exclusion. The consciousness of their decision making and the clarity of their final aim is distinctive. Let us meet these pupils before we proceed any further.

Colin: Fifteen years and ten months old when interviewed. Considered 'immature' by his teachers, Colin had the most striking record of 'acting out' behaviour in school. He started his secondary school career in Parklane Comprehensive, where he remained until the beginning of his fourth year. He was then sent to the Emery Centre where he remained until school leaving age, almost two academic years. Colin showed very negative feelings towards school and teachers, and was very critical of teacher attitude to pupils. He was therefore determined to get out. To that end, he presented problems in every aspect of school life. He fought with pupils, argued with teachers and did not do any work. He was in the special unit the longest and felt at home there. He was quite friendly with adults, but could easily become restless. Colin tried to be cooperative during our chats, but had neither the patience nor the eloquence of Nicola and Jackie.

Jackie: Sixteen years and five months old when interviewed. Characterized in her record as a 'school phobic', Jackie started her secondary career in St Joseph's College, having recently moved to a new area of West Town following her parents to a new council house. As a result, she had no friends from primary school. She managed to find a friend in a girl who was also new in the area, but had serious problems associating with any other pupils. She became very isolated when her only friend left the school. Her school attendance, already poor, became a very serious problem. She was finally sent to the Emery Centre in the middle of her fifth year and ended her school days there. Jackie had some commitment to education and appeared to be getting a lot out of her attendance in the unit.

Nicola: Sixteen years and five months old when interviewed. The most determined of group C pupils, Nicola had neither respect nor fear for school. She started secondary school in Elton College, a private school, which, according to her account was asked to leave near the end of her fourth year because she made clear her intention not to take any exams[1]. She was then sent to Compton Comprehensive where she stayed until the beginning of her fifth year. By that time, Nicola — who was by then 16-years-old, but obliged by law to attend school for two more terms — had decided to become a photographer, and gradually became convinced that school had nothing to offer her. She refused to return to school ever again. The Education Welfare Officer managed to persuade her to attend classes in the Emery Centre until school leaving age. Although very skeptical about the quality of education at the Centre, Nicola liked the atmosphere and attended regularly. She was completely disillusioned with school because she firmly believed that it lacked relevance to her life.

Grouping pupils together is hard. This is particularly true of pupils attending special schools and units, given their widely varied school background and experience[2]. This was also true of the Emery Centre pupils. There were nevertheless experiences shared by all three pupils above, despite the traits peculiar to each one of them. The most striking one was the pupils' alienation from the school system and its people. The importance of good relationships with peers has been well documented in the education literature. (see Hargreaves, 1967, and Lacey, 1970, for the earliest accounts). The disastrous effects of peer rejection have been shown in the study of Burleigh High (see also Woods, 1975). It appears from existing evidence that pupils not partaking in peer sub-culture groups usually subscribe to academic aims and concern themselves with good peer and teacher relationships. In the case of Colin, Jackie and Nicola, none of these aspects of school life was satisfying.

Relationships with Peers

Isolation from peers was a phenomenon peculiar to this group. This was more apparent in Jackie's case:

Jackie: I just couldn't make friends! . . . I tried . . . They just didn't wanna know . . . 'Cause I moved just before I started secondary school, and they'd all been to St Joseph's Primary and I didn't fit in . . .

HP: Do you think that you were expecting not to fit in and you met your expectations?

Jackie: No, I wanted to fit in and I tried . . . but I just didn't get on with them . . . 'Cause they'd already made their friends . . .

Nicola and Colin also had social problems and did not appear to value relationships with peers much. As a result peers did not influence their decision to leave school. They did not work either as an incentive to stay or as a deterrent from leaving.

HP: Did you have any friends at school?

Colin: (nods yes)

HP: Did you miss them when you left?

Colin: (shakes head: no)

Nicola summarizes these feelings in a somewhat more elaborate statement:

> *Nicola:* Even if you got friends, you still got your own problems which . . . with me basically . . . I didn't want to go to school . . . Most of my friends are still there . . .

Lack of supportive friendships is characteristic of the group and offers instant access to the feelings of isolation these pupils must have been experiencing. We shall see this to be a very different situation to that experienced by the other three pupils.

Relationships with Teachers

The pupils' relationships with their teachers varied from indifferent to hostile. One can certainly detect no warmth between the two parties.

> *HP:* Did you use to have any trouble with teachers?
> *Jackie:* No, not really trouble . . . I used to argue with some of them . . . only one . . . she was the head of the girls . . . She was always arguing . . . you know . . . always having arguments. I got on with some of them all right . . . They thought I was a pain in the end . . . (laughs) Cause I was always bunking it . . . and whenever you do that in school, they think you're a pain.

Nicola's account gives no indication of warm relationships either:

> *Nicola:* I think they were indifferent. To me they were anyway . . . They couldn't really care if I was there or not . . .
> *HP:* Did you not have anybody who would sort of . . . miss you when you were not there?
> *Nicola:* I don't think so . . . (laughs)
> *HP:* Did you have any teachers that you really got on with?
> *Nicola:* No.

Colin went even further:

> *HP:* Did you care what the teachers think of you at school?
> *Colin:* No.
> *HP:* Why not?
> *Colin:* 'Cause they are a bunch of (intranscr.). They're stupid! They're spastics! That's why . . .
> *HP:* What does 'spastics' mean?
> *Colin:* (laughs) Sitting in wheelchairs and that . . . They're spastics! They make me sick!
> *HP:* . . . Really, did you not have ANY teachers you could talk to?
> *Colin:* No.

It seems therefore that all three pupils were very isolated and lonely in school. The only thing left that could provide possible satisfaction was work.

Work

Unfortunately this did not happen as there was no feeling amongst group C pupils that school had any role to play in their lives. They either believed that school education was of no relevance to them, as Nicola did[3], or they thought that they could get qualifications elsewhere without having to put up with people and situations they despised. Jackie was of the latter opinion. This was no reflection of limited academic ability, because there was evidence that the pupils were of average ability and they did not face serious difficulties with work.

HP: Didn't you think you were getting something out of school?
Nicola: No.
HP: Would you have learned more if you had stayed at home?
Nicola: Yeah, probably . . . I want to do photography and they don't do that at school . . . So, I mean, I'm not learning anything that I want to. And I don't see what I want to know about what chemicals do this when you mix them . . .
HP: Ah! That's a bad example because you probably need that in photography. Don't you?
Nicola: Yeah, but . . . I mean, you know that. You get to know the bits that you need for that. Mixing developers and staff like that. You know . . .
HP: So at some point you actually stopped getting anything out of it. Did you?
Nicola: Yeah.
HP: When was that?
Nicola: The beginning of last year I would have thought . . .
       I stopped . . . I thought it was a total waste of time because I wasn't getting anything out of it . . .

Jackie appeared to share the same feelings.

HP: Do you think you're losing out by not being in school?
Jackie: No . . . You can usually get . . . like you can get results here really . . . and in night classes you can get results . . .
HP: So you don't regret leaving school . . . If you had the choice again . . .
Jackie: Yeah . . . I'd leave it again . . . What I'd like to do though . . . I'd like to get back to the exams and get some results and that . . . I suppose you could do it . . . That's what my cousin did . . .

Jackie's cousin had a similar history of withdrawn behaviour in school and had informed Jackie about the existence of Emery Centre. Teresa from group D had also known about it from her older brother. Being aware of alternatives to mainstream education through family or friends is not uncommon, and appears to influence pupils' decision making. More research is needed to explore the extent of this influence and help explain why attendance of special schools and units appears to be a 'trend' in some families. Up to now this has been solely attributed to destructive home factors (see Stott, 1956; Galloway, 1976; Laslett, 1977).

Building up Frustration

If relationships with peers, relationships with teachers, and academic goals are the three major circles in pupils' school life-as indicated by the pupils' preoccupation with them during the interviews — and if the pupils of this group had failed in all three — as has been shown — it is not surprising that they wanted to get out of school. Taking the decision to leave was simply taking the situation to its logical conclusion. Nicola summarized these feelings with a comment probably borrowed from her teachers: '*I just don't fit into the system.*'

As time passed with no hope of improvement, the feeling of alienation became increasingly stronger. The pupils began to feel completely disillusioned with school and started questioning the very purpose of being there.

HP: So when did you decide to become a photographer?
Nicola: Say about a year ago. Couple of years ago . . .
HP: Are you saying that the moment you decided to become a photographer and you thought that school was irrelevant to what you wanted to do was when you really started not liking it?
Nicola: Yeah.
HP: But you weren't happy with it before either. Were you?
Nicola: I didn't like it much before, but . . . I used to go . . . you know . . . every single day . . . (smiles) But then, after I decided what I wanted to do, everything just fell apart, I thought there's no point 'cause it's not teaching me anything that's going to be useful to me . . . So . . .
HP: Was that a click? Or was it a slow thing? Was it building up?
Nicola: It was sort of slowish . . . It took quite a few weeks for me to start thinking that obviously what I was doing was just a total waste of time . . .

Perhaps unsurprisingly, before resorting to extreme forms of behaviour all three pupils gave early signals of their problem and tried solving it through 'legitimate' means first, i.e. by talking to their parents or the school authorities.

HP: Were you in Compton Comprehensive since your first year?
Nicola: No, I was at the Elton College first.

HP:	And?
Nicola:	I left there because I told the mistress that I wasn't going to take any exams. So she said basically: 'If you're not gonna take any, piss off . . .', basically . . .
HP:	Why did it matter?
Nicola:	Because . . . you know, Elton College is a private school and they are worried about their exam results and things like that . . . So they wouldn't let me . . .
HP:	So, if you tell them you're not going to take exams they get rid of you. Do they?
Nicola:	Well, they got rid of me. I don't know about other people . . .

Colin on the other hand tried asking his parents for help. It is interesting to note that his parents did not seem to realize the seriousness of his problem and appeared unsympathetic to Colin's request. Colin himself is not in a position to explain their lack of response to his problem.

HP:	Why are your friends there and you here?
Colin:	Because they behaved themselves! That's why!
HP:	Why didn't you?
Colin:	'Cause I didn't like the school . . .
HP:	Then why didn't you ask your parents to take you to a different school?
Colin:	I did.
HP:	And?
Colin:	They said no.
HP:	Why not?
Colin:	They said they didn't want me to change.
HP:	Why not? They liked the people you were with there?
Colin:	No. They just didn't want to . . .

For Jackie the struggle was long and hard as she was trapped between a school which did not understand her problem and a home too scared to help.

Jackie:	We saw everybody about it . . . Saw the headmistress, I saw the deputy head, the head of the girls . . . and no one would do anything . . .
HP:	Even when you told them you wanted to get out of there?
Jackie:	Yeah! And they said I have to keep going to school. So I started going . . . then . . . I don't quite . . . it weren't quite wrong . . . you know . . . and then I saw her about it and she says: No I couldn't go because I seem to be settling down, so I just didn't bother going . . .
HP:	Didn't you tell her why you were settling down?
Jackie:	Well, I just said I wasn't settling down. 'You said if I did go

you'd let me leave' ... you know ... 'You'd let me go to another
school if I started going regularly' ... And she said (imitates
teacher's voice): 'You're settling down now ...' So I thought
... (intranscr)

HP: What did your parents think about all this?

Jackie: What me bunking it? Oh! they went mad ...

HP: Did you not try to talk to them?

Jackie: Well, I was talking to them ... like when I was in the second
year, third year ... but they were on their side because they
couldn't do nothing ... 'cause if they didn't send me, if I didn't
go, they'd go to court and they'd get fined ... but near the end
they changed their mind, you know ... cause it was near my
sixteenth birthday and they started being on my side, they started
to fight against them.

HP: But they could have done something, they could have put pressure on the school to let you go ... Couldn't they?

Jackie: Yes but they wouldn't ... They were too scared to! ...

HP: Of the school?

Jackie: Yeah. They thought they'd go to court and get fined and what
have you ...

It seems that in both Jackie's and Colin's case the parents were not so much
uncaring, as lacking in resources and knowledge of how to help their children[4].
Their inactivity nevertheless led to other developments.

Developing Strategies

Eventually, and apparently after the failure of the concerned parties to understand
and help, the pupils' frustration seems to have turned into overt misbehaviour, and
what had been an expression of unhappiness to start with, appears to have developed
into a strategy, as part of an escape plan.

HP: Did you argue with teachers? Did you sort of stand up and say:
'This is a load of rubbish?'

Nicola: Yes. I did it quite a lot. I used to say: 'This is a total waste of
time!' ... (smiles)

HP: In the lesson?

Nicola: Yeah!

HP: And how did they respond to that?

Nicola: (sigh) They were shocked at first, but then I kept doing it all the
time, or I used to sit there (intranscr.) if they wanted me to do
something that I wouldn't do ... I used to start swearing at them
and things like that ...[5]

HP: When you decided that you didn't really like it, did you start
having trouble at school or did you just stop going?

Nicola:	First, when I decided I didn't like it, I used to go but I didn't like it. But I didn't use to . . . sort of . . . do my homework or anything like that . . . I just used to go . . . Then, when I decided what I wanted to do, I just started bunking it . . .

HP:	Did you always use to skive or only when Sharon left?
Jackie:	Well, me and Sharon used to sometimes do it . . . but not as bad as it'd go when she run off . . . I used to do it most times and then I didn't use to go in at all . . .

The wish to get out of school was by that time so strong that the consequences of one's actions were not weighed much.

HP:	What did you imagine being expelled would be like?
Jackie:	Oh! I just didn't know what it would be like. They would just send me to a different school . . .
HP:	And were you trying to do that?
Jackie:	Yeah.
HP:	Weren't you worried about it?
Jackie:	No.
HP:	So you thought that anything would be better that being there . . .
Jackie:	Mmm!!! (nods yes)

HP:	And where would you go if you left there?
Colin:	Don't know . . . I ended up here. Didn't I?
HP:	Yeah, but did you want to go to a different school?
Colin:	Yeah.
HP:	Well, how would you know how the other school would be?
Colin:	I didn't . . .
HP:	So, you just wanted to take a chance?
Colin:	Yeah.
HP:	Were you not worried about what was going to happen to you? I mean, you didn't know what was going to happen to you by getting in trouble, did you?
Colin:	No.
HP:	Were you not afraid of that?
Colin:	(shakes head: no)
HP:	So, what did you think the worst thing would be? What were you thinking?
Colin:	Nothing. I didn't care . . .
HP:	Did you think that anywhere else would be better than there?
Colin:	(nods yes)
HP:	Was Parklane so horrible?
Colin:	(nods yes)

With no wish to stay in school and no fear of leaving, each pupil set his/her aim and concentrated on achieving it.

Nicola: I just wanted to get out. Couldn't see much point. So, I stopped going on the fourth of November, and I never went again . . .

HP: Were you not suspended from school?

Nicola: No . . . I just stopped going . . .

HP: You just said one nice morning that: 'I don't want to come here any more . . .'

Nicola: Yeah . . . well, I didn't go . . . so, the school got in touch with the Education Welfare Officer . . .

It was not so straight-forward for everybody. For the other two pupils sophisticated strategies had to be invented to help them become expelled.

HP: . . . So, when you were doing the things you were doing, were you actually trying to be expelled from school?

Jackie: Yes. I was trying to get to go into another school and they wouldn't let me. So I thought . . . well, I might as well get expelled . . . But they wouldn't expel me either! . . . I was trying . . . all the way through I was trying to get out of there, but they wouldn't let me go! So I used to bunk it. I used to . . . you know . . . hang around in the loos . . .

HP: And could you stay there for a whole hour?

Jackie: Mmm . . . (nods yes) Sometimes I stayed there for a whole day!

HP: Really? And when people came in . . . did they not see you?

Jackie: No, 'cause it was (intranscr) and they hardly ever go in. You just look as if you're in the loo . . .

HP: And wasn't it smelly or uncomfortable or something?

Jackie: Yeah, a bit . . . but it was better than going to school . . . (smiles)

HP: What were you doing? Were you just sitting there smoking or something?

Jackie: No, I don't smoke (laughs) I was just sitting there. Sometimes I brought a book . . . Or I would listen to the radio . . .

HP: I can't imagine that being better than going to school!

Jackie: Oh! It was!!!

HP: Tell me about when you used to skive from school altogether. Where did you use to go?

Jackie: Well, that was a whole day. If I was just skiving a lesson I would stay in the loos in school . . . just for the lesson, cause you can move about. But sometimes I'd bunk the whole day and I'd go to my sister's. But they'd always find out . . .

HP: Didn't they find out when you were skiving a lesson inside the school?

Jackie:	No.
HP:	Didn't they notice when you were not there?
Jackie:	No.

Jackie's extreme unhappiness in school is evident from this account. As it became increasingly clear that there was no hope of change, the occasional incident developed into persistent truancy, advancing from a mere expression of frustration to strategy. Equally evident is Jackie's determination to avoid school, which pushed her to adopt the most effective truanting method, despite its being the most unpleasant. Jackie's technique although similar to that employed by Nicola, is in fact the most subtle of all[6]. Clearly, it cannot be true that her absence was never noticed when she was within school premises. The more cynical, but more likely explanation is that the school was not seen to be breaking the law by allowing Jackie to remain in the toilets, while it was ultimately responsible for her absence when she was outside school premises. Under such circumstances it is highly questionable why the school did not act earlier to help solve the problem and relieve Jackie of her misery!

Contrast now Jackie's technique to Colin's. Colin's strategy was nothing but an open challenge to the system! His method consisted of creating problems in every aspect of school life, for example, being disruptive in the class, fighting with pupils, not doing homework etc., until the school would run out of patience and want to get rid of him.

HP:	Tell me about the school. Were you glad to leave it?
Colin:	Yeah.
HP:	Why?
Colin:	'Cause I wanted to . . .
HP:	What was wrong with it?
Colin:	Everything! It took me four years . . .
HP:	You mean you tried all these years to get expelled?
Colin:	Yes! (smiles)
HP:	Why?
Colin:	'Cause I wanted to . . .
HP:	Are you telling me that you were getting in trouble on purpose to leave the school?
Colin:	Yeah!
HP:	What sort of trouble did you have?
Colin:	Everything!
HP:	Go on . . . Tell me some things that used to happen to you.
Colin:	Fighting . . .
HP:	Who with?
Colin:	Everyone . . .
HP:	Why? For no reason?
Colin:	No. 'Cause I wanted to . . .
HP:	You like to fight with people . . .
Colin:	No . . .

HP:	Well then?
Colin:	I wanted to get expelled! Didn't I?
HP:	You wanted to . . . Come on! . . .
Colin:	Yeah!
HP:	From the first year 'till the fourth year you were trying to get in trouble, so that you would get out of school?
Colin:	Yeah!

Note the consistency in Colin's argument despite my persistence. In spite of his inability or unwillingness to articulate the reasons for his dissatisfaction with school, to his mind fighting was a strategy, and indeed one that required a lot of effort.

All such efforts seem to have been rewarded by a final exclusion from the mainstream followed by a transfer to a special unit where the disadvantages of mainstream schooling are absent. Teachers are less authoritarian and more approachable, pupils more friendly, and the curriculum more flexible, offering pupils more appropriate choices. The pupils' aim seems to have been achieved, through a careful manipulation of the school system.

The evidence seems to be as overpowering as it is interesting. Special education literature has traditionally ignored the pupils' own point of view[7]. Their cases have been presented through teachers' or researchers' eyes, with a heavy concentration on pathological explanations of their behaviour. Even Grunsell and White's work, although original in presenting the pupils' own views, appears to have the characteristics of mystification[8] evident in early psychological works (such as Wills, 1945; Bettelheim, 1950 and 1955; Shields, 1962), as it presents an insider's view of day-to-day work with children. It appears to be the task of external observers such as Tattum (1982) to put pupils in perspective. Tattum seems to be the first researcher to take accounts of pupils in special units at face value and categorize them. He makes the mistake, however, of applying no criteria to assessing these accounts. This can create problems with some students as we shall see in the next section.

Noting this gap in the literature and taking into account current research trends, this study has focused on the pupils' own point of view. This is done following an interactionist perspective, in order to understand pupil behaviour as they see it, and identify possible differences from the way mainstream pupils see themselves. It is of course inevitable that studies like this have to be conducted retrospectively. This makes teacher confirmation of pupil stories very difficult. What one has instead are the pupils' files, the testimony of the unit teachers, the observation and the pupil interviews. A combination of these can give a global view of pupil behaviour and throw plenty of light on their past. However, given the lack of direct observation of this past, one needs to examine the consistency and coherence of the pupils' accounts in order to evaluate them.

On this criterion, Colin, Nicola and Jackie appeared coherent and sincere. They never contradicted themselves or altered their statements. During recurring informal chats and a long formal interview they repeatedly evaluated their story, and explained again and again how they tried to be listened to, and were ignored. They argued passionately without hesitation. They indicated the unchanged conviction of people who have long thought, fought and suffered, leaving little doubt about the motives of their misbehaviour.

This was not the case with group D pupils. They were different in all respects, and their accounts were not convincing. The internal contradictions and evident exaggerations of these accounts made them suspect, and indicated that they lied. These accounts therefore call for a different kind of explanation.

Conclusion

Although extreme forms of behaviour are common in school, especially among pupils who end up being excluded, there seem to be specific reasons why they were adopted by Colin, Jackie and Nicola. They were their means of achieving their goal which was exclusion from school! Summarizing we can suggest that:

- Unruly behaviour was not used by pupils of group C casually and occasionally, but persistently and on a daily basis for a long time. Jackie skived 'almost every day' and Colin had trouble 'all the time'. Nicola's blunt refusal to ever go back to school again is even more striking. This indicates that the pupils' behaviour was not incidental, but with a purpose.
- In every case the pupil was acting on his/her own, and not under the influence of a gang or a 'mate'. On the one occasion where there was involvement of a friend (Jackie's), this had a positive and not a negative effect. The situation deteriorated dramatically when the friend left. This is proof that the pupil was operating on the basis of a plan, not in a spontaneous and suggestible fashion.
- The types of misbehaviour used were not chosen at random, nor were they designed to provide pleasure. They were instead chosen with a high degree of sophistication to produce maximum results. This is clear in Nicola's use of the school library and Jackie's use of the school toilets, after having tried less effective methods. Colin's strategy was also guaranteed to attract attention and lead to the desired outcome.
- Each child's actions were a more or less open challenge to the school, for no school could ignore such extreme forms of behaviour. As a consequence the school staff were practically forced into dealing with it, which seems to be what all three pupils wanted.
- Finally, all three pupils stated quite clearly that the sole purpose behind their behaviour was to attract school attention and get themselves expelled. There was no hesitation and no regret regarding this matter.

It is the purpose of the next chapter to make the broad comparisons between the various deviant groups inside and outside the mainstream. We can, however, safely conclude here that in group C we have a good example of deliberate use of deviant behaviour for the pupil's own purposes. This is no different from group A's use of deviance in mainstream school. It indicates that there is little difference between deviant pupils in the mainstream and deviant pupils in the special unit, and this is simply a difference in goals.

Clearly, the possibility of deliberate use of misbehaviour has to be taken into account seriously when studying deviant behaviour both within and without mainstream education. We can no longer assume that deliberate use of deviance is a mainstream phenomenon and pupils in special schools or units are simply 'out of control'.

Group D — The Drifters

Meeting the Pupils

Just like the pupils of group C, the pupils of group D, found their way to a special unit before the end of their school career, but the process leading there was very different for them. All three pupils of group D had at least one change of mainstream school in their career. All three were suspended from school and had to leave. For all of them leaving school was marked by a fight with a teacher or a pupil. All accounts indicate that the pupils did not choose to leave school but were forced to. If group C 'got rid' of school, school certainly 'got rid' of group D. Before examining their stories, we first need to meet these pupils:

> **Louise:** Fifteen years and seven months old when interviewed. Louise was the most pleasant and sociable member of group D. Because of her eloquence, she gave the impression that she had thought things over and was in control of her destiny. However, there was a significant discrepancy between her wishes on the one hand, and her school behaviour on the other. She argued that she left her first school, Clarenton, at the end of her third year, because her mother was worried about her friendships there. It appears, however, that she had faced serious problems there, and it is quite possible that she had no choice but to leave the school. She had to leave her second school, Waverley, near the end of her fourth year, because of a fight which resulted in the other girl's injury. She was then out of school for a few months. In the beginning of her fifth year, she was transferred to the Emery Centre, where she remained until school leaving age. Louise appeared to posses an unpredictable temperament, and to be easily impressed and influenced by peers. As a result, she had repeatedly become involved in violent incidents with other pupils. To me she tried very hard to give a good impression leading the conversation to non controversial issues. In the Centre her behaviour improved, and, although in occasional need of counselling, she never became involved in a similar incident again. Instead she was making a sincere effort to take advantage of what the Centre had to offer, by studying typing.

> **Philip:** Fifteen years and six months old when interviewed. Philip, gave an initial impression of a quiet and shy boy — unlike Colin — but handled in the

wrong way could present enormous problems. He started his school career in Boswell Comprehensive, which he was forced to leave at the end of his fourth year after a serious incident with a teacher. He was then transferred to a special school for children with learning difficulties (ESN). It was, however, too late for remedial help. Partly because of that and partly because of the staff's inability to cope with his behaviour[9], he was transferred to the Emery Centre. In the Centre, academic pressure removed, Philip was happy, and developed a special interest in computers. Although his feelings about school were not particularly negative, his behaviour there seems to have been a constant provocation. Not very bright and rather lazy, Philip had enormous problems with school work, and that's where the majority of his troubles stemmed from. It was very difficult to extract any sort of reasoning from him, and he was unable to concentrate for any length of time. His conversational skills were very poor. Philip was generally a pleasant boy and eager to please, but constantly searching for laughs without knowing where to stop.

Teresa: Fifteen years and nine months old when interviewed. Teresa was — like Philip — very slow and quite lazy, and gave very little evidence of thinking about her actions and their consequences. According to her account, she chose to leave her first school, Forester, in the middle of her third year, after being involved in a violent fight with another pupil. It appears, however, that this decision was imposed on her, as it was on Louise. She was then suspended from her second school, Pemberton, in the beginning of her fifth year, for hitting a teacher, and she had to go to the Emery Centre. Despite her unhappy experience in the mainstream, Teresa did not have strong feelings against school. Nevertheless her behaviour exceeded every possible limit, apparently giving schools no alternative but to exclude her. Without being very bright or skilful, Teresa was eager to please. The reason for her continuous involvement in trouble appears to be her inability to understand or influence the circumstances around her. Her biggest weakness was her temper, which appeared to be frequently out of control. She also seemed to be easily influenced by peers. Given her fatalistic approach to life, expulsion from school was finally perceived by her as a heavenly gift, and after the first shock, as the best thing that had happened to her in her school life.

As noted earlier, all six pupils of Emery Centre had unpleasant experiences in the mainstream, but the accounts of group D reveal significantly less alienation from people. While Colin, Nicola and Jackie stood alone and bitter, Philip, Louise and Teresa appear to be reasonably happy with school. This was not due to lack of problems, but rather to the pupils' own perception of their situation. The pupils of group D did not seem particularly affected by their troubles in school. They did not appear to learn from their experiences and they never modified their behaviour. Where pupils of group C spoke of an ever deteriorating situation making life in school unbearable, group D pupils drew a happy picture of school life and pinpointed isolated incidents which caused their exclusion. Group C greeted their transfer to the Emery Centre with relief — if not a sense of achievement. Group D pupils was surprised with the school's overreaction to a single incident. They declared having received unfair treatment and being upset at having to leave. This is a very different group with a different attitude altogether. The following section will concentrate on elaborating the difference more fully. The three spheres of pupil life investigated for group C will also be explored for group D.

Relationships in School — Work

There is no doubt that group D faced enormous difficulties with school work. They seemed to have neither academic aspirations nor commitment to education. Coping with school work was a very hard task for them. From the three spheres of school life used to measure pupil activity, work was the one which suffered most. Philip did not make any effort to hide it, although he tried to deny that this was due to his poor ability.

> *HP:* What sort of trouble did you have?
> *Philip:* Mostly argue with teachers and that . . .
> *HP:* What did you argue about?
> *Philip:* Doing work and that . . .
> *HP:* So that was your main problem. Why didn't you do your work? Didn't you like it?
> *Philip:* Didn't want to . . .
> *HP:* Why though?
> *Philip:* Just didn't want to . . .
> *HP:* Did you find it difficult?
> *Philip:* No. I didn't find it difficult but I just didn't wanna do it. I'd rather laugh and joke![10]

Philip makes a special effort to argue here that he faced no difficulties with work. The truth is however that the enormous difficulties he had with school work was the reason for his initial transfer to an ESN school. These difficulties continued to exist in the Centre, but there, at last, no academic results were required of him.

Teresa attempted to prove herself a nice girl arguing that she was quite good with school work.

> *HP:* How did you do in school work? Did you do well?
> *Teresa:* Yeah.
> *HP:* Were you good in academic lessons?
> *Teresa:* Yeah . . . I was good . . .
> *HP:* Really?
> *Teresa:* Yeah.
> *HP:* Which set were you in?
> *Teresa:* I was in the third . . . (out of three)

Despite her reassurances about academic achievement, Teresa was in fact a pupil of very poor abilities. In Emery Centre she was never interested in doing any work. She was not interested in reading, and played the most mundane games on the computer, avoiding those requiring any form of thinking. She spent most of her time drawing and her pictures were of very poor quality. On this evidence it is very hard to believe, that she was as good in the mainstream as she argued.

Louise probably faced fewer problems, as she was at least able to keep up with the class. This was evident in her statements, but also in her confidence with reading and writing, her subject choices in the Emery Centre, and in her interest in taking a typing exam.

> *Louise:* I am not bright but I can get passed . . .
> I couldn't go to the university or anything like that, but I can get passed exams just about half way . . . you know . . .
> *HP:* So, you coped all right in school . . .
> *Louise:* Yeah . . . With my work . . . It's not my work . . .

It seems therefore that work was a serious problem for at least two of the three pupils. Their low academic ability may well be related to lack of judgment and self-control which affected their relationships in school.

Relationships with Peers

In contrast to group C, peers appear to play an important role in group D's life in school. All three pupils had valued friendships and had made use of behaviour frowned upon in school to earn the acceptance of the 'gang'. Philip repeatedly stated how much he liked 'having a laugh with the boys'.

> *HP:* Didn't you tell me that you hit a teacher?
> *Philip:* Oh yeah! I hit one. That's why they mainly chuck me out.
> *HP:* How did you hit her? You punched her?
> *Philip:* No. She slapped me, so I slapped her back.
> *HP:* Why did she slap you?
> *Philip:* 'Cause I was having a laugh and joke with some of the boys. She hit me, so I hit her back.
> *HP:* I see. And after that they expelled you from the school.
> *Philip:* Yeah.
> *HP:* Would you like to have stayed in the school?
> *Philip:* Yeah.
> *HP:* Why?
> *Philip:* Lots of my mates are there . . . (Compare this with Nicola's replies earlier.)

We shall comment later on Philip's relationships with his teachers. Let's use the quotation here to note how fun-seeking brings Philip in direct confrontation with teachers. This alone does not, of course, explain his involvement in trouble. In order to explain that we will have to look to Philip's inability to distinguish where the limits are.

> *HP:*   Did you ever skive a lesson?
> *Teresa:* Yeah ... (laughs) Ah yeah! Quite often ...
> *HP:*   Where did you go?
> *Teresa:* Oh! Down town ... with my brother and that ... mates ...
> *HP:*   And didn't they miss you at school? Didn't you get in trouble?
> *Teresa:* No, they thought I was ill all right ...
> *HP:*   What did you do? You used to skive all day?
> *Teresa:* Yeah. The whole morning you know ... If I didn't want a les-
>   son, then I'd skive it you know ... and nobody knew ... They
>   wouldn't give you away ...

This example, apart from exposing Teresa's naive view on school authorities[11], clearly shows the importance she placed on her friendships in school. She believed that peers were invaluable for having fun with, and for covering up for skiving or other kinds of misbehaviour (see also Davies, 1979, for peer covering up in truancy). So peers were very important in Teresa's school life, as in Philip's. It was Louise however who made the most sacrifices for her friends.

> *Louise:* That is why I did it (misbehaving). Because I wanted to stay in
>   with the gang, my friends, and the only way to do it was ... to
>   do all their dirty rotten things ...
> *HP:*   ... Why did you fight in the first place?
> *Louise:* I was sticking up for a boy who joined that school when I did ...
>   Her (the girl she had the fight with) boyfriend was gonna beat
>   him up because she was supposed to have gone out with him ...
>   You know what I mean ...

We see that peers played a significant role in these pupils' school life, providing the opportunity for fun, and promising support and cover, without which attempts to 'have fun' would have been unlikely to succeed. Furthermore the majority of serious incidents in which they were involved were directly related to peer issues. Indeed, it is quite possible that their school 'friends' initiated and encouraged Philip, Louise and Teresa's misbehaviour for their own enjoyment[12]. Having fun and keeping in line with their friends cost Louise, Teresa and Philip dearly. And so peers hold a key role in the explanation of their misbehaviour.

Relationships with Teachers

Surprisingly enough, there were some positive relationships between these pupils and their teachers. It is already apparent that although all three pupils had problems with the majority of teachers, none of them entertained the strong anti-teacher feel-ings of Group C. Instead of using harsh language they simply complained about their teachers being boring or unfair. Philip and Teresa even refer to rewarding relation-ships with some of them!

HP:	Tell me, what did you like most about school?
Philip:	The English lessons . . .
HP:	Why?
Philip:	The teacher! She used to be a good laugh . . . She used to help you more and all that . . .[13]
HP:	Did you like English?
Philip:	No, but I didn't mind the lessons . . .
HP:	I see . . . Because she was nice . . .
Philip:	Mmm . . . (nods yes).
Teresa:	(talking about her first school) You could talk to the teachers and that . . .
HP:	How did you get on with them?
Teresa:	I got on all right with a couple of them . . . But one left . . .
HP:	Did you care what the teachers thought about you in school?
Louise:	Yes.
HP:	You did. Did you?
Louise:	Yeah! . . . very much . . .

So overall, it appears that Teresa, Louise and Philip did not feel alienated in school to the extent Jackie, Nicola and Colin did. Unlike them, they maintained enough rewarding relationships to keep them happy in school. Moreover they insisted on wanting to stay in school and expressed a feeling of satisfaction which makes their departure from the mainstream difficult to explain. The answer seems to lie in the discrepancy between the picture the pupils present and their real life in school. We become better acquainted with the latter when we examine the pupils' accounts more closely.

Contradictions

The most striking characteristic of group D seems to be the inconsistency between their expressed attitude towards school, and their behaviour in school. There seems to be no doubt that their behaviour in school was quite unacceptable. Nevertheless, it becomes obvious that this behaviour was not backed by a coherent anti-school philo-sophy. Indeed, there appears to have been very little thinking behind it altogether. The first contradiction is therefore the combination of a fairly conformist attitude with extremely deviant behaviour. The second is a combination of apparent accept-ance of school rules, with manifested breaking of these rules.

An initial impression of Philip was that of a timid child trying to keep out of trouble. He stated that he was quiet in class:

HP: When you were in the classroom what did you like to do?

Philip: (ticks the questionnaire[14] without talking) 'Sit quietly doing only a little work'.

He even appeared to reserve only mild criticism for teachers.

HP: What do you think of the teachers?

Philip: They are boring . . .

HP: You mean they did not have a sense of humour . . . or what?

Philip: Yeah . . . Mostly humour and that. They didn't want to have a laugh and joke and all that . . . while you were doing the work . . .

HP: So if they were like they are here you wouldn't mind . . .

Philip: No.

As the interview progressed serious problems with teachers were revealed. Philip's behaviour towards them could easily be perceived as plainly provocative.

HP: Would you remember the number of detentions you got in the last term?

Philip: No, never done them.

HP: Why not?

Philip: Got things to do.

HP: And did they not do anything to you?

Philip: No, they used to get angry and that . . . Just gave me more detentions that I didn't do.

HP: . . . So what happened? The teachers would say: 'Where is your homework?' and you would say: . . .

Philip: 'I haven't done it . . .' Simple as that . . .

HP: And they would get angry with you?

Philip: Yeah.

HP: But you didn't actually fight with the teachers. Did you?

Philip: No.

And just as he has confirmed his good relationships with teachers:

HP: Why were you expelled from your first school?

Philip: I didn't get on with the teachers . . . Just kept arguing . . .

HP: But was there a specific incident?

Philip: What d'you mean?

HP: Something happened . . .

Philip: Can't remember . . .

HP: Didn't you not tell me that you hit a teacher?

Philip: Oh yeah! I hit one. That's why they mainly chuck me out . . .

Contradiction between attitude and behaviour was also evident in Teresa's account. To this, other contradictions were added, as Teresa appeared to have conflicting feelings about teachers. She initially gave the impression of being very concerned about her image:

HP: How about uniform? Did you wear it when you had to?
Teresa: Yeah . . .
HP: You didn't try to skip that . . .
Teresa: No.
HP: Did you ever bring a radio to school?
Teresa: No, never! You weren't allowed!
HP: Trying to keep the rules of the school. Were you?
Teresa: No . . . well, you had to . . . 'cause then you'd have to sit there and do no work. You'd have to catch up, so you had no choice . . .
HP: (reading the questionnaire) Pupils destroy school property because . . .
Teresa: What me? Destroy property?!
HP: Well pupils . . . Why do they do it? And you can tell me if you have done it or not . . .
Teresa: (laughs) I ain't done it! I don't destroy property! I don't know that answer . . .
HP: Destroy school property might just mean writing on desks . . . writing on walls . . .
Teresa: Oh yeah! They're fun . . . scribbling on desks . . .

And she went on:

HP: About punishment in school now . . .
Teresa: Oh! They come along and hit you! (strongly)
HP: Why do they do it?
Teresa: No reason sometimes, but if you're shouting or talking in the classroom they come along and hit you!
HP: So you think they do it because they want to punish you . . . they want to make you better . . . or what?
Teresa: Oh! They just think it's funny, you know!

There is an evident difficulty here to reason and attribute motives to teachers. And back to a milder attitude . . .

HP: What do you think about teachers in school?
Teresa: Boring . . .
HP: You think they are boring . . .
Teresa: Yeah . . . They don't teach you properly . . .
HP: Why not?
Teresa: 'Cause they don't. They're not doing the job properly . . .[15]

Louise also appeared initially to be a conformist:

> *HP:* You told me your problem was with pupils, not with teachers
> . . .
>
> *Louise:* Yeah . . . I never, never, NEVER! . . . I've answered back to
> teachers, but I've never hit or swore like some people have . . .
>
> *HP:* . . . Why do pupils destroy school property?
>
> *Louise:* I don't know why . . .
>
> *HP:* Have you never done it?
>
> *Louise:* No.
>
> *HP:* Like writing on desks, writing on walls . . . things like that . . .
>
> *Louise:* I might have done a bit like this on the table . . . but I don't call
> that destroying school property . . . (smile) I just call it . . . being
> bored . . . (laughs)

Louise, like the others, had a school change in her school career. She argued that
she tried hard to behave properly in her second school in order to avoid further
trouble.

> *HP:* Did you used to be on report?
>
> *Louise:* Yes, I have been in Clarenton several times but I didn't in
> Waverley.[16]
>
> *HP:* Why is that? Is it because the second school didn't have this
> system or you were much better there?
>
> *Louise:* I was much better there. They had it but I was much better
> there . . . I was behaving myself . . . And then, when one incident
> happened . . . you see . . . they expelled me . . .
>
> *HP:* Why?
>
> *Louise:* Because when I went there, they said that all your warnings have
> now been given. So, if there is any trouble happening, I will be
> immediately expelled . . . And that's what they did. But I was
> good up to then. It was only that one thing . . .
>
> *HP:* So how long did you stay there being quite good?
>
> *Louise:* From September till March . . .

This could, of course, be the most serious of a number of incidents that had
occurred earlier. Whatever the case, Louise appears to have had a pretty good idea
of what was expected of her, and states that she tried to achieve it. However, her
effort did not go very far. Not only did she become involved in the kind of activity
she had been warned against, but also participated in new forms of unacceptable
behaviour, such as skiving.

> *HP:* Did you used to skive?
>
> *Louise:* I didn't at Clarenton. At Waverley I did.
>
> *HP:* When were you at Waverley?

Louise: Beginning of my fourth year . . .
HP: So that's the last school you went to . . .
Louise: Yeah . . . that's my last school.

Louise's inability to avoid new fights with pupils is a clear example of another phenomenon common to group D, lack of self-control. In retrospect, it is difficult to distinguish whether pupil behaviour is a result of bad judgment or inability to control him/herself. In this case however the possible consequences of a new fight had been made very clear to Louise, and failure to avoid fighting cannot be attributed to lack of judgment. Inability to control her temper, in view of well-known and feared consequences, is a more likely reason for her misbehaviour. This inability is characteristic of the group.

Self Perception and Self Judgement

We have seen so far that unlike Colin, Jackie and Nicola, who declared hating school and wanting to escape, Louise, Teresa and Philip professed liking it and trying hard to succeed. Yet their behaviour resulted in outcomes which surprised and upset them. Their disappointment is more easily understood when their self-perception becomes clear.

It seems, perhaps, obvious to an outsider that this behaviour would not recommend these pupils to their teachers. The pupils themselves did not share this view. Indeed they were quite confused on this issue. While Nicola, Colin and Jackie stated that they were disliked by their teachers because of their behaviour, Teresa, Louise and Philip initially argued that they were liked, only to change their story later.

After naming a number of teachers that had sent her out of the classroom, Teresa went on to suggest that teachers thought of her as 'quite helpful'.

HP: What did you think the teachers thought of you?
Teresa: Some thought I was helpful . . .
HP: Did they?
Teresa: Yeah . . .
HP: In Pemberton?[17]
Teresa: Yeah! Some did! Some thought I was helpful!

And again a little later . . .

Teresa: Most teachers in school thought I was helpful . . .
HP: What opinion did they have of you? Did they think you were all right?
Teresa: All right . . . sometimes . . .
HP: They didn't think of you as a troublemaker . . .
Teresa: No, not all the time . . .

And Philip says exactly the same, after describing how difficult his behaviour was:

> *HP:*   What did the teachers think of you? Did they think you were helpful?
> *Philip:* Sometimes . . . (smiles and ticks 'quite helpful')
> *HP:*   That was in school . . .
> *Philip:* Yeah.
> *HP:*   They thought you were quite helpful . . .
> *Philip:* Yeah!

Not long after he goes back on it:

> *HP:*   What opinion did teachers have of you in school? What did they think about you?
> *Philip:* Horrible.
> *HP:*   Did they?
> *Philip:* Yeah.
> *HP:*   Because you gave them trouble?
> *Philip:* Yeah.
> *HP:*   But were they justified?
> *Philip:* Yeah.

Louise was more realistic about her teachers' opinion of her, although she entertained some illusions.

> *Louise:* Well, there (the mainstream schools) my teachers thought I was most unhelpful . . . but here (Emery Centre) I'm been . . .
> *HP:*   You said they thought you were a troublemaker . . .
> *Louise:* Yes, that's what I thought they thought of me . . .
> *HP:*   In both schools?
> *Louise:* Yes . . . No, not in Waverley. Though I didn't really know the teachers at Waverley . . . But at Clarenton they used to hate me all the time, call me a troublemaker and everything . . .

The way the pupils viewed their behaviour in school is also very interesting. It is already clear from Philip's responses how unproblematic he found his behaviour. He appeared unable to grasp the seriousness of the incidents he instigated and the importance of their consequences. The same way of thinking was evident in the girls' statements.

> *HP:*   Why did you leave Forester?
> *Teresa:* 'Cause I hit a girl. And they were gonna expel me.
> *HP:*   Why did you fight with her?
> *Teresa:* Ah! She got on my nerves and that . . .
> *HP:*   Was it just an isolated incident or hadn't you liked each other for quite a long time?

Teresa:	No, we liked each other and that . . . but she just started on me and that . . . and she winds me up you know . . .
HP:	Do you remember exactly what happened? To give me an idea . . .
Teresa:	Yeah, I was coming through the school and she started laughing at me and that . . . in front of my mates . . . She just started call- ing me slut and that . . .
HP:	Out of the blue?
Teresa:	Yeah.
HP:	No previous argument or anything?
Teresa:	No.
HP:	Something outside the school?
Teresa:	No. She started on me . . . She knows what I'm like, so I just beat her up. And the teacher had to call me off.
HP:	What do you mean she knows what you're like?
Teresa:	She knows what I'm like 'cause I'm really good friends with her, but . . . you know she winds me up a lot.
HP:	So, did you slap her or what?
Teresa:	Ah! I kicked her straight in the privates . . . (laughs)
HP:	Really?
Teresa:	Yeah . . . (still laughing) 'Cause she bit me and I don't like that . . . (becomes serious)
HP:	Oh! She started first!
Teresa:	Yeah! So I knocked her against the wall and she bit me, so I kicked her privates and she went down . . .
HP:	So the teachers came to separate you . . .
Teresa:	Yeah. And then I hit the teacher . . .
HP:	Did you? Why?
Teresa:	I was in a mood and that . . . and in the argument . . . and she grabbed me and I pushed her out of the way . . .

While describing this violent incident, Teresa kept smiling and laughing. This might have been partly due to embarrassment, but she showed no regret, and appeared unable to fully appreciate the seriousness of her action. Instead of apologizing, she tried to shift the responsibility onto the other girl. The excuse she put forward was her uncontrollable mood. This indicates Teresa's inability to control herself and expectation that others will control her. Once provoked she declares herself unable to control her temper and accept responsibility for her actions. Her inability to appreci- ate the graveness of the situation is obvious in her description of the consequences of this incident. She appeared to think she had suffered gross injustice and was vindicated only by her mother's support. Interestingly, there is no sign of regret or apology anywhere.

HP:	And what happened? They said they were going to expel you . . .
Teresa:	Yeah . . . they were . . . They said they could have . . . could have led to court and that . . . and they were going to get the police

around . . . you know . . . So the next day I went in with my
mum and I said: 'I'm leaving this school . . .'[18] That day me and
my mum went up and they couldn't do nothing much . . . Me
and my mum had a fag in the school . . .

A similar blend of inability to estimate the seriousness of the situation, and an effort
to minimize the importance of the incident was characteristic of Louise.

HP: Why did you leave Clarenton?
Louise: My mum didn't like the people I was mixing with . . .
HP: So you were not expelled, it was your mother . . .
Louise: I had been suspended from there about three times . . .
HP: Why?
Louise: Ah! Odd bits and things you know . . . They sent letters at
           home . . . Just stupid things you know . . . Never used to swear at
           a teacher. Never used to hit a teacher or anything, but it was silly
           little things with other people, you know what I mean? And then
           the teachers would sort of be awful to me for what I've
           done to another pupil . . .
HP: You didn't tell me why you were expelled from your last school.
           What was the incident . . .
Louise: I had a fight with a girl and her mother said that she was going
           to take us to court . . . (meaning Louise and her parents)
HP: Was it a bad fight?
Louise: I was supposed to have hit her in the back and she was supposed
           to have scratches . . . Well, she came in crying and all that . . . and
           I asked my friend the next day . . . I rang up and said: 'Has Mary
           got any scratches on her back?' And my friend said 'no'. 'Cause
           that was why her mum was taking me to court . . .

The words 'stupid', 'silly' and 'little' seem to be used in an effort to minimize the
importance of Louise's actions. Very carefully she avoids giving a detailed account
of her 'sins' in the first school and the fight in the second. This is another technique
aiming at minimizing these incidents, which also deprives us of the opportunity to
form an independent judgment. However, we know from Teresa's account how
violent fights between pupils can be, and have no reason to believe that Louise's
behaviour had been dissimilar, and not as harmless as she would like us to believe;
especially if the incident had been considered serious enough to be taken to court.

Rationalizing

Resorting to self-perception as the wronged party is not enough. There is the added
need to persuade others that you have been wronged. In any case it is not always
easy to persuade yourself. To help solve this problem a very clever technique was

devised by pupils of group D: Rationalizing! Rationalizing comprises the epitome of the pupils' self-righteousness and is particularly interesting as a defence method. It is characteristic of group D, and represents the most sophisticated technique these pupils employed. Therefore it deserves particular attention.

Its ultimate purpose was the justification of one's behaviour. In order to achieve that each pupil was prepared to accuse almost everybody but him or herself for his or her actions[19]. This behaviour is specific to group D, and not confined to accusations against school authorities. The pupil's failure seems to be blamed indiscriminately on everyone but the pupil him/herself. This is one reason why these accounts are not taken at face value. Another reason is that although the facts related in the interviews have a true basis, as indicated by school records and teacher interviews, the pupils' accounts appear to be exaggerated, and give ground for doubts about their ability to accurately perceive and truthfully relate what happened. The inconsistencies and contradictions observed so far give more reason for critical examination. This is not to suggest that the pupils lie on purpose. They simply present facts as they perceived and experienced them. What is in question is not their honesty but rather their judgment.

Blaming the teachers was the most common way of rationalizing. With that the pupils tried to prove that they suffered because of a specific teacher's unfairness or personal dislike to them, and not because they did anything wrong.

Teresa: I was just sitting in geography and I was getting my work out and she comes along and says: 'You're not doing that no more, you can just sit there and do whatever you like . . .' you know . . . . . . And I got kicked out of biology . . .

HP: What was that for?

Teresa: Oh! She thought I was a troublemaker[20] and she didn't like me. She don't like none of my family[21].

HP: Had you ever caused her any trouble?

Teresa: No! She just don't like me . . . you know . . . and that . . .

HP: Just by seeing you in the lesson?

Teresa: Yes! Only cause we used to sit there and talk and that . . . she didn't like it. She thought I was a troublemaker so she kicked me out.

Blaming the system is an effort to indiscriminately accuse all teachers of being nasty or unfair and the school system of being unjust.

HP: So you went to the new school and . . . how were things there?

Teresa: Oh! They just . . . you know . . . it was all right for a while, and then the teachers started picking on me and that . . . you know . . .[22] And then I got chucked out of several lessons and that . . . they just kept pick, pick, pick . . . you know . . .

HP: Why did they pick on you?

Teresa: They just started . . . they thought . . . you know . . . they start on just several people and that . . . that they don't like . . .

HP: But how did it start that they didn't like **you**?

Teresa: I don't know . . . It's just that they thought I was just a trouble-maker and that . . .

HP: Why? What were you doing to them?

Teresa: Nothing! I was just sitting there getting on with my work . . .

HP: You said that you were standing up for yourself . . .

Teresa: Yeah . . . I was. 'Cause a lot of people . . . you know . . . you know what boys are like, they pick on you and that . . . at school and that . . . And when you retaliate back you get picked on, you know, and they watch you . . .

HP: The teachers?

Teresa: Yeah . . .

Although Teresa had difficulty explaining why she was continually picked upon for no reason, there was clearly no doubt in her mind that she had been treated unfairly[23].

Louise felt the same way and she offered some suggestions about how teachers should treat pupils.[24]

Louise: Half of that time I hadn't done anything . . . But they didn't be-lieve me because I'd been in trouble previously . . .

(talking about Colin) . . . But at school, if he was behaving like he did there, (an instant in Emery Centre) they say: 'get out of the class!'.
And that's not the way to go about it! You say: 'Can you stop misbehaving?' If he don't, say it a bit louder, then if he don't send him out. That's the way to go about it. Not send him out straight away . . .

HP: Did they not do that?

Louise: No! They used to just chuck you out . . .

Louise seems to be judging each incident on its own merit here, and is unable or unwilling to appreciate that a pupil with a long history of problems has been given these warnings repeatedly and is likely to be treated more harshly than an 'average' pupil[25].

Blaming one's peers was also used to help the pupil get out of a difficult position and give a reasonable explanation for his/her behaviour.

Teresa: (answering the question about what she prefers to do in the classroom) Get on with my work!

HP: In school? Did you?

Teresa: Yeah! But you can't really, 'cause children around you are making

a lot of noise, and the teacher is having a go at you, that you
can't . . . You try your hardest but you can't . . .

This is also evident in Louise's description of the difference between her first
school, Clarenton, and her second, Waverley, and the corresponding changes in her
behaviour.

HP: Why was there such a big difference between the two schools?

Louise: I think that they're city children and they were village people
and that . . . and I think that these people have to live with them
in the village . . . So they were friendlier . . . I had more friends
in Waverley than I ever did in Clarenton. Because everyone was
acting friendly there, (Waverley) I was . . . and because everyone was acting bitchy there, (Clarenton) I was . . .

HP: That is including pupils and teachers, is it?

Louise: Yes, teachers and pupils. But over there (Waverley) it's half
teachers. But over there (Clarenton) it's half teachers and never
pupils . . . you know . . . (being friendly)

As is obvious by now, Louise was very eloquent with her excuses, so much so that
they did not sound like excuses, and appeared to have thought about school more
than the other two pupils had. However she too did not hesitate to blame her friends
in order to excuse herself.

Blaming one's self: sometimes the pupils could not shift the blame anywhere
else, so they accepted it for themselves. However this was very rarely a straight
forward acceptance of responsibility. They simply blamed their temper or mood,
and thus indirectly the people who, in full knowledge of their problem, had provoked them. On these rare occasions when the pupils accepted the blame for themselves, they always attempted to minimize the significance of their actions.

HP: Do you think you are a troublemaker?

Teresa: No!

HP: So, why did she? (talking about a teacher)

Teresa: I might have been a bit of a nuisance you know . . . talking and
that . . . but I got on with my work and that . . . I weren't the
only one who got kicked out anyway . . .

HP: So there were other people too . . .

Teresa: Oh! Yeah! There was another girl that got kicked out . . .

HP: . . . But you don't swear here . . .

Teresa: I do if I lose my temper but . . . it's only in my
temper . . . you know . . .

HP: I don't think I've ever seen you losing your temper . . .

Teresa: No! (laughs) You wouldn't want to . . . I'm terrible . . .

HP: Does it happen often?

Teresa: Oh no! It used to, when other people used to wind me up and that . . . I used to go mad!

HP: Really?

Teresa: It's just when I'm getting wound up, you know . . . But now I'll just walk out . . . you know . . . in the fresh air . . . and cool down . . .

HP: So that's better. Is it?

Teresa: Yeah! It's a lot better!

HP: . . . So you think that all this childish behaviour is actually provoked by teachers . . .

Louise: Yeah! They make you . . . they get you all worked up . . . they say things they know is gonna make you all worked up and so they do it. And you blow your top! D'you know what I mean?

Occasionally rationalizations were not aimed at anyone in particular, but were simply well presented, rationalized excuses. Below are two examples of that:

HP: Did you smoke?

Louise: In my previous school . . . Well, yeah . . . it wasn't allowed . . .

HP: But you used to smoke . . .

Louise: Everyone did . . . you know . . .
It wasn't really a lot . . . It wasn't every day . . . It was about three times a week . . .

HP: Do you smoke here?

Louise: Yes. But that is allowed. There is no rule here . . .

HP: Did you enjoy going to school in the morning?

Teresa: (ticks 'No, not very much')

HP: That is to do with school. Not with getting up early . . . Because you said that doesn't bother you . . .

Teresa: It don't bother me . . . But I didn't . . . you know . . . like going to that place . . . 'cause I had to walk a hell of a long way and I didn't look forward to it . . .

There is finally here a fine example of rationalization, quite indicative of the technique. It demonstrates the ingenious sophistication used to weave different excuses until there was no one — but the pupil — left without blame.

HP: Why did the teachers pick on you? Why not someone else?

Louise: Because I probably did one thing wrong and . . . I probably did quite a few things wrong and so teachers got (intranscr.) . . . you know what I mean . . . They decided they found the good ones and the bad ones . . . When you first walk into a new lesson with

	a new teacher . . . I don't know . . . but then you can show . . . then the other children will play up and you'll play up with them . . .
HP:	What do you do that for?
Louise:	Because your friends do . . . That's why I did it, because I wanted to stay in the gang, my friends, and the way to do it was to be their . . . in other words to do their dirty, rotten things . . .
HP:	So your mum was right. It was the people you were mixing with that caused all the trouble . . .
Louise:	Yes . . . and part of it was my own fault.
	I must admit that . . . yes . . . Some of it was my fault. But then again I don't think they dealt with it fairly! I mean . . . it takes two to have a fight and they don't bother about it . . .

This method of self-defence indicates the pupils' need to find some support and also a scapegoat for their behaviour. Through the systematic use of these comments they have first convinced themselves about their innocence and are now attempting to convince others, in this case me. Throughout our discussions there was a naive and somewhat childish effort to take me on their side, and to have me sympathize with the injustice they had suffered in school. This was attempted by the use of a defensive conversation tone, repetition of confidential remarks (you know, you know what I mean), and an effort to please me by agreeing with my remarks without even examining them:

HP:	What did you dislike most about school?
Teresa:	Teachers. Most of the teachers.
HP:	Why did you dislike them?
Teresa:	Don't know . . . 'Cause they picked on you . . .
HP:	You think they're unfair. Do you?
Teresa:	Yeah!
HP:	Do they do it just for fun? Are they not reasonable?
Teresa:	Oh they do! No! They're not reasonable . . .
HP:	Mmm . . . So, why did they do it? Is it because they can't be bothered to sit down and think whose fault it is and find out . . .
Teresa:	No, they don't bother . . .
HP:	. . . or is it because they're nasty . . .
Teresa:	They're nasty! Oh yeah! They're really nasty!

This phenomenon, although understandable and quite common[26] was quite unlike anything group C did. The clear explanations and the harsh and confident tone used by those pupils, indicated their unchanged conviction of having done the right thing and their indifference to anybody else's opinion or sympathy.

It is probably because of the special way they perceived and explained their own behaviour, that group D pupils were able to go through school without seriously questioning their status. As a consequence, they were unable to articulate the problems they were facing.

In Pursuit of Fun

We have so far established that life in school had not been as idyllic as Louise, Teresa and Philip tried to present it, and they had faced serious problems there[27]. We have also witnessed how they perceived their own behaviour, and the techniques used to rationalize their actions. Nevertheless the reason for the pupils' misbehaviour in school remains unclear. The purpose of this section is to explain why these pupils misbehaved in school and why they were finally transferred into the special unit.

If the main purpose behind Nicola's, Colin's and Jackie's misbehaviour was to get themselves expelled, the main reason behind the misbehaviour of group D was to have fun[28]. These pupils were not trying to attract school attention to their misbehaviour. On the contrary, they tried to hide it and often were under the illusion that school authorities had no knowledge of it. Their aim was to make school life more exciting and to 'have some laughs' compensating for their difficulties in school work.

HP: Why do pupils destroy school property?

Philip: Because they want to . . . I've done that . . . I . . . yeah . . . I used to do that . . .

HP: What did you use to do?

Philip: Nick the books . . .

HP: The books?

Philip: Yeah . . . Used to take them at home . . .

HP: Why?

Philip: The writing books . . . Scrap paper at home . . .

HP: I see . . . So you did it because you wanted them and you didn't have money to buy or what?

Philip: Oh no! I could have bought, but I preferred the school ones.

HP: Just for fun?

Philip: Yeah!

HP: And do you do it here? (In the Emery Centre)

Philip: No.

HP: Why?

Philip: Not worth doing it here. 'Cause you don't pay. They give you it. You've only got to ask them.

HP: What about school?

Philip: No! If you asked them they wouldn't give you it. They wouldn't let you have the school paper and what have you . . .

Their preoccupation with 'having fun' and their idealized self-perception inhibited the pupils' understanding of context and led to lack of appreciation of the consequences of their actions. Consequently they had no reason to expect a breakdown in their life in school. When it came, it surprised and upset them. Their first reaction was not wanting to leave the school.

HP: So you were upset when they sent you away ...
Philip: No, I wasn't upset, but ...
HP: Would you have stayed there if they had given you a chance?
Philip: Yeah.
HP: You didn't want to leave it ... (school)
Philip: No ...

Louise: (talking about Waverley, her second school) It was a very nice school. I'd like to have gone back, but ... I don't know ...
HP: So you were not pleased when they expelled you. You didn't want to leave ...
Louise: No, I cried and cried ... I must have cried a whole week ... but ... I just couldn't help it after that ... (the fight)
HP: If you had the choice then would you have stayed?
Louise: Yeah ...
HP: You said you cried ... You were very upset about it ...
Louise: Yeah. I didn't want to come here (Emery Centre). I wanted to go back to school ...

However with the exclusion procedure under way there was little the pupils could do, except become used to the idea of transfer, and perhaps rationalize again.

Louise: ... But then, when I thought it over, and I thought of what the people think of me there, you now ... I thought that they were going to be bad, they were going to be awful to me, I thought I'd come here. Because all the people here are mostly the same as me ...

Leaving the Mainstream: A Conscious Choice?

Having established that the aim of the pupils' misbehaviour was 'to have fun' and they were unwilling to leave school, we finally need to discuss in some detail the possible reasons for their transfer.

There is no indication of a conscious wish out of school. The pupils stated their intention to do well in school and the interviews showed that they found enough rewards to keep them happy there. It is of no relevance if relationships with peers and teachers were not in reality as the pupils suggested. The pupils themselves perceived them as such, and were satisfied. Their language related with their transfer also indicated this to be a decision forced on them:

Philip: They made me come here 'cause I didn't get on in school ... They chuck me out ...
Teresa: They expelled me ... You know ... they got rid of me ...

> *Louise:* They wouldn't have me back . . .
> I think they just wanted to get me out of there . . .

These pupils were transferred by force, not by choice. The decision was forced on them due to their failure to reach the behaviour standards required in school. Their repeated involvement in trouble exceeded, at last, their schools' tolerance. This failure lays, it seems, with the pupils' lack of judgment and poor self-control. This is a particularly disadvantageous combination as it provided no means of coping. Consequently they were often unable to judge a situation properly and foresee a crisis coming. Furthermore, they appeared unable to control their behaviour and avoid further complications once involved in an incident. This phenomenon was clearly visible in crisis situations such as fights with other pupils or arguments with teachers. Misled by appearances, and preoccupied with immediate gratifications, they proved unable to receive warning messages and adapt their behaviour accordingly. Having attracted attention and punishment, they failed to see their behaviour in context and learn from their mistakes. This led to repetition of mistakes and recurrence of punishment, and finally rejection from school. Mainstream data from previous chapters provide more direct access to classroom decision making, and can assist in formulating a clear picture of how lack of judgment and control manifested itself in the classroom for Teresa, Philip and Louise.

Conclusion

To summarize, we shall address the five points that helped outline the behaviour of group C earlier.

- Misbehaviour used by group D was simply a means of providing fun in school. Far from trying to provoke the school, the pupils tried to hide it, and often made the mistaken assumption that the school was unaware of their misconduct.
- The goal of 'having fun' was supported by the fact that misbehaviour occurred in groups. Far from being isolated, the pupils acted out with the help, or under the influence, of their school friends. High suggestibility and strong peer influence appear to have been major forces behind their misbehaviour.
- The methods employed were highly unsophisticated. The pupils seem to have been acting on the spur of the moment. There was no consistent development in their misbehaviour, or at least none that they were aware of. They just appeared to fall in and out of trouble without any particular pattern. They were unaware of the school's constant surveillance, and its reaction took them by surprise.
- There was an apparent discrepancy between their declared aims and their proven behaviour in school. This indicates even more strongly the

lack of thinking behind their actions. They failed in their plans to do well in school, and were unable to understand and explain that failure. They simply made a last effort to rationalize:

> *Teresa:* . . . I wasn't doing it on purpose. I am like that: if some-
> one picks on me, I pick on them . . .
>
> *Louise:* I don't actually know why I got in trouble . . . Most of
> the time it was because a teacher was blaming me for
> something I didn't do . . . They treat you like babies . . .
> Babies and children lie, don't they? And that's why I
> think you lie . . .[29]

Comparison between Group C and Group D

We have now concluded the examination of deviant pupils in the special unit. Two distinct deviant groups were identified. The pupils of both groups were initially seen to perform similar deviant acts such as fighting with pupils, arguing with teachers, misbehaving in the classroom, skiving etc. The differences between them were found to lie in their motivation.

The pupils of group C, the determined, were seen to consciously use these forms of behaviour as a means of attracting attention and instigating exclusion from school, and transfer to another place. The reasons for their dislike of school appeared to be specific to each individual and related to disapproval of the school ethos.

The pupils of group D, the drifters, did not appear to use their behaviour as a means to a goal. They were seen to behave on impulse and be largely unaware of the possible consequences of their actions. The motive behind their misbehaviour was argued to be a wish for an enjoyable time in school. They were seen to be particularly susceptible to peer group pressure and influence. Lack of accurate and timely judgment alongside poor behaviour control while attempting to emulate shrewder peers in fun seeking activities was seen to cause repeated involvement in trouble, and finally rejection from the mainstream.

It will be the task of the next part to bring together the pupils of the mainstream school, Burleigh High, and the special unit, Emery Centre, and to try and draw parallels which will complete our understanding of deviant pupils and facilitate further interpretations of their behaviour.

Postscript

It is harsh having to judge the pupils' stories and justify some of them while rejecting others. It is, however, necessary for our purposes to establish exactly what happened and this requires this assessment in order to identify which ones willingly took the road to exile and which ones did so unwillingly. Sympathy and empathy for all the pupils remains unaffected.

Notes

1 Nicola was the only Emery Centre pupil from a public school, the rest of them having attended state schools. Her transfer to the state sector, as provided by her account, raises some interesting questions about needs and procedures in the private sector.

2 This is partly the reason for the concentration of special education literature on case studies, and its traditional emphasis on individuality (Wills, 1945; Redl and Wineman, 1951; Rothenberg, 1960; Shields, 1962; Galloway, 1976; Wakefield, 1977; Grunsell, 1980a and 1980b; Cooper, 1993; Wade and Moore, 1993).

3 Pupils are often known to express similar feelings (Davies, 1979), without going so far as to decide to leave school.

4 This phenomenon of parent confusion and helplessness is very clearly demonstrated elsewhere: (Hargreaves, 1967; Booth, 1978; Tomlinson, 1981a). Middle class parents appear to be much more successful in protecting their child within school (Riddell, 1994), although knowledge of the way the system functions and how it can be manipulated is also the privilege of parents who have gone through it themselves (Sewell, 1981).

5 The teachers' shock and their inability to cope with Nicola's behaviour is very clearly portrayed here. It is perhaps unsurprising that teachers faced with this phenomenon named Nicola's behaviour 'bizarre' and suggested that she 'needed help'.

6 It is interesting to note the lack of direct challenge Jackie's strategy involved. More research could show if there is a particular gender bias in the kind of strategies developed by boys and girls in this situation. We already know that there is a sex differentiation in the strategies used by mainstream pupils (Delamont, 1976; Davies, 1979 and 1984).

7 There are a few exceptions to this in the last fifteen years: White and Brocklington, 1978; White, 1980; Grunsell, 1978, 1980a and 1980b; Tattum, 1982; Cooper, 1993; Wade and Moore, 1993. Some of these writers are more radical than others, but they all touch on the subject.

8 Tomlinson (1982) introduces the notion of 'mystification' when she suggests that psychologists have tried to, and succeeded in, surrounding special schools and pupils with a kind of mystery that has for a long time discouraged researchers of other disciplines from studying them.

9 Tomlinson (1982) clearly draws the distinction between ESN and 'maladjusted' children, and comments on referral to the appropriate school.

10 The abrupt tone of Philip's comments was a reflection of his limited conversation skills, and not a consequence of his relationship with me, which was excellent. Given the limited range of Philip's conversational skills, the girls' accounts will be used more extensively in this section. Their statements were far more elaborate than Philip's and give a much clearer picture of the situation.

11 Compare with Jackie's: 'They'd always find out!'.

12 This is a well known phenomenon as we have seen in Burleigh High with Mark and Peter.

13 There is a distinct similarity between this statement and those of Mark in Burleigh High, which seems to indicate an acute need for attention and help in the classroom.

14 The questionnaire was used as a basis for the interview.

15 A statement like this could be due to serious work problems, which we have already seen to exist.

16 Clarenton was Louise's first school and Waverley her second.

17 Pemberton was Teresa's second school.

18 This version of **choosing** to leave the school after an incident like the one described above, has to be treated with caution, not least because Teresa contradicts it herself:

> *HP:*   Didn't they have any problems taking you? (in her second school) Because they knew about . . .
>
> *Teresa:* (interrupting me) Oh no! They didn't have any problems. They took me straight in! They didn't know what it was . . . It (the school record) just went on 'expelled', you know . . . no reason . . .

Evidently, she was simply asked to leave the school.

19 Hargreaves (1967) deals with the process of rationalizing deviance too. Tattum (1982) also describes five ways deviant pupils in his study used to explain their behaviour. They were: (a) 'It was the teacher's fault'; (b) 'Being treated with disrespect'; (c) 'Inconsistency of rule application'; (d) 'We were only messing — having a laugh'; (e) 'It's the fault of the school system'. In their accounts those pupils also attempt to shift the blame on teachers and the school system. Tattum treats these responses as 'vocalizations' rather than rationalizations but provides no evidence to support his claim that these are not just well-rationalized excuses.

20 Grunsell (1980b) and Bird (1980) mention similar pupil complaints. Woods (1975) suggests that given the amount of 'policing' teachers have to do, mistakes are inevitable. Moreover, hesitation in punishing a pupil could lose the teacher the respect of the class (also Hargreaves, 1967; and Lacey, 1970). It seems therefore that it is the pupil's responsibility to avoid giving grounds for deviant reputation. This is something Teresa, Louise and Philip seem unable to grasp.

21 The 'sibling phenomenon' is clearly portrayed in Seaver's work (1973).

22 Pollard (1984) deals in great length with the notion of 'picking on' by teachers, and pupils' reactions to it.

23 Nash (1976) considers 'fair-unfair' to be one of the dimensions teachers are judged on by their pupils.

24 Also remember Louise's statement about 'having been good' until 'this one thing happened'.

25 As Tattum (1986a) puts it, 'Not all pupils are treated the same by teachers, for there is the human practice of rewarding those who conform most closely to the ideal pupil role as the teacher perceives it, and punishing those who deviate most prominently from perceived expectations'.

26 See Phtiaka (1994) for a similar technique used by teachers.

27 The data from Burleigh High indicates how relationships with peers and teachers might have really been for group D while in the mainstream. However it is important to have the picture as seen by the pupils themselves, in order to understand their rationalizations.

28 This can explain partial acceptance of school rules not directly interfering with their enjoyment.

29 Being treated like a child is a common complaint amongst pupils (Woods, 1975; Tattum, 1982).

Part IV

Comparisons and Conclusions

This part of the book attempts to draw together the findings from the two areas of fieldwork and presents the similarities and the differences between the various deviant groups of pupils from the mainstream school and the special unit. On the basis of these comparisons, the main question of the study, regarding the necessity for the division between mainstream and special school deviance, is answered. Questions are consequently raised about the need for special provisions for deviant pupils, the efficiency of such provisions, and the ethics involved. Alternative suggestions are also made.

Chapter 7

What Then?

Burleigh High and Emery Centre: Comparing Deviance

Having examined closely each deviant group in Burleigh High and Emery Centre and having compared the different groups within the two places, it is now time to summarize and make comparisons between the mainstream school and the special unit.

Burleigh High group A pupils (the fun-seekers), despite presenting an initial strong impression of deviant behaviour backed by a coherent philosophy, proved to have retained some faith in the value of school and to be seriously interested in staying there. To this end they had devised very sophisticated patterns of behaviour that offered them the right balance between enjoying themselves and retaining their 'street credibility' in school on the one hand, and ensuring their remaining within the acceptable mainstream limits on the other. Deeper belief in school values appeared to be partly due to parental support.

Burleigh High group B pupils (the troubled ones) were shown to lack this degree of sophistication and to be relatively confused about their aims in school. They too were interested in having a good time in school and maintaining a good reputation amongst peers, but appeared unable to achieve either of these aims. This failure was seen to be the result of lack of judgment in classroom situations while seeking fun under the influence of their peers. They also appeared to lack the ability to learn from their mistakes and avoid similar hazards in the future. These problems appeared to invite intolerance from teachers and contempt from peers, with the result of isolating these pupils.

The pupils of the Emery Centre group C (the determined ones) appeared to equal in sophistication and clarity of aims Burleigh High group A pupils. They were also similar in their ability to achieve their aims by an equally clever manipulation of the school system. But they did not appear to share the fun-seekers' concern to stay in school. These pupils had serious objections to certain aspects of the school ethos and were not particularly convinced that school had anything to offer them. Consequently, their efforts had been concentrated on getting themselves expelled, rather than on keeping the right balance required in school. The reasons for their conviction about the school's faults or irrelevance appeared to be individualistic, a combination of home influence and personal experience in school.

The pupils of Emery Centre group D (the drifters), like those of Burleigh High group B, appeared to have difficulty in clearly defining and achieving their aims in school. They also appeared to be very susceptible to peer influence. They seemed unable to exercise their judgment and sustain a level of behaviour acceptable in the mainstream, a fault that was seen to be the main reason for their expulsion from school.

From this evidence it would appear that there are two types of deviant pupil within Burleigh High (mainstream) directly comparable to the two types of deviant pupil in the Emery Centre (special unit). The first type appears to be of average intelligence and well developed social skills who consciously, and within the existing limits, takes decisions that influence his/her career in school. These decisions seem to be a product of careful consideration based on the pupil's long-term aims in school. The second type is a pupil who lacks the maturity, social skill and intelligence of the previous group, and who, as a consequence, is prone to outside influences. S/he appears to have no long term goals, but is easily impressed and influenced, and his/her behaviour is not the result of prior thinking, but a product of impulsive acting in an effort to impress or an attempt to imitate fellow pupils.

Questions Arising

It was stated in the beginning of this book that the nature of this study was genuinely exploratory. Nevertheless, the deviant pupils were expected to be found very similar across the dividing line, their actions resulting from pre-meditation and thinking. The pupils' own will was expected to be the force behind their behaviour, and their school career was seen as the outcome of a decision-making process. In this context it can be argued that the deviant groups B and D were an unexpected finding. The existence of two diverse deviant types of pupils seems nonetheless to satisfy points raised in the first chapter by both disciplines interested in school deviance, without completely justifying either.

It is very interesting to have arrived at the conclusion that the deviant pupils within a mainstream school and a special unit are very similar. For there evidently are striking similarities between groups A and C and groups B and D, with groups A and C having clarity of short and long-term aims regarding school and being successful in manipulating the school system and achieving them, and groups B and D lacking long term goals with regards to school and failing to achieve even their short term aim of 'having a laugh' without jeopardizing their career in school.

Having established that there is a number of similarities in the behaviour of deviant pupils within and without mainstream education, it is necessary to show what the differences are between the two areas, before going on to draw any further conclusions[1].

For groups A and C it is the pupils' own choice which determines their transfer or otherwise to a special unit. The fun-seekers are in the mainstream because, although they might not present the picture of an ideal pupil, they are still to an extent committed to school. They believe that school has some value, and are interested in making good use of it without compromising too much of their freedom. In fact, the exciting and challenging life they lead in school as a result of this balancing act contributes to their commitment. On the other hand, the determined have been led in the unit by a very strong conscious wish to get out of school. They have decided that school is completely irrelevant to their lives and has nothing to offer them. It is furthermore a place which makes them unhappy because of the restrictions it imposes on them. They have concluded therefore that anything would be better than school, and they have concentrated their skill and efforts on being expelled. The 'out of school' wish seems to have been a choice for a better future and appears to have paid off, leading the pupils to a place where they can be free from the restrictions of the traditional school and so happier[2]. The reasons for one group A's commitment to school and group C's disillusion, cannot be fully discussed on the strength of this data. They appear to depend heavily on home and school factors and on each pupil's personal school experience. It seems that the pupils' overall view of school, its relevance and its importance to their life determines their long-term goals, and leads to a specific pattern of decision making. This in turn results in retaining the pupils within the mainstream system, or alienating them from it.

The differences between the pupils of group B and those of group D are not so clearly defined. It would appear that in the case of these two groups, the pupils' school career has not been decided by the pupils, but rather their schools. Their transfer appears to be not only involuntary, but also unwanted and initially opposed[3]. Being ruled by impulse rather than reason, the pupils of these two groups would seem to be at the mercy of school tolerance and policy. The fact that the troubled pupils remained in the mainstream appears to be more a reflection of Burleigh High's tolerant policy, rather than a result of differences between their behaviour and that of the drifters. The transfer of the drifters on the other hand does not point to a kind or degree of misbehaviour uniformly unacceptable. Instead it indicates the level of behaviour tolerance in their mainstream schools, since it seems to be a decision taken by the individual school on the basis of its policy. Neither is there clear evidence that this transfer has been proposed on the basis of the pupils' particular needs. The differences appear to lie with the schools which have instigated the transfer and not with the pupils. The pupils within (group B) as well as without (group D) the mainstream, seem to be very similar in behaviour, and in genuine need of help. They are all exactly the kind of pupil who needs the special attention and help a special unit can sometimes offer. It is therefore all the more disturbing to see pupils like them (group B), deprived of this help.

It has been established so far that there is indeed very little difference between the behaviour of the fun-seekers and that of the determined pupils, and no apparent difference between the troubled ones and the drifters. It has also been argued that the difference which does exist in the former case is only a matter of degree controlled by the pupils themselves, and based on their perception of school. It seems that the special unit was not catering for a very distinct deviant population, but rather for pupils with very similar behaviour patterns to those of some mainstream pupils. It appears therefore, as an answer to the main question of the study, that *behaviour differences between the pupils were not enough to justify their division on either side of the dividing line*. The distinction then between mainstream and special school deviance seems in this case to be rather pointless and unnecessary.

The next section will examine questions relating to the effectiveness and the efficiency of the special unit.

Special versus Mainstream: Practice and Ethics

Having established that the division between special and mainstream deviance was not necessary, it is now time to examine if it was — at least — of any use[4], and to discover which group — if any — had its interests best served by the division.

For the determined pupils the Emery Centre had been a conscious choice as an alternative to an inadequate mainstream school. It would appear thus that the unit was serving the purpose of this group, by allowing them to aim for it in their dissatisfaction. However the unit curriculum did not help them acquire an education in any way comparable to that of their colleagues graduating from a mainstream school; and so, in reality, the Emery Centre did not serve their interests well. If such units did not exist, pupils such as those of group C would still try to be expelled, but would have to be transferred to another school which they might have found easier to accept. There they could still have the opportunity to continue their education. The existence of the unit appeared to deprive them of this option, and to render this plan impracticable. The pupils, who for various reasons had come to deny school, were thereby denying themselves a variety of possibilities that were only available within mainstream education.

It is apparent, on the other hand, that the unit was to the advantage of pupils such as those of group D, for it provided them with some of the support and the self-confidence they desperately needed. Had they remained in the mainstream these pupils would most probably have completely wasted the last years of their schooling. So it appears that a genuine need was met by the Emery Centre in their case[5]. Not without cost however. For what has been argued about the inadequacy of the curriculum in the case of group C is also true in this case. Furthermore, it would seem that while some of the pupils in need (group D) were catered for by the unit, others who could also benefit from such help (group B), were excluded as the criteria for transfer appeared to be rather arbitrary[6], and set by individual schools. Moreover, before allowed access to this assistance which they desperately needed, the pupils had to be stigmatized by the process of exclusion from school[7]. The interests of group D, were therefore not well served by the Emery Centre, and the interests of group B were not served at all. Summarizing, one has to conclude that no group's interests were fully and without reservation catered for by the unit; for not all needy pupils received support and the ones who did were both stigmatized and denied a variety of other possibilities.

It is not the need for a support system that is in question here, but rather the format of this support system. The Emery Centre had indeed a task to perform, offering real life education to pupils in need of it[8], and improving their social skills[9]. The need for the existence of a support system is therefore evident and justifiable. However, it must be pointed out that because of reasons which have already been offered, this need is not best met by units such as the Emery Centre.

Efforts to improve special units, an argument that can be presented here, would direct attention away from the mainstream. For if a friendly atmosphere and a relevant curriculum[10] were on offer within the mainstream, pupils of the disposition of those of group C, or any disposition indeed, would not have to make a choice; and pupils such as those in group D would be able to receive the help they needed without being moved away from their peers. Moreover, this help would be available to all pupils in need, and would not simply exist as a privilege for a small number only. Emery Centre was undoubtedly of some service, but only because the mainstream schools had failed to be. Special attention and individualized instruction seems to be what the mainstream schools ought to have given all their pupils. It is therefore argued that, useful service as the special units might on occasion provide, it is in the best interest of a pupil to remain in the mainstream school. It is consequently suggested that efforts for improvement should be directed towards the mainstream system.

A Lesson for the Future?

The purpose of this study was to evaluate the existence of special provisions for deviant pupils in the secondary school. Two main arguments, put forward by two different disciplines in the beginning of the book supported two diametrically opposed views on the subject. An attempt was made to take into account views from both disciplines in the effort to investigate the need or otherwise for the existence of these provisions. The approach adopted has been unique, not only because it has used methods from both psychology and sociology, but also because it has presented an in depth case study of a mainstream school, and a special unit, crossing for the first time the boundary between mainstream and special education. It was my belief that this approach would be the most appropriate to assess the differences between pupil behaviour on either side of this boundary, and effectively evaluate the division between pupils. Although the study was exploratory, initial expectations were somewhat biased towards a sociological viewpoint, the pupils being expected to be in control of their own behaviour and destiny. The findings showed that views which have traditionally been put forward by psychologists also bear some validity, as a number of pupils appeared to be unaware of the consequences of their behaviour, and so, in a way, 'out of control'.

Coming as they do from a comparison across the dividing line, the results are important as well as interesting, and can lead to useful conclusions. They appear to convey two main messages.

The first is that there are a number of pupils who are unhappy in school and need help. Some of them are able to cope with their unhappiness and find satisfactory solutions inside or outside the mainstream school system. However it would be desirable if all these pupils were happy in school and made the best possible use of what it has to offer for their future life. It is the responsibility of the school system to safeguard the happiness of all its pupils. To this end, more research is needed to discover the reasons behind the pupils' dissatisfaction and make suggestions about how they might be helped. The findings also suggest that there are pupils who, though very unhappy with school, remain passive not knowing how to improve their life there. They too are in urgent need of help, and it is the school's duty to help them. The combined information from Burleigh High and Emery Centre points specifically to two problems: Low academic performance and poor social skills. Academic assistance and social skills training seem to be needed urgently, although the confidence arising from the first will most certainly benefit the second too.

The second message refers to the way in which this assistance should be given. The findings of this study appear to support the claim that special units are not the ideal place for providing pupils with the help required[11]. Attempting to prevent the need for special units appears to be wiser than trying to meet it. It would therefore seem sensible to try to provide the opportunities of a less pressured environment and of caring teacher-pupil relationships within mainstream schools. This would allow more pupils to be helped avoiding problems which arise from peer separation. It is not the purpose of this study to describe in detail how this would be manifested[12], but rather to point out that school ethos ought to be in the centre of the argument for effective assistance and support in the mainstream. A long tradition of special education in the UK has provided the expertise on how to deal with problem pupils. What is now needed is the shifting of this knowledge and skill onto the problem school[13].

It is therefore crucial to conclude this book emphasizing the importance of the mainstream school as an educational venue for all children. Modifying schools to achieve personalized teaching and maximize everybody's potential by offering special education to all, would make special schools and units unnecessary. This would benefit everyone concerned, and would help us 'in developing a vision of the kind of society in which we want to live' (Barnes and Oliver, 1995). This may well 'prove to be one of the most difficult challenges we will ever face' (ibid), but we can handle it . . .

Postscript

Much has changed in special education, especially in its policy (DES, 1994; Lewis, 1995) since these lines were first written. And yet the answer to the central question of the study has not been given, nor indeed has the question been asked. Policy changes following the 1988 Education Act (DES, 1988) and the establishment of the National Curriculum have helped reverse the positive flow that could have followed the 1981 Education Act (DES, 1981) had it been given more time to be implemented. Recent work such as Gillborn's (1995), Garner's (1994) and Lewis' (1995) indicate only too clearly how 'fashionable' exclusions and special units for behaviour problems continue to be, notwithstanding the evidence presented here (and elsewhere) that the distinction between acceptable and unacceptable deviance in the mainstream is arbitrary, given that most of the time there are no behaviour differences. Where there are, the deciding factor is either pupil decision making based on school ethos, or school ethos pushing the pupil to a certain direction. Unacceptable behaviour, this is to say, is created, maintained and defined by the school itself. How is it possible that in the face of such overwhelming evidence produced by sociologists and educationists for years now, we continue in good faith to separate, prejudge and stigmatize pupils? This is a painful question I cannot in all honesty answer.

Notes

1 Generalizing from Burleigh High to mainstream education, although Burleigh High is a typical provincial comprehensive, is presumptuous enough, but generalizing from Emery Centre to special education provisions for deviant pupils, would be even more arbitrary. Special education provisions, even those of the same kind, like behaviour units, differ significantly, as they are often established with distinctly different aims. (Topping, 1983; Emerson, 1984; Leavold, 1984; Lloyd-Smith, 1984b; McDermott, 1984). Generalizing is therefore not easy. It is, however, necessary here, in order to make the comparison and suggest new possibilities and explanations. Naturally, much more research is needed into special schools and units, if one is to become familiar with their inhabitants and be in a position to generalize more freely.

2 It has been argued (Whitty, 1984) that 'normal' mainstream pupils are in fact disadvantaged for they never have the opportunity of entering a special unit, as well as being unlucky in having the deviant pupils, who are potential agents of change, removed from the mainstream. No pupil in Emery Centre appeared to want to go back to the mainstream, and although this could well be a rationalization, it appears that there were good enough reasons in their school history to make them prefer the Emery Centre to a mainstream school. This preference on the part of the pupils is also clearly indicated in Leavold (1984), but is very much unlike the pupil reactions reported by McDermott (1984), where returning to a 'normal' school seemed to be the pupils' ultimate wish. This is an interesting difference, due perhaps to the different policies of the units, the unit reported by McDermott having reintegration into the mainstream as a primary aim.

3 Pupils of this kind appear to be unable to take positive steps towards been expelled, even when they reach a breakdown in their relationship with school. The case of Mark from Group B in Burleigh High, who was transferred to a special school before the end of the fieldwork, clearly indicates this point. Even when he had developed a clear hatred for school, Mark appeared to make no conscious effort to get out of it. Instead he appeared to surrender to his fate. When the transfer came, it was initiated by the school.

4 This is by no means a criticism directed to the Emery Centre. The staff of the Centre deserve wholehearted respect and support for coping very successfully with a hard and demanding task. The Centre is simply used here as an example of the existing system. It is this system which is being criticized.

5 It has been argued that occasionally segregation from the mainstream and attendance of such a unit is the lesser of two evils for a pupil, because it provides access to educational experiences and special relationships the pupils had no opportunity of achieving in the mainstream (Sewell, 1981). It would be unfair to deny that a number of individual pupils have benefited to a great extent by attending special units such as the Emery Centre (McDermott, 1984).

6 Sewell (1981) indicates very clearly just how arbitrary these criteria can be.

7 Sewell (1981) points out that this process of transfer is also occasionally harmful.

8 Its success was evident from the pupils' favourable attitude and good attendance record.

9 The notion of social skills training has been severely criticized by sociologists (Tomlinson, 1982), as a means of social control. The question has therefore arisen as to why should certain skills be regarded as 'appropriate', the argument being that it is doctors, psychologists and teachers who have the power to decide what is 'appropriate' behaviour for a child. Since I am implying here that this kind of training is desirable and beneficial, I need to support my claim.

It is suggested here that the benefit is derived from the aquisition of a wide repertoire of behaviours, and the skill to choose patterns of behaviour fitted to a particular situation, and to be able to carry them through. This cannot but be an improvement over a situation where the pupil is not presented with this choice, and is unable to act in accordance with the possible consequences of his/her actions. It is my belief that this choice was not available to the pupils of groups B/D, and that they lacked insight into other people's behaviour and awareness of the consequences of their own actions. This lack of skills was shown to have been very harmful to them.

It is, of course, necessary to avoid using behaviour modification techniques as a form of social control. And this can be avoided if the pupil, after been provided with the ability to choose, is left to make his/her own choices (see also Strivens, 1981, for a similar argument regarding use of behaviour modification).

10 The establishment of the National Curriculum has possibly altered the situation. Before this can be said, however, more research is needed to show how the National Curriculum is applied in special units today.

11 They are, of course, as suggested earlier, the lesser of two evils, and better than a mainstream school without the proper organization and facilities, and this is the reason why improvement of mainstream education is of crucial importance.

12 Researchers such as Lewis (1991) attempt that in their own work.

13 This would also benefit 'ordinary' mainstream pupils as the teachers' attention would no more be constantly dedicated to the few 'difficult' children in the class, and they would have more time for the pupils who have to 'fight it out for the remaining teachers and resources' (see Bird, 1984). This shift would, in the long-term, provide financial as well as educational rewards.

Appendices 1–14

Appendix 1: Burleigh High-school Rules

1 Pupils are expected to act with courtesy at all times towards each other and towards adults. We expect them to observe rules at school, when representing the school and while travelling to and from school.

2 Pupils must always wear the approved dress. *Outdoor clothing must not be worn inside the classrooms.*

3 Radios and cassette recorders must not be brought to school.

4 Every pupil must provide him/herself with a pen, pencil and ruler.

5 Cycles must be left inside the cycle parks and be locked at all times.

6 No smoking.

7 Keep to the left when moving around the school and do not run.

8 Pupils must observe all out of bounds areas.

9 Pupils must arrive punctually at school and to lessons. No pupil is allowed to leave school during lesson time without permission and must sign out and in at the Pupil Welfare Office.

10 Pupils who stay at school for lunch may not leave the premises without permission. Packed lunches must be eaten at the set times in the school dining hall. Litter must be placed in the bins provided.

Appendix 2: Letter to the Parents

Dear parent,

As part of a research project looking at pupils' feelings and attitudes towards school, the fourth year pupils will be asked to complete a questionnaire. The questions asked will relate to the pupils' attitude towards school, their opinions about it, as well as some home background information.

If you object to your child participating in this research project, please contact the fourth year tutor. The information obtained will of course be *strictly confidential*.

Thank you.

Appendix 3

Name:

Form:

Sex:

SECTION A

1 Do you like school in general?

- [0] Yes, a lot.
- [1] Yes, I quite like it.
- [2] Sometimes yes, sometimes no.
- [3] No, not very much.
- [4] No, I hate it.

2 Do you work hard at school?

- [0] All the time.
- [1] Most of the time.
- [2] About half the time.
- [3] Sometimes.
- [4] Hardly ever or never.

3 Do you care what teachers think of you?

- [0] Yes, very much.
- [1] Yes, quite a bit.
- [2] Not particularly.
- [3] No, not very much.
- [4] No, I don't care.

4 Do you enjoy coming to school in the morning?

- [0] Yes, a lot.
- [1] Yes, I quite enjoy it.
- [2] Sometimes yes, sometimes no.
- [3] No, not very much.
- [4] No, I hate it.

5 When in the classroom do you prefer to:

- [0] Get on with your work.
- [1] Do part of your work and then have a chat.

2 Sit quietly doing only
  a little work.
3 Talk rather than work.
4 Mess around with your friends.

6 Do your close friends at school like school work?

0 Yes, they work as hard
  as they can.
1 Yes, they work fairly hard.
2 Not particularly.
3 No, they don't like it.
4 No, they hate it.

7 Will you be glad when you have finally left school?

4 Yes, very much.
3 Yes, quite a bit.
2 Not particularly.
1 No, not really.
0 No, I'll miss it.

SECTION B

1 Are you ever late for registration or lessons?

4 Yes, all the time.
3 Yes, quite often.
2 Sometimes.
1 No, not often.
0 Never.

2 Do you always wear the school uniform?

0 Yes, always.
1 Yes, most of the time.
2 About half the time.
3 Sometimes.
4 Hardly ever.

3 Do you always carry a pen, pencil and ruler with you in school?

0 Yes, always.
1 Yes, most of the time.
2 About half the time.
3 No, not often.
4 Hardly ever.

4 Do you ever bring a radio to school?

4 Yes, all the time.
3 Yes, quite often.
2 Sometimes.
1 Seldom.
0 No, never.

5 Do you ever deliberately miss a lesson when you are at school?

4 Yes, very often.
3 Yes, quite often.
2 Sometimes.
1 Seldom.
0 No, never.

6 Do you ever smoke on the school premises?

4 Yes, a lot.
3 Yes, very often.
2 Sometimes.
1 No, not often.
0 No, never.

7 Do you ever leave school at lunchtime when you are not supposed to do so?

4 Yes, all the time.
3 Yes, quite often.
2 Sometimes.
1 No, not often.
0 No, never.

SECTION C

1 (a) Have you had a detention this term?

☐ Yes.
0 No.

(b) If yes, how many?

☐ once   two three   four six
    2   3   4

2 (a) Have you been on report this term?

☐ Yes.
0 No.

(b) If yes, how many times?

☐ once   two three   four six
    2   3   4

3 How many times did you have to see your year tutor this term:
(a) for poor work?
(b) for bad behaviour?

☐ once   two three   four six
☐ 2   3   4

4 Since September have you been excluded:
(a) from a lesson?

2 Yes.
0 No.

(b) from school?

3 Yes.
0 No.

5 Do you think your teachers think your behaviour towards them is:

0 Very helpful.
1 Quite helpful.
2 Neither helpful, nor unhelpful.

3 Often unhelpful.
4 Most unhelpful.

6 In school work do you do well?

0 Always.
1 Usually.
2 About half the time.
3 Not usually.
4 Hardly ever.

SECTION D

Please complete the following sentences in your own words.

1 I think teachers are ....

....

2 Teachers here think of me as ....

....

3 Pupils destroy school property because ....

....

4 Teachers punish pupils because ....

....

5 What I like most about school is ....

....

6 What I dislike most about school is ....

....

7 When I leave school I am going to ....

....

Once again, thank you very much for helping me with my research.

Appendix 4: Pupil Questionnaire Section D Marking Technique

QUESTION 1: I THINK TEACHERS ON THE WHOLE ARE . . .

(a)   Positive (and enthusiastic) praise e.g. 'They are friendly and always ready to help you.' : **0**

(b)   Positive comment without much emphasis. Perhaps a restriction in numbers or frequency. No negative comment. e.g. 'All right.' : **1**

(c)   Ambivalent comment, or split of the teachers in categories. No strong words used. e.g. 'All right but they don't always listen to you', 'Not too bad.' : **2**

(d)   Negative comment. Not very strong words. No nasty feelings. Possibly a fair comment. e.g. 'Mostly boring.', 'Nosey.' : **3**

(e)   Negative comment. Strong adjectives used. Obvious hostility. e.g. 'Stupid' : **4**

QUESTION 2: MOST TEACHERS THINK OF ME AS . . .

(a)   Positive comment. Enthusiasm. Many favourable adjectives. e.g. 'Hard working and hopefully helpful, friendly and good.' : **0**

(b)   Positive comment. Varying behaviour between teachers or lessons. e.g. 'Good worker but could do better if she tried.' : **1**

(c)   Varying behaviour with emphasis on, or details of, good behaviour. A negative word but not a strong one. e.g. 'A pupil who can work but usually doesn't.', 'A bit lazy.' : **2**

(d)   Varying behaviour with strong adjectives used to emphasize the negative side. e.g. 'A person who does work, then mucks about.' : **3**

(e)   Negative comments. Strong adjectives used, two or even three for emphasis. e.g. 'Stupid, always in trouble, thick and stingy.' : **4**

QUESTION 3: PUPILS DESTROY SCHOOL PROPERTY BECAUSE . . .

(a) Blame of the pupils, negative adjectives used to describe them. e.g. 'They have no brains.', 'They are not civil human beings.' : **0**

(b) No clear explanation. No reason behind the action. e.g. 'They feel like it. I don't think they have a reason.' : **1**

(c) Boredom or lack of occupation given as a reason. e.g. 'They have nothing better to do.', 'They get bored.' : **2**

(d) Frustration, annoyance, attention seeking or not liking school given as a reason. e.g. 'They might be fed up with school.' Combination of boredom and dislike for school. e.g. 'They are bored, have nothing to do and they are fed up with school,' : **3**

(e) Hate for school given as a reason. Use of strong negative adjectives. Evidence of anger or enjoyment in doing so. e.g. 'They are angry and upset.', 'It's a laugh.', 'They think it's hard.' : **4**

QUESTION 4: TEACHERS PUNISH PUPILS BECAUSE . . .

(a) The pupils are in the wrong, they deserve punishment. Punishment will 'do them good'. Teachers are well motivated, they try to teach the pupils, they know it is good for them. e.g. 'They've been bad and they deserve to be punished.' : **0**

(b) Pupils are in the wrong, they have been naughty, they have misbehaved, have broken rules. e.g. 'they don't get on with their work and play about.' : **1**

(c) The teachers want to teach the pupils a lesson. They do it to avoid repetition of the misbehaviour. e.g. 'So that they don't misbehave again.' : **2**

(d) The teachers are blamed as unfair, but in a form of complaint rather than hostility. e.g. 'They (the pupils) do not do anything.' : **3**

(e) Teachers are nasty, they enjoy punishing pupils, they do it for the fun of it. e.g. 'They enjoy it.' : **4**

QUESTION 5: WHAT I LIKE MOST ABOUT SCHOOL IS . . .

(a) The best thing in school is teachers and/or lessons. School is good fun altogether. e.g. 'I learn a lot of things.', 'The good teachers that you can have a laugh with. : **0**

(b) Mixed preferences, the friendly atmosphere, lunch time. e.g. 'Dinner time and break, plus active lessons.', 'Art and practical cooking, friends.' : **1**

(c) Mostly social reasons, meeting new people, making friends. e.g. 'Meeting my friends, and breaks.' : **2**

(d) Only break and holiday time, hometime. e.g. 'Summer holidays and Christmas time off.' : **3**

(e) Nothing at all. Total dislike of the place. e.g. 'Nothing!' : **4**

QUESTION 6: WHAT I DISLIKE MOST ABOUT SCHOOL IS . . .

(a) Nothing. The pupil likes everything about the school. No complaints at all. Pupils who misbehave. e.g. 'Not a lot really.', 'The children that won't be bothered to work.' : **0**

(b) The school dinners, waiting in the queue, getting up in the morning, e.g. 'Coming early in a morning on a winter's day.' : **1**

(c) Homework : **2**

(d) Boring lessons. Criticism of teachers presented as complaints rather than accusations. e.g. 'Biology.', 'Teachers accuse you of things you haven't done.' : **3**

(e) All lessons. Teachers as a whole, or specific teachers. e.g. 'The way some teachers boss you about.' : **4**

QUESTION 7: WHEN I LEAVE SCHOOL I AM GOING TO . . .

(a) Plans to go to University or College. : **0**

(b) Plans to go to a college of Further Education or plans for a specific job. : **1**

(c) No specific plans. Any job. : **2**

(d) The pupil does not have nay plans yet. : **3**

(e) 'Doss around' or join the dole queue. : **4**

Appendix 5: Burleigh High: Pupil Questionnaire

Dear Fourth Year Pupil,

This is a questionnaire which I have made especially for the pupils of the BURLEIGH HIGH.

With this I want to give you a chance to talk about your true feelings and attitudes to school.

There are no right or wrong answers; the questions are asking what is the way *you personally* feel. Nobody, apart from me, will know what you have said, and I am only going to use this information for my research, so there is no reason for you to worry.

I hope that you will enjoy filling the questionnaire, and that you will be happy to help me.

Thank you.

Helen Phtiaka

University of Cambridge,
Department of Education,
17 Trumpington Street,
Cambridge, CB2 1PT.

SECTION A

1 Do you like school in general?

☐ Yes, a lot
☐ Yes, I quite like it
☐ Sometimes yes sometimes no
☐ No, not very much
☐ No, I hate it

2 Do you work hard at school?

☐ All the time
☐ Most of the time
☐ About half the time
☐ Sometimes
☐ Hardly ever or never

3 Do you care what teachers think of you?

☐ Yes, very much
☐ Yes, quite a bit
☐ Not Particularly
☐ No, not ver much
☐ No, I don't care

4 Do you enjoy coming to school in the morning?

☐ Yes, a lot
☐ Yes, I quite enjoy it
☐ Sometimes yes, sometimes no
☐ No, not very much
☐ No, I hate it

5 When in the classroom do you prefer to:

☐ Get on with you work
☐ Do part of your work and then have a chat
☐ Sit quietly doing only a little work
☐ Talk rather than work
☐ Mess around with you friends

6 Do your close friends at school like school work?

☐ Yes, they work as hard as they can
☐ Yes they work fairly Hard
☐ Not particularly
☐ No, they don't like it
☐ No, they hate it

7 Will you be glad when you have finally left school?

☐ Yes, very much
☐ Yes, quite a bit
☐ Not particularly

☐ No, Not really
☐ No, I'll miss it

SECTION B

1 Are you ever late for registration or lessons?

☐ Yes, all the time
☐ Yes, quite often
☐ Sometimes
☐ No, not often
☐ Never

2 Do you always wear the school uniform?

☐ Yes, always
☐ Yes, most of the time
☐ About half the time
☐ Sometimes
☐ Hardly ever

3 Do you always carry a pen, pencil and ruler with you in school?

☐ Yes, always
☐ Yes, most of the time
☐ About half the time
☐ No, not often
☐ Hardly ever

4 Do you ever bring a radio to school?

☐ Yes, all the time
☐ Yes, quite often
☐ Sometimes
☐ Seldom
☐ No, never

5 Do you ever deliberately miss a lesson when you are at school?

☐ Yes, very often
☐ Yes, quite often
☐ Sometimes
☐ Seldom
☐ No, never

6 Do you smoke on the school premises?

☐ Yes, a lot
☐ Yes, very often
☐ Sometimes
☐ No, not often
☐ No, never

7 Do you ever leave school at lunchtime when you are not supposed to do so?

☐ Yes, all the time
☐ Yes, quite often
☐ Sometimes

☐ No, not often
☐ No, never

SECTION C

1 (a) Have you had a detention this term? ☐ yes
                                                  ☐ No

   (b) If yes, how many? No ☐

2 (a) Have you been on report this term? ☐ Yes
                                                ☐ No

   (b) If yes, how many times? No ☐

3 How many times have you had to see your year tutor this term? (if none please put 0)
   (a) For poor work No ☐
   (b) For bad behaviour No ☐

4 Since September have you been excluded:
   (a) From a lesson? ☐ Yes
                          ☐ No

   (b) From school? ☐ Yes
                         ☐ No

5 Do you think your teachers think your behaviour towards them is:
   ☐ Very helpful
   ☐ Quite helpful
   ☐ Neither helpful nor unhelpful
   ☐ Often unhelpful
   ☐ Most unhelpful

6 In your school work do you do well?
   ☐ Always
   ☐ Usually
   ☐ About half the time
   ☐ Not usually
   ☐ Never

SECTION D

Please complete the following sentences in your own words.

1 I think teachers on the whole are ....

....

2 Most Teachers here think of me as ....

....

3 Pupils destroy school property because ....

....

4 Teachers punish pupils because ....

....

5 What I like most about school is ....

....

6 What I dislike most about school is ....

....

7 When I leave school I am going to ....

....

Once again, thank you very much for helping me with my research.

Helen Phtiaka

Appendix 7: Research Diary Specimen

WEDNESDAY 6 February 1985
Awful weather. Drizzle all day.

9.10: Arrival at school. Chat with Miss Raw and Mr Harris until the bell goes.

1st/2nd: Maths. Class not very noisy. Mark absent. Lots of sweets are going around, but some kids are exceptionally quiet.

tea break: Chat with David and Jason in the fourth year area.

3rd/4th: English. A very interesting lesson. Lisa and Daniel more excited than ever before in a lesson, when the discussion comes to gender differences. A quite nice Mark makes useful comments, not too silly today. Peter is absent, just when I was expecting him to tell me about the interview.

lunch break: Quick lunch and preparation of the video room. Interview with Dean. He is very shy, he even stutters and blushes. We soon run out of topics. He is too good for my purposes. No technical problems and no disturbances. I am happy with the interview and I ask Dean to feel free to come and talk to me any time. I say it is easier for them to do so than it is for me (with them being in groups). He replies: 'That's what you think!'.

5th/6th: Physics. Jason is skiving and Robin is absent. Only two of my pupils here, quite apart from each other in every sense. I talk to the teacher for a while, and I seriously consider changing my timetable.

coffee break: Very short because of the weather. No time for anything.

7th/8th: Art. The exam is going well. The teacher tells me that he has rearranged the tables in case the pupils want to sit alone. The kids are working hard and keep quiet. Clare says that she will bring me the letter on Monday.

Appendix 8

1

21/1–15/2

	Period 1	Period 2	Period 3	Period 4	Period 5	Period 6	Period 7	Period 8
M O N	English — Mrs NE		Art — Mr HO		T.D. — Mr HD		Commerce — Mr RO	
T U E S	Biology — Mrs HO		Computer studies — Mr HA		Careers — Mr RO		—	
W E D	Maths — Mr HA		English — Mrs M-H		Physics — Mr HU		Art — Mr IL	
T H U R S								
F R I								

2 25/2–15/3

	Period 1	Period 2	Period 3	Period 4	Period 5	Period 6	Period 7	Period 8
MON								
TUES	Art Mr HO			Commere Mr RO	Careers Mr RO		—	
WED		Maths Mr HA	English Mr Mc		Biology Mrs HO		Art Mr IL	
THURS		Maths Mrs MA	T.D. Mr HD		Biology Mrs HO		English Mrs M-H	
FRI								

3   25/3–29/3

	Period 1	Period 2	Period 3	Period 4	Period 5	Period 6	Period 7	Period 8
MON								
TUES	Art Mr HO		Commerce Mr RO		Careers Mr RO		—	
WED	Maths Mr HA		English Mr Mc		Biology Mrs HO		Art Mr IL	
THURS	Maths Mr MU		T.D. Mr Hd		General science Mrs FO		English Mrs M-H	
FRI								

Appendix 9: Letter to the Parents

Dear parent,

I am a research student at the University studying pupils' feelings and attitudes towards school. I have been carrying out my research in Burleigh High since the beginning of this academic year.

During this term I hope to conduct tape-recorded interviews with pupils, to discuss their opinions and views. As your child is to be included in my study, I would like to ask for your permission before I conduct the interview. The information I obtain will of course be held in the strictest confidence.

If you are willing to allow your child to be interviewed, could you please sign the statement below and ask him/her to bring it back to school?

Thank you very much for your cooperation.

Helen Phtiaka
Research Student

I allow my child to be interviewed.

Signature ....

Date ....

Appendix 10: Letter to the Teachers

Dear teacher,

As you probably know, the special interest of my research is the pupils' behaviour in school. During the last few months I have identified, through the questionnaire and the observation, a number of fourth year pupils who disrupt the classroom with their behaviour.

If it is convenient and you have some time, could you please help me by naming up to five pupils that YOU consider the most disruptive in the fourth year groups you teach, explaining in a sentence why you think so?

Ideally, I would have liked to talk to all of you in person about this matter, but as this is not possible owing to lack of time, I have to contact you in this impersonal way.

Thank you very much for your cooperation.

Sincerely yours,

Helen Phtiaka

P.S. Please leave the sheet in Mr Daff's pigeon hole.

Appendix 11: Trouble in the Classroom

Please write a small essay describing an incident you had with a teacher inside the classroom. It must be an unpleasant situation where the teacher and you were disagreeing about something, or you were asked to do something you did not want to do.

Describe how it all started, what the teacher did, what you did, what were the words you exchanged, what you were thinking at the time, both about yourself and about the teacher. Explain how serious it was, and give your judgement about who was in the right (maybe you both were).

Conclude by saying what the consequences were for you and whether you regretted it after it was finished. Try to be as precise as possible and to give a clear picture of what happened.

Thank you.
Helen.

Appendix 12

Form

Sex

1 Please list the members of your family living at home with you.

Father   Mother
Stepfather   Stepmother
Fosterfather   Fostermother
Other (Please explain)   Other (Please explain)
....

Brother/s   Sister/s
Stepbrother/s   Stepsister/s
Fosterbrother/s   Fostersister/s

Other (Please explain)
....

2 (a) How many brothers and sisters do you have altogether? (Do not
        include yourself).
        Brothers ....   Sisters ....
   (b) How many of them are older than you?   ....

3 What country were you born in?   ....

4 What country were your parents born in?   Father...............................
                                                     Mother...............................

Thank you very much once again.

Helen Phtiaka

Appendix 13: Emery Centre: Pupil Questionnaire

Dear Pupil,

This is a questionnaire which I have made especially for the pupils of the EMERY CENTRE.

With this I want to give you a chance to talk about your true feelings and attitudes to school.

There are no right or wrong answers; the questions are asking what is the way *you personally* feel. Nobody, apart from me, will know what you have said, and I am only going to use this information for my research, so there is no reason for you to worry.

I hope that you will enjoy filling the questionnaire, and that you will be happy to help me.

Thank you.

Helen Phtiaka

University of Cambridge,
Department of Education,
17 Trumpington Street,
Cambridge, CB2 1PT.

SECTION A

1   Do you like school in general?

☐ Yes, a lot
☐ Yes, I quite like it
☐ Sometimes yes sometimes no
☐ No, not very much
☐ No, I hate it

2   Did do you work hard at school?

S   U

☐ All the time ☐
☐ Most of the time ☐
☐ About half the time ☐
☐ Sometimes ☐
☐ Hardly ever or never ☐

3   Did do you care what teachers think of you?

S   U

☐ Yes, very much ☐
☐ Yes, quite a bit ☐
☐ Not particularly ☐
☐ No, not very much ☐
☐ No, I don't care ☐

4   Did do you enjoy coming to school in the morning?

S   U

☐ Yes, a lot ☐
☐ Yes, I quite enjoy it ☐
☐ Sometimes yes sometimes no ☐
☐ No, not very much ☐
☐ No, I hate it ☐

5   When in the classroom did do you prefer to:

S   U

☐ Get on with your work ☐
☐ Do part of your work and then have a chat ☐
☐ Sit quietly doing only a little work ☐
☐ Talk rather than work ☐
☐ Mess around with your friends ☐

6   Did do your close friends at school like school work?

S   U

☐ Yes, they work as hard as they can ☐
☐ Yes, they work fairly hard ☐
☐ Not particularly ☐

☐ No, they don't like it ☐

☐ No, they hate it ☐

7 Were will you be glad when you have finally left school? left school?

S   U

☐ Yes, very much ☐

☐ Yes, quite a bit ☐

☐ Not particularly ☐

☐ No, not really ☐

☐ No, I'll miss it ☐

SECTION B

1 Were Are you ever late for registration or lessons?

S   U

☐ Yes, all the time ☐

☐ Yes, quite often ☐

☐ Sometimes ☐

☐ No, not often ☐

☐ Never ☐

2 Did you always wear the school uniform?

☐ Yes, always

☐ Yes, most of the time

☐ About half the time

☐ Sometimes

☐ Hardly ever

3 Did you always carry a pen, pencil and ruler with you in school?

☐ Yes, always

☐ Yes, most of the time

☐ About half the time

☐ No, not often

☐ Hardly ever

4 Did you ever bring a radio to school?

☐ Yes, all the time

☐ Yes, quite often

☐ Sometimes

☐ Seldom

☐ No, never

5 Did you ever deliberately miss a lesson when you are at school?

S   U

☐ Yes, very often ☐

☐ Yes, quite often ☐

☐ Sometimes ☐

☐ Seldom ☐

☐ No, never ☐

6 Did do you smoke on the school premises?

☐ Yes, a lot
☐ Yes, very often
☐ Sometimes
☐ No, not often
☐ No, never

7 Did you ever leave school at lunchtime when you are not supposed to do so?

☐ Yes, all the time
☐ Yes, quite often
☐ Sometimes
☐ No, not often
☐ No, never

SECTION C

1 (a) Have you had a detention last term?
    In school?
  (b) If yes, how many?

☐ Yes
☐ No
No ☐

2 (a) Have you been on report last term?
  (b) If yes how many times?

☐ Yes
☐ No
No ☐

3 How many times have you had to see your year tutor last term? (if none please put 0)
  (a) For poor work
  (b) For bad behaviour

No ☐
No ☐

4 During your last term in school have you been excluded
  (a) From a lesson?

☐ Yes
☐ No

  (b) From schoool?

☐ Yes
☐ No

5 Do you think your teachers think your behaviour towards them is/was:

S

☐ Very helpful
☐ Quite helpful
☐ Neither helpful nor unhelpful
☐ Often unhelpful
☐ Most unhelpful

U

☐
☐
☐

☐
☐

6   In your school work did/do you   S   U
    do well?   ☐ Always   ☐
                                         ☐ Usually   ☐
                                         ☐ About half the time   ☐
                                         ☐ Not usually   ☐
                                         ☐ Never   ☐

SECTION D

Please complete the following sentences in your own words.

1   I think teachers on the whole are ....

    ....

2   Most teachers here think of me as ....

    ....

3   Pupils destroy school property because ....

    ....

4   Teachers punish pupils because ....

    ....

5   What I like most about school is ....

    ....

6   What I dislike most about school is ....

    ....

7   When I leave school I am going to ....

    ....

Once again, thank you very much for helping me with my research.

                                                                            Helen Phtiaka

Appendix 14: Emery Centre Timetable

	MON	TUES	WED	THURS	FRI
10–12:	Squash	Computer Studies	Pre-Employment	Table Tennis	Wood-work
	Basic Skills	Typing/ Office Skills	—	Indoor Games	Cookery
12–1:	LUNCH BREAK				
1–3:	Building Maintenance	Swimming	Art	Photography/ Art	Meetings
	—	Craft	Cookery	Computer Studies	—

Bibliography

AINSCOW, M. (1993) 'Beyond special education: Some ways forward', in VISSER, J. and UPTON, G. (Eds) *Special Education in Britain after Warnock*, London, David Fulton Publishers Ltd.

ARMSTRONG, D., GALLOWAY, D. and TOMLINSON, S. (1993) 'Assessing special educational needs: The child's contribution', *British Educational Research Journal*, **19**, 2, pp. 121–31.

ATKINSON, P., SHONE, D. and REES, T. (1981) 'Labouring to learn? Industrial training for slow learners', in BARTON, L. and MEIGHAN, R. (Eds) (1979) *Schools, Pupils and Deviance*, Driffield, Nafferton Books.

BALDWIN, J. (1972) 'Delinquent schools in Tower Hamlets — A critique', *British Journal of Criminology*, **12**, pp. 299–340.

BALL, S.J. (1980) 'Initial encounters in the classroom and the process of establishment', in WOODS, P. (Ed) *Pupil Strategies: Explorations in the Sociology of the School*, Beckenham, Croom Helm.

BALL, S.J. (1981) *Beachside Comprehensive: A Case Study of Secondary Schooling*, Cambridge, Cambridge University Press.

BANDURA, A. (1971) *Principles of Behavior Modification*, New York, Holt, Rinehart and Winston.

BARNES, C. and OLIVER, M. (1995) 'Disability rights: Rhetoric and reality in the UK', *Disability & Society*, **10**, 1.

BARTON, L. (1988) *The Politics of Special Educational Needs*, London, Falmer Press.

BARTON, L. (Ed) (1989) *Disability and Dependency*, London, Falmer Press.

BARTON, L. (1993) 'Labels, markets and inclusive education', in VISSER, J. and UPTON, G. (Eds) *Special Education in Britain after Warnock*, London, David Fulton Publishers Ltd.

BARTON, L. and MEIGHAN, R. (Eds) (1979) *Schools, Pupils and Deviance*, Driffield, Nafferton Books.

BARTON, L., MEIGHAN, R. and WALKER, S. (Eds) (1980) *Schooling, Ideology and the Curriculum*, London, Falmer Press.

BARTON, L. and MOODY, S. (1981) 'The value of parents to the ESN(M) school: An examination', in BARTON, L. and TOMLINSON, S. (Eds) *Special Education: Policy, Practices and Social Issues*, London, Pitman Press.

BARTON, L. and TOMLINSON, S. (Eds) (1981) *Special Education: Policy, Practices and Social Issues*, London, Pitman Press.

BARTON, L. and WALKER, S. (Eds) (1981) *Schools, Teachers and Teaching*, London, Falmer Press.

BARTON, L. and WALKER, S. (Eds) (1983) *Race, Class and Education*, Beckenham, Croom Helm.

BARTON, L. and WALKER, S. (Eds) (1984) *Social Crisis and Educational Research*, Beckenham, Croom Helm.

BECKER, H.S. (1963) *Outsiders: Studies in the Sociology of Deviance*, New York, Free Press.

BERNSTEIN, B. (1970) 'Education cannot compensate for society', *New Society*, 29 February, pp. 344–7.

BETTELHEIM, B. (1950) *Love is Not Enough*, Glencoe, Illinois, Free Press.

BETTELHEIM, B. (1955) *Truants from Life*, Glencoe, Illinois, Free Press.

BEVERIDGE, S. (1993) *Special Educational Needs in Schools*, London, Routledge.

BIRD, C. (1980) 'Deviant labelling in school — The pupils' perspective', in WOODS, P. (Ed) *Pupil Strategies: Explorations in the Sociology of the School*, Beckenham, Croom Helm.

BIRD, C. (1984) 'The disaffected pupil: A suitable case for treatment', in LLOYD-SMITH, M. (Ed) *Disrupted Schooling: The Growth of the Special Unit*, London, John Murray.

BIRD, C., CHESSUM, R., FURLONG, J. and JOHNSON, D. (1981) *Disaffected Pupils: A Research Report*, Uxbridge, Brunel University.

BLAU, P.M. (1954) 'Cooperation and Competition in a bureaucracy', *American Journal of Sociology*, May, **6**, pp. 530–5.

BOOTH, T.A. (1978) 'From normal baby to handicapped child', reprinted in SWANN, W. (Ed) (1981) *The Practice of Special Education: A Reader*, Oxford, Basil Blackwell with the Open University Press.

BOOTH, T.A. (1981) 'Demystifying integration', in SWANN, W. (Ed) *The Practice of Special Education: A Reader*, Oxford, Basil Blackwell with the Open University Press.

BOOTH, T.A. (1982) *Handicap is Social*, Mitton Keynes, Open University Press.

BOOTH, T.A. and POTTS, P. (1983) *Integrating Special Education*, Oxford, Basil Blackwell.

BOOTH, T.A. and STATHAM, J. (1982) *The Nature of Special Education: A Reader*, Beckenham, Croom Helm with the Open University Press.

BOWERS, A.J. (Ed) (1984) *Management and the Special School*, Beckenham, Croom Helm.

BOWERS, A.J. (1986) 'Interpersonal skills and conflict management', in TATTUM, D.P. (Ed) *Management of Disruptive Pupil Behaviour in Schools*, Chichester, John Wiley & Sons.

BOWMAN, I. (1981) 'Maladjustment: A History of the category', in SWANN, W. (Ed) *The Practice of Special Education: A Reader*, Oxford, Basil Blackwell with the Open University Press.

BRENNAN, W.K. (1985) *Curriculum for Special Needs*, Milton Keynes, Open University Press.

BRIDGELAND, M. (1971) *Pioneer Work with Maladjusted Children*, London, Staples Press.

BURGESS, R.G. (1982) *Field Research: A Sourcebook and Field Manual*, London, George Allen & Unwin Ltd.

BURGESS, R.G. (1984a) *In the Field: An Introduction to Field Research*, London, George Allen & Unwin Ltd.

BURGESS, R.G. (Ed) (1984b) *The Research Process in Educational Settings: Ten Case Studies*, London, Falmer Press.

BURNS, R.B., CHANAN, G. and DELAMONT, S. (Eds) (1978) 'The relative effectiveness of various incentives and deterrent as judged by pupils and teachers, frontiers of classroom research', *Educational Studies*, **4**, 3, pp. 229–43.

CAMPBELL, A. (1991) *The Girls in the Gang*, Oxford, Blackwell.

CARLEN, P., GLEESON, D. and WARDHAUGH, J. (1992) *Truancy: The Politics of Compulsory Schooling*, Buckingham, Open University Press.

CLARRICOATES, K. (1980) 'The importance of being Ernest . . . Emma . . . Tom . . . Jane', in DEEM, R. (Ed) *Schooling for Women's Work*, London, RKP.

COHEN, A.K. (1955) *Delinquent Boys: The Sub-culture of the Gang*, Glencoe, Illinois, Free Press.

COHEN, A.K. (1965) 'The sociology of the deviant act: Anomie theory and beyond', *American Sociological Review*, **30**, 1, pp. 5–14.

COHEN, L. and MANION, L. (1980) *Research Methods in Education*, Beckenham, Croom Helm.

COOPER, P. (1993) *Effective Schools for Disaffected Students*, London, Routledge.

COOPER, P., SMITH, C. and UPTON, G. (1994) *Emotional and Behavioural Difficulties: Theory to Practice*, London, Routledge.

CORBETT, J. (1996) *Bad-Mouthing: The Language of Special Needs*, London, Falmer Press.

CORBETT, J. and BARTON, L. (1992) *A Struggle for Choice — Students with Special Needs in Transition to Adulthood*, London, Routledge.

CORRIE, M., HAYSTEAD, J. and ZAKLUKIEWICZ, S. (1982) *Classroom Management Strategies: A Study in Secondary Schools*, London, Hodder and Stoughton fro the Scottish Council for Research in Education.

CORRIGAN, P. (1979) *Schooling the Smash Street Kids*, London, Macmillan.

COULBY, D. (1984) 'The creation of the disruptive pupil', in LLOYD-SMITH, M. (Ed) *Disrupted Schooling: The Growth of the Special Unit*, London, John Murray.

DAVID, S., DERALD, S. and STANLEY, S. (1994) *Understanding Abnormal Behaviour*, Boston, MA, Houghton Mifflin.

DAVIE, R. (1993) 'Implementing Warnock's multi-professional approach', in VISSER, J. and UPTON, G. (Eds) *Special Education in Britain after Warnock*, London, David Fulton Publishers Ltd.

DAVIES, L. (1979) 'Deadlier than the male? Girls' conformity and deviance in school', in BARTON, L. and MEIGHAN, R. (Eds) *Schools, Pupils and Deviance*, Driffield, Nafferton Books.

DAVIES, L. (1983) 'Gender, resistance and power', in WALKER, S. and BARTON, L. (Eds) *Gender, Class and Education*, London, Falmer Press.

DAVIES, L. (1984) *Pupil Power: Deviance and Gender in School*, London, Falmer Press.

DEEM, R. (1978) *Women and Schooling*, London, RKP.

DEEM, R. (Ed) (1980) *Schooling for Women's Work*, London, RKP.

DEEM, R. (Ed) (1984) *Co-education Revisited*, Milton Keynes, Open University Press.

DELAMONT, S. (1976a) 'Beyond Flanders fields: The relationship of subject matter and individuality to classroom style', in STUBBS, M. and DELAMONT, S. (Eds) *Explorations in Classroom Observation*, Chichester, John Wiley & Sons Ltd.

DELAMONT, S. (1976b) *Interaction in the Classroom*, London, Methuen.

DELAMONT, S. (1980) *Sex Roles and the School*, London, Methuen.

DELAMONT, S. (Ed) (1984) *Readings on Interaction in the Classroom*, London, Methuen.

DELAMONT, S. (1992) *Fieldwork in Educational Settings: Methods, Pitfalls and Perspectives*, London, Falmer Press.

DELAMONT, S. and HAMILTON, D. (1976) 'Classroom research: A critique and a new approach', in STUBBS, M. and DELAMONT, S. (Eds) *Explorations in Classroom Observation*, Chichester, John Wiley & Sons Ltd.

DELAMONT, S. and HAMILTON, D. (1984) 'Revisiting classroom research: A continuing cautionary tale', in DELAMONT, S. (Ed) *Readings on Interaction in the Classroom*, London, Methuen.

DES (1975) *Reports on Education: The First Years After RSLA*, London, HMSO.

DES (1978a) *Behavioural Units: A Survey of Special Units for Pupils with Behavioural Problems*, London, HMSO.

DES (1978b) *Truancy and Behavioural Problems in Some Urban Schools*, London, HMSO.

DES (1979) *Reports on Education No 95 ROSLA Four Years On*, London, HMSO.

DES (1981) *Education Act 1981*, London, HMSO.

DES (1983) *Police Liaison with the Education Service*, London, Collins and Wilson Ltd for the HMSO.

DES (1984) *Slow Learning and Less Successful Pupils in Secondary Schools* (Evidence from HMI visits), London, HMSO.

DES (1988) *Education Reform Act 1988*, London, HMSO.

DES (1989) *Children Act 1989*, London, HMSO.

DES (1990) *National Health Service and Community Care Act 1990*, London, HMSO.

DES (1992) *Further and Higher Education Act 1992*, London, HMSO.

DES (1993a) *Education Act 1993*, London, HMSO.

DES (1993b) *Circular*, London, HMSO.

DES (1994) *Code of Practice on the Identification and Assessment of Special Educational Needs*, London, HMSO.

DES (Welsh Office) (1985) *The Educational System of England and Wales*, Linneys CP for HMSO.

DENSCOMBE, M. (1980) 'Pupil strategies in the open classroom', in WOODS, P. (Ed) *Pupil Strategies: Explorations in the Sociology of the School*, Beckenham, Croom Helm.

DENSCOMBE, M. (1984) 'Keeping 'em quiet: The significance of noise for the practical activity of teaching', in DELAMONT, S. (Ed) *Readings on Interaction in the Classroom*, London, Methuen.

DITTON, J. (1977) 'Alibis and aliases: some notes on the "motives" of fidding bread salesmen', *Sociology*, **11**, 2, pp. 233–55.

DOCKAR-DRYSDALE, B. (1968) *Therapy in Child Care*, London, Longmans, Green & Co Ltd.

DOCKAR-DRYSDALE, B. (1971) *The Management of Violence in Disturbed Children*, London, Longmans, Green & Co Ltd.

DOCKRELL, W.B., NISBET, J., NUTTALL, D.N., STONES, E. and WILCOX, B. (1986) *Appraising Appraisal*, London, BERA Publications.

DOWNES, D. and ROCK, P. (1988) *Understanding Deviance: A Guide to the Sociology of Crime and Rule Breaking*, Oxford, Clarendon Press.

DURKHEIM, E. (1968) *Suicide: A Study in Sociology*, London, RKP.

DURKHEIM, E. (1977) *The Evolution of Educational Thought*, London, RKP.

EISENBERG, L., CONNORS, K. and SHARPE, L. (1965) 'A controlled study of the differential application of out-patient psychiatric treatment for children', *Japanese Journal of Child Psychiatry*, **6**, pp. 125–32.

EMERSON, T. (1984) 'Developing a policy for a support unit', in LLOYD-SMITH, M. (Ed) *Disrupted Schooling: The Growth of the Special Unit*, London, John Murray.

FORD, J., MONGON, D. and WHELAN, M. (1982) *Special Education and Social Control: Invisible Disasters*, London, RKP.

FRASIER, N. and SADKER, M. (1973) *Sexism in School and Society*, London, Harper and Row.

FRIEL, J. (1995) *Young Adults with Special Needs: Assessment, Law and Practice — Caught in the Act*, London, Jessica Kingsley Publishers.

FULCHER, G. (1989) *Disabling Policies? A Comparative Approach to Education Policy and Disability*, London, Falmer Press.

FULLER, M. (1980) 'Black girls in a London comprehensive school', in DEEM, R. (Ed) *Schooling for Women's Work*, London, RKP.

FURLONG, V.J. (1976) 'Interaction sets in the classroom: Towards a study of pupil knowledge', in STUBBS, M. and DELAMONT, S. (Eds) *Explorations in Classroom Observation*, Chichester, John Wiley & Sons.

FURLONG, V.J. (1984) 'Black resistance in the liberal comprehensive', in DELAMONT, S. (Ed) *Readings on Interaction in the Classroom*, London, Methuen.

FURLONG, V.J. (1985) *The Deviant Pupil*, Milton Keynes, Open University Press.

FURLONG, V.J. and BIRD, C. (1981) 'How can we cope with Karen?', *New Society*, **56**, 959, pp. 12–14.

GALLOWAY, D.M. (1976) *Case Studies in Classroom Management*, London, Longman Group Ltd.

GALLOWAY, D.M. (1981) 'Institutional change or individual change? An Overview', in GILLHAM, B. (Ed) *Rethinking the Problem*, Beckenham, Croom Helm.

GALLOWAY, D.M. (1985) 'Meeting special educational needs in the ordinary school? Or Creating them', *Maladjustment and Therapeutic Education*, **3**, 3, pp. 3–10.

GALLOWAY, D.M. and GOODWIN, C. (1979) *Educating Slow Learning and Maladjusted Children: Integration or Segregation?*, London, Longman Group Ltd.

GALLOWAY, D. and GOODWIN, C. (1987) *The Education of Disturbing. Children: Pupils with Learning and Adjustment Difficulties*, Longman, New York.

GALWAY, J. (1979) 'What pupils think of special units', *Comprehensive Education*, winter, **39**, pp. 18–20.

GANNAWAY, H. (1976) 'Making sense of school', reprinted in HAMMERSLEY, M. and WOODS, P. (Eds) (1984) *Life in School: The Sociology of Pupil Culture*, Milton Keynes, Open University Press.

GARNER, P. (1994) 'Advocacy and the young person with special educational needs', *International Journal of Adolescence and Youth*, **5**, pp. 47–60.

GASCOIGNE, E. (1995) *Working with Parents as Partners in SEN: Home and School, A Working Alliance*, London, David Fulton Publishers Ltd.

GILLBORN, D. (1995) 'Racism and exclusions from school: Case studies in the denial of educational opportunity', paper presented at the European Conference on Educational Research, Bath, September.

GILLHAM, B. (1981a) *Problem Behaviour in the Secondary School*, Beckenham, Croom Helm.

GILLHAM, B. (1981b) *Rethinking the Problem*, Beckenham, Croom Helm.

GIPPS, C. (1982) *Warnock's Eighteen Percent*, London, Falmer Press.

GLASER, B.G. and STRAUSS, A.L. (1964) 'The social loss of dying patients', *The American Journal of Nursing*, **64**, 6, pp. 119–21.

GLASER, B.G. and STRAUSS, A.L. (1967) *The Discovery of Grounded Theory: Strategies for Qualitative Research*, Adline Publishing Company.

GOFFMAN, E. (1968) *Asylums*, London, Penguin.

GOLBY, M. (1984) 'Special units: Some underlying issues', in LLOYD-SMITH, M. (Ed) *Disrupted Schooling: The Growth of the Special Unit*, London, John Murray.

GOLD, M. (1963) *Status Forces in Delinquent Boys*, Ann Arbor, MI, University of Michigan.

GRACE, G. (1978) *Teachers, Ideology and Control*, London, RKP.

GROSS, J. (1993) *Special Educational Needs in the Primary School: A Practical Guide*, Buckingham, Open University Press.

GRUNSELL, R. (1978) *Born to be Invisible*, London, Macmillan.

GRUNSELL, R. (1980a) *Absent from School*, London, Writers and Readers (with Chameleon Books).

GRUNSELL, R. (1980b) *Beyond Control? Schools and Suspension*, London, Writers and Readers (with Chameleon Books).

GULLIFORD, R. (1971) *Special Educational Needs*, London, RKP.

GULLIFORD, R. (1992) 'Learning difficulties', in GULLIFORD, R. and UPTON, G. (Eds) *Special Educational Needs*, London: Routledge.

GULLIFORD, R. and UPTON, G. (1992) *Special Educational Needs*, London, Routledge.

HALL, S. and JEFFERSON, T. (1976) *Resistance through Rituals: Youth Sub-cultures in Post-war Britain*, London, Hutchinson & Co Ltd.

HAMMERSLEY, M. and WOODS, P. (Eds) (1976) *The Process of Schooling: A Sociological Reader*, London, RKP with the Open University Press.

HAMMERSLEY, M. and WOODS, P. (Eds) (1984) *Life in School: The Sociology of Pupil Culture*, Milton Keynes, Open University Press.

HARGREAVES, A. and Woods, P. (Eds) (1984) *Classrooms and Staffrooms: The Sociology of Teachers and Teaching*, Milton Keynes, Open University Press.

HARGREAVES, D.H. (1967) *Social Relations in a Secondary School*, London, RKP.

HARGREAVES, D.H. (1979) 'Durkheim, deviance and education', in BARTON, L. and MEIGHAN, R. (Eds) *Schools, Pupils and Deviance*, Driffield, Nafferton Books.

HARGREAVES, D.H., HESTER, S. and MELLOR, F. (1975) *Deviance in Classrooms*, London, RKP.

HEGARTY, S. (1987) *Special Needs in Ordinary Schools: Meeting Special Needs in Ordinary Schools*, London, Cassell.

HEGARTY, S. and POCKLINGTON, K. with LUCAS, D. (1981) *Educating Pupils with Special Needs in the Ordinary School*, London, NFER-Nelson.

HEGARTY, S. and POCKLINGTON, K. with LUCAS, D. (1982) *Interaction in Action: Case Studies in the Interaction of Pupils with Special Needs*, London, NFER-Nelson.

HINDE, R.A. (1973) 'On the design of check-sheets', *Primates*, **14**, 4, pp. 393–406.

HODGSON, A., CLUNIES-ROSS, L. and HEGARTY, S. (1984) *Learning Together: Teaching Pupils with Special Educational Needs in the Ordinary School*, London, NFER-Nelson.

HOFFMAN, L., PARIS, S. and HALL, E. (1994) *Developmental Psychology Today*, New York, McGraw Hill, Inc.

HOLMAN, P. and LIBRETTO, G. (1979) 'The on-site unit', *Comprehensive Education*, **39**, pp. 10–12.

HUMPHRIES, S. (1981) *Hooligans or Rebels? An Oral History of Working Class Childhood and Youth 1889–1939*, Oxford, Basil Blackwell.

HUNT, N. (1994) *The Story of Lucy and Nell*, Boston, MA, Houghton Mifflin.

HUNT, N. and MARSHALL, K. (1994) *Exceptional Children & Youth: An Introduction to Special Education*, Boston, MA, Houghton Mifflin.

ILEA RESEARCH AND STATISTICS REPORT (1984) *Characteristics of Pupils in Special Schools RS 962/84*, London, ILEA.

ILEA SCHOOLS SUPPORT UNIT DIVISION 5 (1983) *Evaluation: Phase II*, London, ILEA.

JAMIESON, M., PARLETT, M. and POCKLINGTON, K. (1977) *Towards Integration: A Study of Blind and Partially Sighted Children in Ordinary Schools*, Slough, NFER Publishing Company.

JOHNSON, A.C. (1942) 'Our schools make criminals', *Journal of Criminal Law and Criminology*, **33**, pp. 310–15.

JONES, N. and DOCKING, J. (1992) *Special Educational Needs and the Education Reform Act*, Stoke on Trent, Trentham Books.

JONES, V.F. (1986) 'Classroom management in the United States: Trends and critical issues', in TATTUM, D.P. (Ed) *Management of Disruptive Pupil Behaviour in Schools*, London, John Wiley & Sons.

KANDEL, I.L. (1951) *Raising the School Leaving Age (1965), Schools Council Working*, paper No 2, London, HMSO.

KEDDIE, N. (1984) 'Classroom knowledge', in HARGREAVES, A. and WOODS, P. (Eds) *Classrooms and Staffrooms: The Sociology of Teachers and Teaching*, Milton Keynes, Open University Press.

KIRK, S.A., GALLAGHER, J.J. and ANASTASIOW, N.J. (1993) *Educating Exceptional Children*, Boston MA, Houghton Mifflin.

KITSUSE, J.C. (1962) 'Social reactions to deviant behaviour: Problems of theory and method', *Social Problems*, **9**, pp. 247–57.

KOUNIN, J.S. (1970) *Discipline and Group Management in Classrooms*, London, Holt, Rinehart and Winston.

KYRIACOU, C. (1980) 'High anxiety', *Times Educational Supplement*, 6 June.

KYRIACOU, C. and SUTCLIFFE, J. (1977) 'Teacher stress: A review', *Educational Review*, **29**, 4, pp. 299–304.

LACEY, C. (1970) *Hightown Grammar*, Manchester, University of Manchester Press.

LACEY, C. (1975) 'Choice and constraint and the possibility of autonomous behaviour', reprinted in BARTON, L. and MEIGHAN, R. (Eds) (1979) *Schools, Pupils and Deviance*, Driffield, Nafferton Books.

LAMBART, A.M. (1976) 'The sisterhood', in HAMMERSLEY, M. and WOODS, P. (Eds) (1976) *The Process of Schooling: A Sociological Reader*, London, RKP with the Open University Press.

LASSLETT, R. (1977) *Educating Maladjusted Children*, London, Crosby Lockwood Staples.

LASSLETT, R. (1982) *Maladjusted Children in the Ordinary School*, Stratford Upon Avon, National Council for Special Education.

LASLETT, R. and SMITH, C. (1984) *Effective Classroom Management: A Teacher's Guide*, Beckenham, Croom Helm.

LAZARSFELD, P.F. and BARTON, A.H. (1951) 'Qualitative measurement in the social sciences: Classification, typologies and indices', in LERNER, D. and LASSWELL, H.D. (Eds) *The Policy Sciences: Recent Developments in Scope and Method*, Palo Alto, CA, Stanford University Press, p. 3.

LEAVOLD, J. (1984) 'A sanctuary for disruptive pupils', in LLOYD-SMITH, M. (Ed) *Disrupted Schooling: The Growth of the Special Unit*, London, John Murray.

LEMERT, E.M. (1951) *Social Pathology*, New York, McGraw Hill.

LEMERT, E.M. (1967) *Human Deviance, Social Problems and Social Control*, Englewood Cliffs, Prentice Hall.

LERNER, D. and LASSWELL, H.D. (Eds) (1951) *The Policy Sciences: Recent Developments in Scope and Method*, Palo Alto, CA, Stanford University Press.

LERNER, J. (1993) *Learning Disabilities: Theories, Diagnosis & Teaching Strategies*, Boston, MA, Houghton Mifflin.

LEVITT, E.E. (1957) 'The results of psychotherapy with children: An evaluation', *Journal of Consulting Psychology*, **21**, pp. 189–96.

LEVITT, E.E. (1963) 'Psychotherapy with children: A further evaluation', reprinted in WILLIAMS, P. (Ed) *Behaviour Problems in School: A Source Book of Readings*, London, University of London Press.

LEWIS, A. (1991) *Primary Special Needs and the National Curriculum*, London, Routledge.

LEWIS, A. (1995) *Children's Understanding of Disability*, London, Routledge.

LLEWELLYN, M. (1980) 'Studying girls in school', in DEEM, R. (Ed) *Schooling for Women's Work*, London, RKP.

LLOYD-SMITH, M. (1984a) 'Disaffected pupils in special units', in LLOYD-SMITH, M. (Ed) *Disrupted Schooling: The Growth of the Special Unit*, London, John Murray.

LLOYD-SMITH, M. (Ed) (1984b) *Disrupted Schooling: The Growth of the Special Unit*, London, John Murray.

LLOYD-SMITH, M. (1984c) 'Introduction: The growth of special units for disaffected pupils', in LLOYD-SMITH, M. (Ed) *Disrupted Schooling: The Growth of the Special Unit*, London, John Murray.

LLOYD-SMITH, M. (1993) 'Problem behaviour, exclusions and the policy vacuum', *Pastoral Care in Education*, **11**, 4, December, pp. 19–24.

MCDERMOTT, J. (1984) 'A disruptive pupil unit: Referral and reintegration', in LLOYD-SMITH, M. (Ed) *Disrupted Schooling: The Growth of the Special Unit*, London, John Murray.

MCGUINESS, J. (1993) *Teachers, Pupils and Behaviour: A Managerial Approach*, London, Cassell.

MCGREW, W.C. and PHTIAKA, H. (1984) 'A simple and direct method of assessing dominance in young children', *Human Ethology Newsletter*, **4**, 2, pp. 2–4.

MACINTYRE, S. (1977) *Single and Pregnant*, Beckenham, Croom Helm.

MCMANNUS, M. (1989) *Troublesome Behaviour in the Classroom: A Teacher's Survival Guide*, London, Routledge.

MCROBBIE, A. and GARBER, J. (1976) 'Girls and sub-cultures', in HALL, S. and JEFFERSON, T. (Eds) *Resistance through Rituals: Youth Sub-cultures in Post-war Britain*, London, Hutchinson & Co Ltd.

MAHONY, P. (1985) *Schools for the Boys? Co-education Reassessed*, London, Hutchinson & Co Ltd.

MAYCHELL, K. and SMART, D. (1990) *Beyond Vision: Training for Work with Visually Impaired People*, Windsor, NFER-NELSON Publishing Company Ltd.

MEASOR, L. (1983) 'Gender and the sciences: Pupils' gender-based conceptions of school subjects', reprinted in HAMMERSLEY, M. and WOODS, P. (Eds) (1984) *Life in School: The Sociology of Pupil Culture*, Milton Keynes, Open University Press.

MEASOR, L. and WOODS, P. (1984) *Changing Schools: Pupil Perspectives on Transfer to a Comprehensive*, Milton Keynes, Open University Press.

MERTON, R.K. (1957) *Social Theory and Social Structure*, New York, Free Press.

MEYENN, R.J. (1980) 'School girls' peer groups', in WOODS, P. (Ed) — which one?

MILLS, R.W. (1992) *Observing Children in the Primary Classroom: All in a Day*, London, Routledge.

MINISTRY OF EDUCATION (1955) *Report of the Committee on Maladjusted Children* ('The Underwood Report), London, HMSO.

MITCHELL, S. and ROSA, P. (1981) 'Boyhood behaviour problems as precursors of criminality: A fifteen year follow-up', *Journal of Child Psychology and Psychiatry*, **22**, pp. 19–33.

MITTLER, P. (1993) 'Special needs in the crossroads', in VISSER, J. and UPTON, G. (Eds) *Special Education After Warnock*, London, David Fulton Publishers Ltd.

MORRISH, I. (1970) *Education Since 1800*, London, George Allen & Unwin Ltd.

NASH, R. (1976) 'Pupils' expectations of their teachers', in STUBBS, M. and DELAMONT, S. (Eds) *Explorations in Classroom Observation*, Chichester, John Wiley & Son.

NATIONAL ASSOCIATION OF SCHOOLMASTERS (NAS) (1973) 'ROSLA report', *The New Schoolmaster*, October.

NORWICH, B. (1993) 'Has "special educational needs" outlived its usefulness?', in VISSER, J. and UPTON, G. (Eds) *Special Education After Warnock*, London, David Fulton Publishers Ltd.

OPEN UNIVERSITY (????) *Social Sciences: A Third Level Course Research Methods in Education and the Social Sciences* (DE 304 Block 4), Milton Keynes, Open University Press.

OPEN UNIVERSITY (1982a) *Special Needs in Education: E241 Handicap is Social*, Milton Keynes, Open University Press.

OPEN UNIVERSITY (1982b) *Special Needs in Education: E241 Special Biographies*, Milton Keynes, Open University Press.

PARK, C.C. (1990) *The Siege, The First Eight Years of an Autistic Child with an Epilogue Fifteen Years Later*, Boston, MA, Little Brown.

PARTINGTON, J.A. and HINCHLIFFE, G. (1979) 'Some aspects of classroom management', *British Journal of Teacher Education*, **5**, 3, pp. 231–341.

PHTIAKA, H. (1988) 'School deviance: An evaluation of the division between mainstream and special education at secondary school level, with special reference to deviant behaviour: A critical analysis of two case studies', unpublished PhD thesis, University of Cambridge.

PHTIAKA, H. (1994) 'What's in it for us?', *International Journal of Qualitative Studies in Education*, **7**, 2, pp. 155–64.

PHTIAKA, H. (1995) The Beginning of a Beautiful Friendship? The School Library and the GCSE, Library and Information Research Report 93, London, British Library Research and Development Department.

PHTIAKA, H. (1996a) 'Each to "his own"? Home school relations in Cyprus, 1996', *Forum in Education*, **50**, 3, spring.

PHTIAKA, H. (1996b) 'Are we ready to meet the challenge?; Integration, inclusive education and children with special educational needs', paper presented at the British Educational Research Association annual conference, September, Lancaster.

POLLARD, A. (1979) 'Negotiating deviance and "getting done" in primary school classrooms', in BARTON, L. and MEIGHAN, R. (Eds) *Schools, Pupils and Deviance*, Driffield, Nafferton Books.

POLLARD, A. (1984) 'Goodies, jokers and gangs', in HAMMERSLEY, M. and WOODS, P. (Eds) *Life in School: The Sociology of Pupil Culture*, Milton Keynes, Open University Press.

POTEET, J.A. (1974) *Behaviour Modification: A Practical Guide for Teachers*, London, University of London Press.

POWER, M.J., ALDERSON, M.R., PHILLIPSON, C.M., SHOENBERG, E. and MORRIS, J.N. (1967) 'Delinquent schools', *New Society*, 19 October, p. 542.

PRITCHARD, D.G. (1963) *Education of the Handicapped 1760–1960*, London, RKP.

PYE, J. (1989) *Invisible Children: Who Are the Real Losers at school?*, Oxford, Oxford University Press.

REDL, F. and WINEMAN, D. (1951) *Children Who Hate*, New York, Free Press.

REX, J. and TOMLINSON, S. with the assistance of HEARNDEN, D. and RATCLIFFE, P. (1979) *Colonial Immigrants in a British City: A Class Analysis*, London, RKP.

REYNOLDS, D. (1976) 'The delinquent school', in HAMMERSLEY, M. and WOODS, P. (Eds) *The Process of Schooling: A Sociological Reader*, London, RKP with the Open University Press.

REYNOLDS, D. and SULLIVAN, M. (1979) 'Bringing schools back in', in BARTON, L. and MEIGHAN, R. (Eds) *Schools, Pupils and Deviance*, Driffield, Nafferton Books.

REYNOLDS, D. and SULLIVAN, M. (1981) 'The effects of school: A radical faith re-stated', in GILLHAM, B. (Ed) *Rethinking the Problem*, Beckenham, Croom Helm.

RIDDELL, S. (1994) 'Parental power and special educational needs', paper presented at the CEDAR International Conference 'Changing Educational Strustures: Policy and Practice', University of Warwick, April.

RIDDELL, S. and BROWN, S. (1994) *Special Educational Needs Policy in the 1990s — Warnock in the Market Place*, London, Routledge.

ROBERTSON, J. (1981) *Effective Classroom Control*, London, Hodder and Stoughton.

ROBINS, L.N. (1966) *Deviant Children Growing Up*, Baltimore, Williams and Wilkins.

ROBINS, L.N. (1972) 'Follow-up studies on behaviour disorder in children', in QUAY, H.C. (Ed) ??

ROSSER, E. and HARRE, R. (1976) 'The meaning of trouble', in HAMMERSLEY, M. and WOODS, P. (Eds) *The Process of Schooling: A Sociological Reader*, London, RKP with the Open University Press.

ROTHENBERG, M. (1960) *Children with Emerald Eyes: Working with Deeply Disturbed Boys and Girls*, New York, Souvenir Press.

RUBINSTEIN, D. (1969) *School Attendance in London 1870–1904: A Social History*, Hull, University of Hull Publications.

RUTTER, M. (1967) *Children's Behaviour Questionnaire*.

RUTTER, M. (1975) *Helping Troubled Children*, London, Penguin.

RUTTER, M. (1977) *Cycles of Disadvantage*, London, Heinemann.

RUTTER, M., MAUGHAN, B., MORTIMORE, P. and OUSTON, J. (1979) *Fifteen Thousand Hours*, London, Open Books.

SCHOOLS COUNCIL (1963) *Working Paper No 2: Raising the School, Leaving Age: A Co-operative Programme of Research and Development*, London, HMSO.

SEAVER, B.W. (1973) 'Effects of naturally induced teacher expectancies', *Journal of Personality and Social Psychology*, **28**, 3, pp. 334–42.

SCIFERT, K.I. and HOFFNUNG, R.J. (1994) *Child & Adolescent Development*, Boston, MA, Houghton Mifflin.

SEWELL, G. (1981) 'The microsociology of segregation: Case studies in the exclusion of children with special needs from ordinary schools', in BARTON, L. and TOMLINSON, S. (Eds) *Special Education: Policy, Practices and Social Issues*, London, Pitman Press.

SHARP, R. (1976) *Just Like a Girl: How Girls Learn to be Women*, London, Penguin.

SHARP, R. and GREEN, A. (1975) *Education and Social Control: A Study in Progressive Primary Education*, London, RKP.

SHAW, J. (1980) 'Education and the individual: Schooling for girls or mixed schooling — A mixed blessing?', in DEEM, R. (Ed) *Schooling for Women's Work*, London, RKP.

SHIELDS, R.W. (1962) *A Cure of Delinquents*, London, Heinemann.

SLEE, R. (Ed) (1993) *Is There a Desk with my Name on it?: The Politics of Integration*, London, Falmer Press.

SLEE, R. (1995) *Changing Theories and Practices of Discipline*, London, Falmer Press.

SMITH, C. (1992) 'Management of special needs', in GUILIFORD, R. and UPTON, G. (Eds) *Special Educational Needs*, London, Routledge.

SOLITY, J. (1992) *Special Education*, London, Cassells.

SOLITY, J. and RAYBOULD, E. (1988) *A Teacher's Guide to Special Needs: A Positive Response to the 1981 Education Act*, Milton Keynes, Open University Press.

SQUIBB, P. (1977) 'Some notes towards the analysis of the social construction of the "less able" or "backward" child', *Journal of Further and Higher Education*, **1**, 3, pp. 76–8.

SQUIBB, P. (1981) 'A theoretical structuralist approach to special education', in BARTON, L. and TOMLINSON, S. (1981) *Special Education: Policy, Practices and Social Issues*, London, Pitman Press.

STEBBINS, R.A. (1980) 'The role of humour in teaching: Strategy and self expression', in WOODS, P. (Ed) *Teacher Strategies: Explorations in the Sociology of the School*, Beckenham, Croom Helm.

STOTT, D.H. (1956) *Unsettled Children and Their Families*, London, University of London Press.

STOTT, D.H. (1966) *Bristol Social Adjustment Guides.*

STOTT, D.H. (1982) *Helping the Maladjusted Child*, London, University of London Press.

STRIVENS, J. (1981) 'The use of behaviour modification in special education: A critique', in BARTON, L. and TOMLINSON, S. (Eds) *Special Education: Policy, Practices and Social Issues*, London, Pitman Press.

STUBBS, M. and DELAMONT, S. (Eds) (1976) *Explorations in Classroom Observation*, Chichester, John Wiley & Sons.

SWANN, W. (Ed) (1981) *The Practice of Special Education: A Reader*, Oxford, Basil Blackwell with the Open University Press.

TATTUM, D.P. (1982) *Disruptive Pupils in Schools and Units*, Chichester, John Wiley & Sons Ltd.

TATTUM, D.P. (1985) 'Disruptive pupil behaviour: A sociological perspective', *Management and Therapeutic Education*, **3**, 2, pp. 12–18.

TATTUM, D.P. (1986a) 'Consistency management: School and classroom concerns and issues', in TATTUM, D.P. (Ed) *Management of Disruptive Pupil Behaviour in Schools*, Chichester, John Wiley & Sons Ltd.

TATTUM, D.P. (Ed) (1986b) *Management of Disruptive Pupil Behaviour in Schools*, Chichester, John Wiley & Sons Ltd.

TAYLOR, M., MILLER, J. and OLIVEIRA, M. (1979) 'The off-site unit', *Comprehensive Education*, Winter, **39**, pp. 13–17.

TOMLINSON, S. (1981a) *Educational Sub-normality: A Study in Decision-making*, London, RKP.

TOMLINSON, S. (1981b) 'The social construction of the ESN(M) child', in BARTON, L. and TOMLINSON, S. (Eds) *Special Education: Policy, Practices and Social Issues*, London, Pitman Press.

TOMLINSON, S. (1982) *A Sociology of Special Education*, London, RKP.

TOMLINSON, S. (1983) *Ethnic Minorities in British Schools: A Review of the Literature 1960–1982*, London, Heinemann.

TOPPING, K. (1983) *Educational Systems for Disruptive Adolescents*, Beckenham, Croom Helm.

TOPPING, K. (1986) 'Consultative enhancement of school-based action', in TATTUM, D.P. (Ed) *Management of Disruptive Pupil Behaviour in Schools*, Chichester, John Wiley & Sons Ltd.

TURNBURY, R. (1978) *Changing Urban School*, London, Methuen.

TURNER, G. (1983) *The Social World of the Comprehensive School: How Pupils Adapt*, Beckenham, Croom Helm.

UPTON, G. (1992) 'Emotional and behavioural difficulties', in GUILIFORD, R. and UPTON, G. (Eds) *Special Educational Needs*, London, Routledge.

VISSER, J. (1993) 'A broad, balanced, relevant and differentiated curriculum?', in VISSER, J. and UPTON, G. (Eds) *Special Education in Britain after Warnock*, London, David Fulton Publishers Ltd.

VISSER, J. and UPTON, G. (Eds) (1993) *Special Education in Britain after Warnock*, London, David Fulton Publishers Ltd.

WADE, B. and MOORE, M. (1993) *Experiencing Special Education: What Young People with Special Educational Needs Can Tell Us*, Buckingham, Open University Press.

WAKEFIELD, T. (1977) *Special School*, London, RKP.

WAKEFORD, J. (1969) *The Cloistered Elite: A Sociological Analysis of the English Public School*, Basingstoke, Macmillan and Co Ltd.

WALKER, S. (1984) *Learning Theory and Behaviour Modification*, London, Methuen.

WALKER, S. and BARTON, L. (Eds) (1983) *Gender, Class and Education*, London, Falmer Press.

WANG, M.C., REYNOLDS, M.C. and WALBERG, H.J. (Eds) (1990) *Special Education Research and Practice: Synthesis of Findings*, Oxford, Pergamon Press.

WARE, L.P. (1994) 'Contextual barriers to collaboration', *Journal of Educational and Psychological Consultation*, **5**, 4, pp. 339–57.

WARNOCK, M. (1993) 'Foreword', in VISSER, J. and UPTON, G. (Eds) *Special Education in Britain after Warnock,* London, David Fulton Publishers Ltd.

WASISCO, M.M. and ROSS, S.M. (1982) 'How to create discipline problems', *The Clearing House,* December, **56**, pp. 149–52.

WEBB, L. (1967) *Children with Special Needs in the Infant School,* London, Fontana.

WEBB, L. (1969) *Special Needs in the Infants' School,* Glasgow, Collins Sons & Co.

WEBER, K.J. (1978) *Yes They Can!: A Practical Guide for Teaching the Adolescent Slow Learning,* Milton Keynes, Open University Press.

WEBER, K.J. (1982) *The Teacher in the Key: A Practical Guide for Teaching the Adolescent with Learning Difficulties,* Milton Keynes, Open University Press.

WERTHMAN, C. (1963) 'Delinquents in schools: A test for the legitimacy of authority', reprinted in HAMMERSLEY, M. and WOODS, P. (Eds) (1984) *Life in School: The Sociology of Pupil Culture,* Milton Keynes, Open University Press.

WESTWOOD, P. (1993) *Commonsense Methods for Children with Special Needs,* London, Routledge.

WHITE, R. (1980) *Absent with Cause: Lessons of Truancy,* London, RKP.

WHITE, R. and BROCKINGTON, D. (1978) *In and Out of School,* ROSLA Community Education Project, London, RKP.

WHITTY, G. (1984) 'Special units in a changing climate: Agencies of change or control?', in LLOYD-SMITH, M. (Ed) *Disrupted Schooling: The Growth of the Special Unit,* London, John Murray.

WHITTY, G. (1985) *Sociology and School Knowledge: Curriculum Theory, Research and Politics,* London, Methuen.

WILLIAMS, P. (Ed) (1974) *Behaviour Problems in School: A Source Book of Readings,* London, University of London Press.

WILLIS, P.E. (1977) *Learning to Labour: How Working Class Kids get Working Class Jobs,* Hampshire, Gower (Reprinted of 1983).

WILLS, W.D. (1945) *The Barns Experiment,* London, George Allen & Unwin.

WILSON, M. and EVANS, M. (1980) *Education of Disturbed Pupils,* London, Schools Council Publications.

WOODHEAD, M. and McGRATH, A. (Eds) (1988) *Family, School & Society: A Reader,* London, Hodder and Stoughton in association with the Open University.

WOODS, P. (1975) 'Showing 'em up in secondary school', in CHANAN, G. and DELAMONT, S. (1975) *Frontiers of Classroom Research,* Windsor, NFER Publishing Company.

WOODS, P. (1976) 'The myth of subject choice', reprinted in HAMMERSLEY, M. and WOODS, P. (Eds) (1984) *Life in School: The Sociology of Pupil Culture,* Milton Keynes, Open University Press.

WOODS, P. (1979) *The Divided School,* London, RKP.

WOODS, P. (Ed) (1980a) *Pupil Strategies: Explorations in the Sociology of the School,* Beckenham, Croom Helm.

WOODS, P. (Ed) (1980b) *Teacher Strategies: Explorations in the Sociology of the School,* Beckenham, Croom Helm.

WOODS, P. (1980c) 'The development of pupil strategies', in WOODS, P. (Ed) *Pupil*

Strategies: Explorations in the Sociology of the School, Beckenham, Croom Helm.

WOODS, P. (1983) *Sociology and the School: An Interactionist Viewpoint*, London, RKP.

WOOLFE, R. (1981) 'Maladjustment in the context of the local authority decision making', in BARTON, L. and TOMLINSON, S. (Eds) *Special Education: Policy, Practices and Social Issues*, London, Pitman Press.

WRIGHT, D.M., MOELIS, I. and POLLACK, L.J. (1976) 'The outcome of individual child psychotherapy: Increments at follow-up', *Journal of Child Psychology and Psychiatry*, **17**, pp. 275–85.

YOUNG, P., STEED, D. and LAWRENCE, J. (1980) 'Local education authorities and autonomous off-site units for disruptive pupils in secondary schools', *Cambridge Journal of Education*, **10**, 2.

YSSELDYKE, J.E. and ALGOZZINE, B. (1995) *Special Education: A Practical Approach for Teachers*, Boston, MA, Houghton Mifflin.

Index